LEGENDARY LOCALS

OF

# WILLINGBORO

## NEW JERSEY

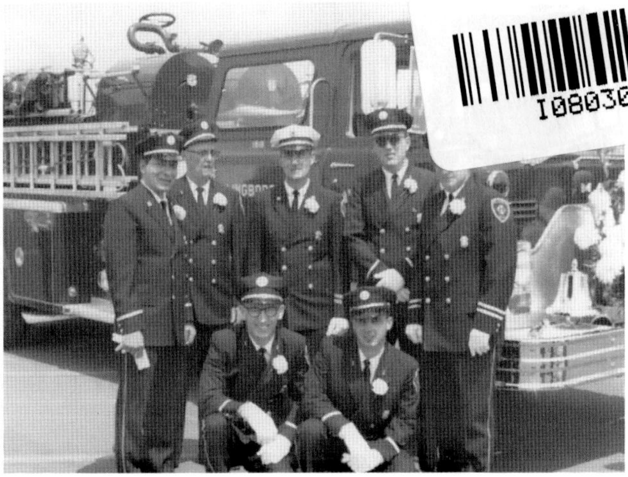

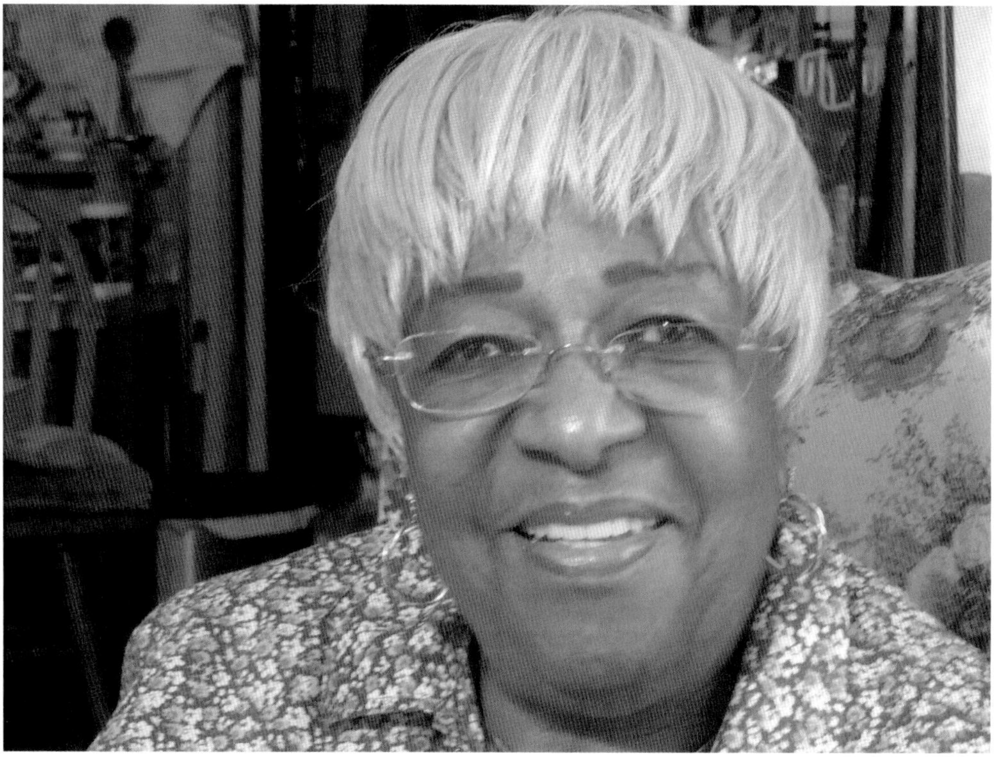

**Addie Hatten**

A native of South Carolina and graduate of one of the first integrated classes of the Women's Army Corps, Addie Hatten and her husband, Fred, moved to Willingboro's Hawthorne Park neighborhood in 1968. A mother of three, she became accounting and finance officer at nearby McGuire Air Force Base. Seeing few or no African Americans on township governing boards, Addie joined the Political Action Coalition of Willingboro, a group that sought to create political awareness among minorities and communicate issues important to them. She was appointed to the township's human relations commission, mentoring troubled children and encouraging them to stay in school. Addie served as a Girl Scout cadet leader and organized a local chapter of the Eta Phi Beta sorority, a national business and professional women's group. She was a regular attendee at township council and school board meetings, frequently questioning elected officials. "I made myself part of the community," she said. (Author's collection.)

**Page 1: Willingboro Fire Department**

Members of the Willingboro Fire Department prepare for a parade at the Willingboro Plaza. (Courtesy Willingboro Fire Department.)

LEGENDARY LOCALS

OF

# WILLINGBORO

## NEW JERSEY

JOSH BERNSTEIN

LEGENDARY LOCALS

ISBN 978-1-4671-0090-8

Legendary Locals is an imprint of Arcadia Publishing
Charleston, South Carolina

Printed in the United States of America

Library of Congress Control Number: 2013932586

For all general information, please contact Arcadia Publishing:
Telephone 843-853-2070
Fax 843-853-0044
E-mail sales@arcadiapublishing.com
For customer service and orders:
Toll-Free 1-888-313-2665

Visit us on the Internet at www.arcadiapublishing.com

**Dedication**
*To Angie, Isa, and Ben, whose love and support made this project possible.*

**On the Front Cover:** Clockwise from top left:
Harry McFarland, recreation director (courtesy Harry McFarland; see page 20); William Franklin, Royal Governor of New Jersey (courtesy Willingboro Public Library, see page 11); Crystal Langhorne, professional basketball player (courtesy NBA Photos, see page 50); Carl Lewis, Olympic track and field athlete (courtesy the Philadelphia Inquirer, see page 53); Henry Rowan, industrialist and philanthropist (courtesy Rowan University/Craig Terry, see page 116); Millie Gama, longtime chamber of commerce executive director (courtesy Burlington County College, see page 36); Kevin Sbraga, chef and restaurateur (courtesy Sbraga/Wagstaff Worldwide, see page 72); Karen Abdul Malik, professional storyteller and educator (courtesy Karen Abdul-Malik/Walter Petrule, see page 78); William Levitt, developer (courtesy Willingboro Public Library, see page 12).

**On the Back Cover:** From left to right:
Madison Thomas, kinsman; Ed Kelly, county clerk; and Paul Krane, councilman (Courtesy Willingboro Library, see pages 16, 23 and 24), Willingboro High School Jazz Band (courtesy Jeffrey Lesser, see page 80).

# CONTENTS


Acknowledgments 6

Introduction 7

CHAPTER ONE Growing the Community: Civic Leaders and Volunteers 9

CHAPTER TWO On the Ball: Athletes and Sports Heroes 49

CHAPTER THREE Born to Shine: Arts and Letters 71

CHAPTER FOUR Healing the Community: Mind, Body, and Spirit 89

CHAPTER FIVE To Serve and Protect: Willingboro's First Responders 99

CHAPTER SIX Economic Drivers: Business and Commerce 115

Index 127

# ACKNOWLEDGMENTS

I would like to express my deepest appreciation to my wife, Angie, and children, Isa and Ben, for their encouragement, support, and understanding while I worked on this book, including the "vacation without Daddy," as well as my parents for their unending love. I would like to thank, for their cooperation, the administration and staff of the Willingboro Public Library, David Nelinson of the Willingboro Emergency Squad and Fire Department, Lt. Joseph Dey of the Willingboro Police Department, Lourdes Health System, and the Westampton Historical Society for granting me for open use of their archives, as well as Jackie Rose at the *Philadelphia Inquirer*, Burlington County College, and Rowan University. For sharing their personal photographs and stories, I thank Harry McFarland, John Tegley, Sally and Victor Friedman, Lavonne Johnson, Jim Ayrer, William McGrath, Tyrone Belford, Jeffrey Lesser, Dr. Bernard Blank, Micha Alston, Addie Hatten, Celeste Whittaker, Jeff Gammage, Gervase Peterson, Bill Probsting of Westfield Friends School, Kelly Logan, and many others.

Unless otherwise noted, all images are from the author's collection.

# INTRODUCTION

Willingboro holds a unique place in American history. A quiet farming community for most of its existence, it experienced a dramatic transformation with the development of thousands of homes. Between 1950 and 1970, the population catapulted from 852 to 43,386 as the township became a model American suburb.

This volume reveals the story of this transformation through the people who lived it, celebrating their contributions to the community and beyond.

"Our family moved to Willingboro in 1960, and thinking back, watching this new community grow and taking part in the growth was an exciting time," said Sue Woodward, whose mother, Marion Huddleston, is profiled in these pages. "There were new homes, new families and friends, and new organizations developing over the years. These gave all of us a sense of creativity and community."

The area's original inhabitants were Lenape Indians, though there were few permanent settlements. In the 1670s, two Quakers purchased land once belonging to the Duke of York. They chose William Penn to lead the colonization effort in West Jersey. In 1677, Quakers sailed from England to West Jersey aboard the ship *Kent*. Among the contingent was Thomas Olive, who named his portion of land after his hometown of Wellingborough. In 1688, the constabulary of Wellingborrow (the spelling of the town name varied over the years) was established, becoming one of Burlington County's 11 original municipalities.

Willingboro was 15 square miles and stretched from the Delaware River to the village of Rancocas. As early as 1695, a ferry was transporting people and goods from Dunks Ferry (in what is now Beverly) to Pennsylvania. Dunks Ferry was an important transportation link in both the Revolutionary War and Civil War.

Willingboro's most famous early resident was Royal Governor William Franklin. Primarily used as a summer residence, the 525-acre estate known as Strawberry Hill included a large Georgian-style house, English gardens, and a deer park. In 1776, Colonial revolutionaries arrested Franklin at his house in Perth Amboy. Franklin never returned to Willingboro, and the house burned in 1839.

Life remained fairly quiet until 1859, when a dispute between Beverly "city dwellers" and farmers over taxes led to a division of the township. All land west of Route 130 became Beverly.

The town buzzed again in 1954 as a New York developer began to purchase acres of farmland. By 1956, the developer, Levitt and Sons, had spent $8 million on 4,500 acres—90 percent of the township. That same year, the state legislature changed the township's boundaries to accommodate the builder. About 450 acres Levitt owned in Burlington Township were annexed by Willingboro, and Rancocas Village was transferred to Westampton. Unlike Levitt's namesake communities in Long Island and Bucks County, Levittown, New Jersey (residents changed the name from Willingboro to Levittown in 1959, then back to Willingboro in 1963), would be a single physical and political entity.

Farms and centuries-old homesteads were cleared to make way for rancher, Cape Cod, and Colonial–style houses. Each neighborhood, or park, had a school and swimming pool, with winding streets that opened onto broad, landscaped parkways. The first letter of each street was the same as the park name. Somerset Park opened first in 1958. Leo and Joan Mount occupied the first house at 51 Sussex Drive.

The new Levittown, however, was segregated. It was not until after Rev. Willie James, a soldier at Fort Dix, sued that Levitt relented. Charles and Vera Williams were the first African Americans to settle in town. Today, a majority of Willingboro residents are African American.

Early residents recall a town filled with promise. "Everybody felt young," said writer Sally Friedman. "There was a spirit and a sense of caring about the place. We were so proud."

Willingboro became a popular place to reside, attracting baseball players like Garry Maddox and Jim Bunning and wrestler Gorilla Monsoon.

"I love Willingboro. Back in the day, it was *the* place to live," said reality show star Gervase Peterson. "You could play in the street. Every park had a basketball court and a swimming pool. How cool was that?"

"There were 50 kids on your block, always out," added businessman Jeff Fante. "You were never bored."

Three hundred twenty-five years after its founding, Willingboro has left a mark on the American landscape, from its transformation from farmland to model suburb to the contribution of residents like Carl Lewis, Marie White Bell, Lizzie Morris, William Kearns, Paul Krane, Ed Kelly, Adam Blackstone, and many more.

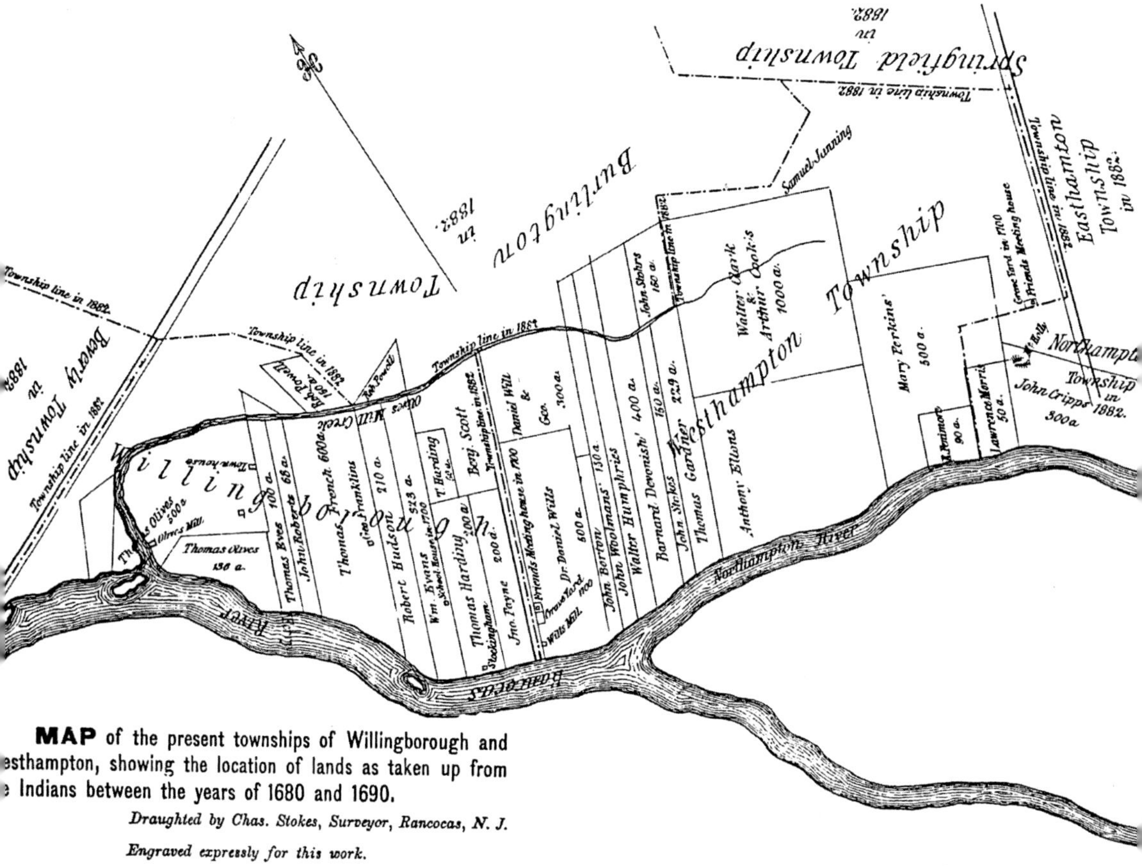


**MAP** of the present townships of Willingborough and esthampton, showing the location of lands as taken up from Indians between the years of 1680 and 1690.

*Draughted by Chas. Stokes, Surveyor, Rancocas, N. J.*

*Engraved expressly for this work.*

### Thomas Olive

Traditionally regarded as the founder of Willingboro, Thomas Olive came to America in 1677. A member of the Society of Friends, Olive is described as being "a man wise in council, energetic in business, and distinguished in public life." He served the General Free Assembly of the colony of West New Jersey as governor and speaker. This map shows Olive's 636 acres of land, upon which he built a large house and mill, and some of the other original landholders of the constabulary of Wellingborough. They include Thomas French (whose land was later occupied by Royal Governor William Franklin), Thomas Harding, Thomas Green, John Payne, William Evans, Thomas Eves, Robert Hudson, and John Roberts. (Courtesy Willingboro Library.)

# CHAPTER ONE

# Growing the Community

## Civic Leaders and Volunteers

Lizzie Morris was a force of nature. From making homemade meals for first responders to gathering signatures for a liquor referendum to serving on various township committees, Morris seemed to be everywhere.

From original West Jersey landowner William Penn, to civil rights activist Rev. Willie James, who helped desegregate modern Willingboro, people like Morris have stepped up to shape and grow the community.

Take J. Cresswell Stuart. A farmer who sold most of his land to Levitt and Sons, he was chairman of the planning board and insisted the developer give residents a say in the construction of their community. Stuart served on the school board for 27 years and as a county freeholder, as well as helping to found the Beverly and Willingboro Rotary Clubs.

Priscilla Anderson, a teacher and guidance counselor, served three terms on township council and became the first black legislator from Burlington County to serve in the state assembly. Anderson had a special interest in young people and established the Willingboro Youth Achievement Awards to recognize their service to the community. Anderson published *The History and Contributions of Black Americans to the Development of Willingboro*, which has become a resource for historians and sociologists.

Harry McFarland came from New England in 1968 to serve as recreation department director. Working with Levitt and Sons, McFarland helped to develop Fairmount, Broido, and Mill Creek parks, whose playgrounds, tennis courts, fields, and hiking trails are enjoyed by thousands of township residents each year.

Kelly Logan turned the tragic death of his teenage daughter into a crusade against violence. A former football player and law enforcement officer, Logan established Stop, Drop Your Gun, Inc., a nonprofit group dedicated to nonviolence and gun awareness. Logan spreads his message at schools, churches, and other organizations across the region, getting young people comfortable talking with their parents and law enforcement about violence, guns, gangs, and bullying to help prevent future tragedies.

During her years teaching, Marilyn Marshall recognized that some students need assistance to succeed, whether it be pens and paper, or simply someone to share their feelings. Still seeing a need after she retired, Marshall established the Hold On To Education Foundation. Today, the group provides scholarships, school supplies, and workshops for youth in the community.

Ron Dash considers himself part St. Francis of Assisi and part Lone Ranger, caring for the less fortunate while staying out of the spotlight. Awarded the Purple Heart for wounds received in Vietnam, Dash is a staunch advocate for veterans. But his generosity doesn't stop there. For 25 years, he distributed food baskets at the holidays. Wishing to reach more people, Dash recently started organizing Thanksgiving dinners at the Kennedy Center for those with nowhere else to go. "Protecting and defending those who are not quite capable of doing so, that's who I am," he told a reporter.

These individuals and others truly make up the fabric of life in Willingboro.

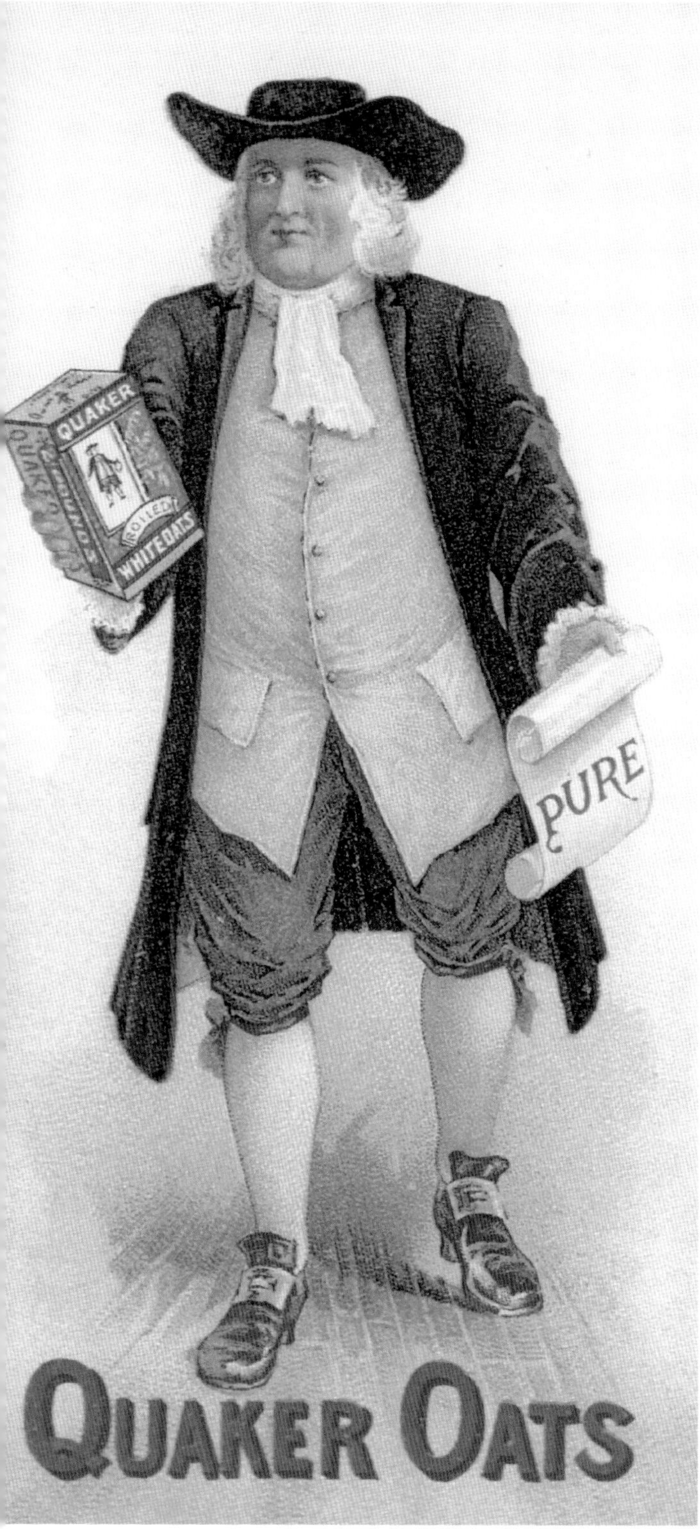


**William Penn**
While best known as the founder of Pennsylvania and Philadelphia, William Penn played an important role in the settlement of New Jersey. In 1675, Lord Berkeley sold his portion of New Jersey (which he had obtained 10 years earlier from the Duke of York) to two Quakers, Major John Fenwick and Edward Byllenge. But a financial dispute between Fenwick and Byllenge led Penn and two fellow prominent Quakers to take over the new colony of West New Jersey. Penn was chosen the leader of the colonization. Penn's *Concessions and Agreements of the Proprietors, Freeholders, and Inhabitants of the Province of West New Jersey* established liberties later found in the US Constitution, including the rights to trial by jury, religious freedom, security in home and property, and the ability to redress grievances against the government. In 1677 and 1678, Penn's "Holy Experiment" attracted 800 Quaker immigrants, including Thomas Olive, who named his property after his hometown of Wellingborough. (Courtesy Westfield Friends School.)

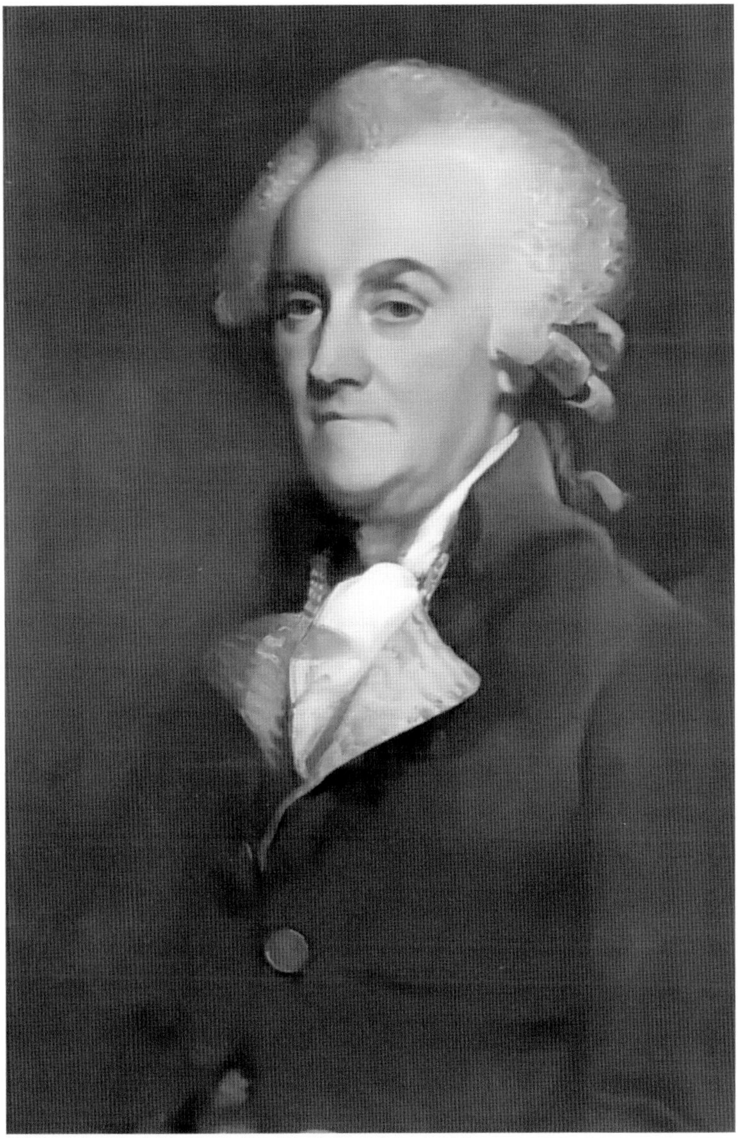

**William Franklin**

The illegitimate son of Benjamin Franklin, William assisted in his father's famed kite experiment in 1752. Through his father's influence with the British prime minister, William Franklin was appointed the Royal Governor of New Jersey in 1763. In 1766, he signed the charter for Queen's College, later to be called Rutgers University. While Franklin's primary residence was at Green Bank in Burlington—entertaining guests such as George Washington—he acquired a Wellingborough Township farm with 525 acres and a large Georgian-style house known as Strawberry Hill. Franklin and his wife, Elizabeth, expanded the house and created elaborate English gardens, including a park with 40 deer, and a profitable farm. Life did not remain rosy. Franklin's support of British rule did nothing to endear him to the public emboldened with revolutionary spirit, and in January 1776 he was placed under house arrest in Perth Amboy. Released in a prisoner exchange in 1778, Franklin led the loyalist community in New York City. He returned to England in 1782 and died in 1813. Tragically, Franklin's home burned in 1839. (Courtesy Willingboro Public Library.)

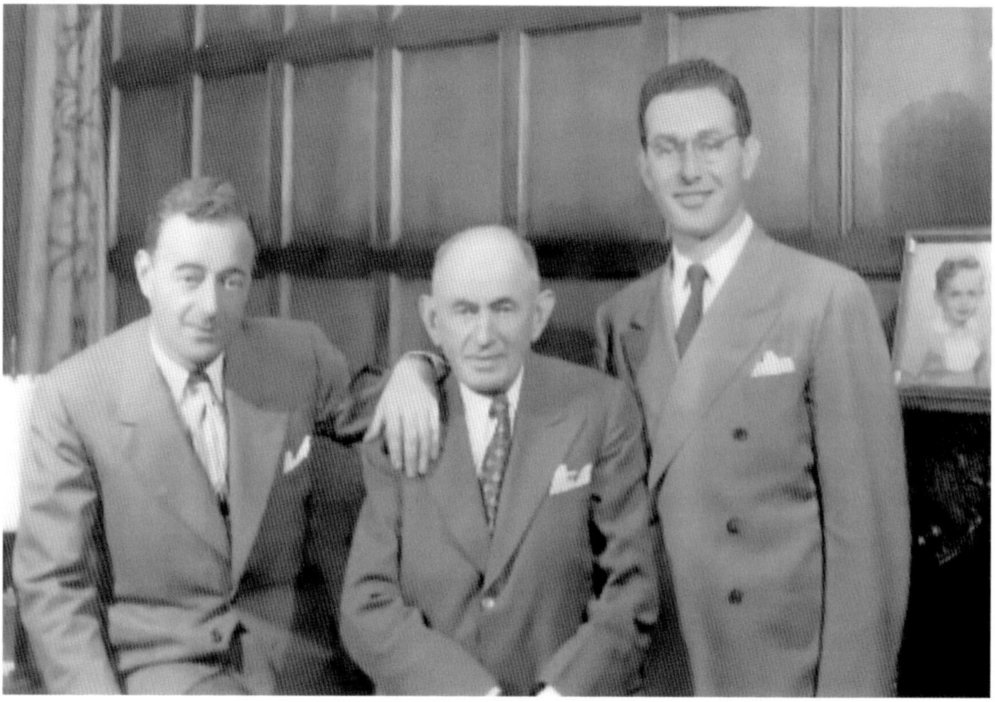

**Levitt and Sons**

Perhaps no other family played as significant a role in Willingboro's history as the Levitts. Founded in 1929 by real estate attorney Abraham Levitt (center), sons William (left) served as president and Alfred (right) as chief architect. From Long Island to Willingboro to Belair, Maryland, Levitt and Sons is credited with creating the modern American suburb through the use of mass-production techniques to construct large developments of houses. Communities like Willingboro were designed from the ground up, with affordable homes, parks, schools, and utilities. Neighborhoods, or "parks," were constructed with internal streets and cul-de-sacs. Each park encircled an elementary school and swimming pool. Key streets led to broad parkways that connected the other neighborhoods. The streets in each neighborhood all had the same first letter—for example, streets in Pennypacker Park all started with *P*—providing a sort of identity and pride to residents. Originally, Levitt and Sons agreed to fund all schools. But after residents voted in 1963 to change the town name back to Willingboro, Levitt stopped the donations. Plans to make Willingboro the firm's international headquarters also were shelved. Levitt built its last neighborhood in 1972. In total, 11,000 of 15,000 planned homes were built, the last in 1972. Abraham Levitt died in 1962; Alfred in 1966. William Levitt sold the company in 1968, and through other companies he founded continued to build communities, including one near Orlando, until his death in 1994. (Courtesy Willingboro Public Library.)

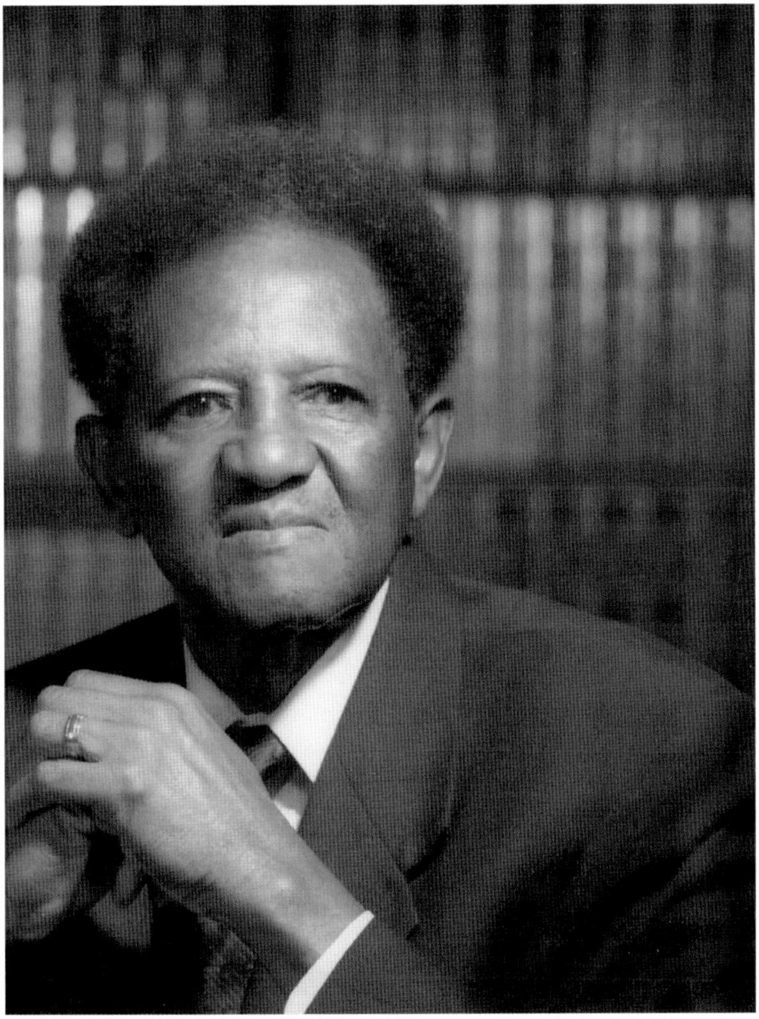

**Rev. Willie James**

The civil rights movement was still in its infancy when Levitt and Sons began developing the new Levittown. New Jersey had a law prohibiting housing discrimination, but it had not been tested. Willie James, an African American from Vidalia, Louisiana, and a US Army officer at nearby Fort Dix, applied to purchase a new Levittown home. He was denied, being told the new development would be an all-white community. James and the Burlington County branch of the National Association for the Advancement of Colored People (NAACP) sued. The New Jersey Supreme Court ruled in favor of James in 1960, and he and his family moved into Millbrook Park in 1960. James led the Burlington County NAACP from 1963 to 1974, working to desegregate the nearby Holiday Lake recreation area and negotiating with store owners to ensure that African Americans were employed at the Willingboro Plaza shopping center. He also filed a complaint with the US Pipe Company in Burlington for maintaining separate shower facilities for African Americans and failing to hire and promote blacks. James was active in the Kinsmen, a black civic group in Willingboro, and was a founder of the Burlington County Community Action Program to assist needy residents. James was transferred to Rhode Island in 1974. While there, he became an ordained minister. Rev. James returned to the area in 1996 and helmed the Willingboro NAACP. He worked with the national NAACP to try to reduce the number of minorities in prison. In 2001, the Willingboro Board of Education renamed the Pennypacker Park Elementary School in his honor. (Courtesy Willingboro Public Library.)

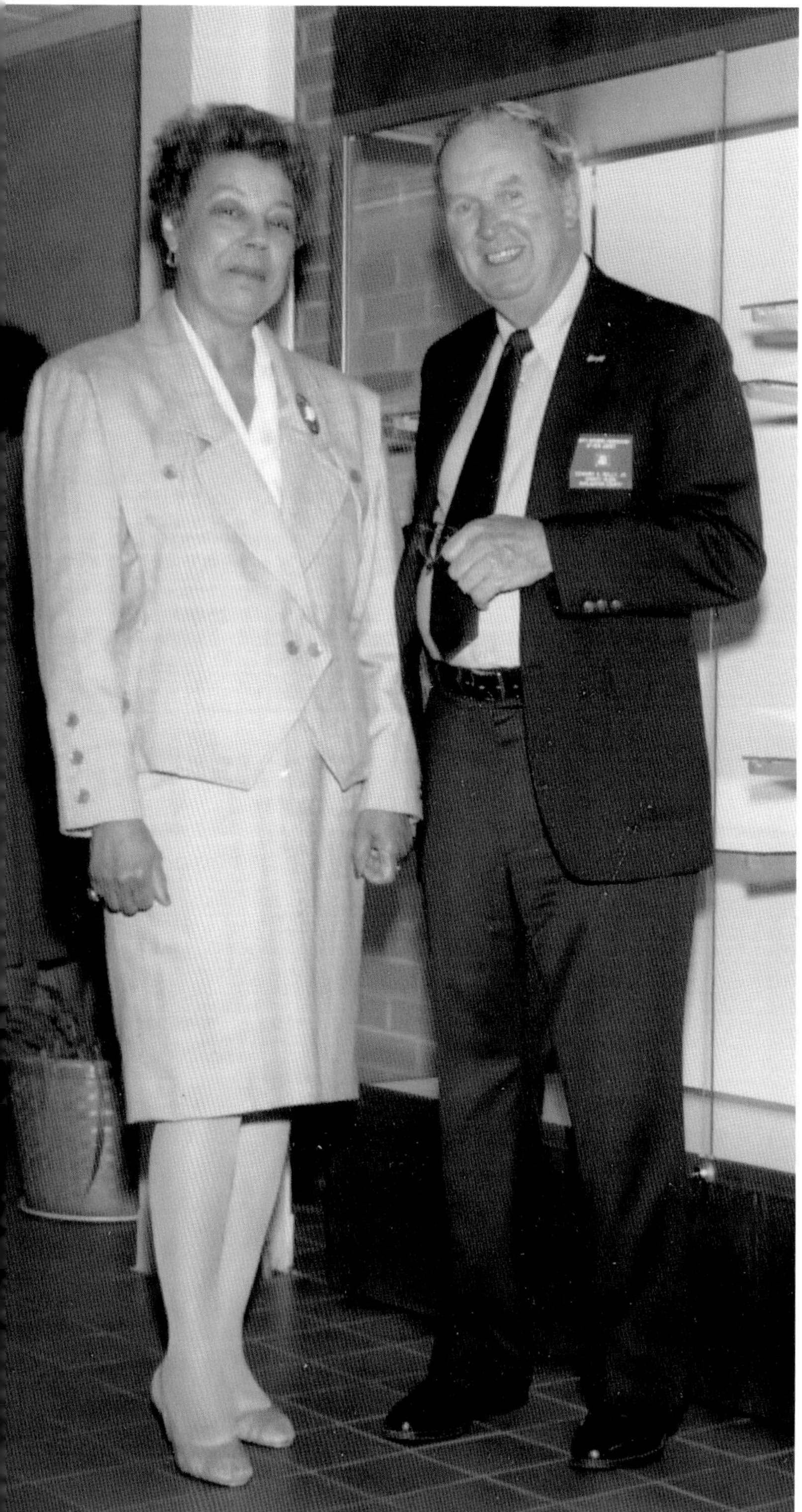

**Vera and Charles Williams**
Vera (seen here with former mayor Edward Kelly) and Charles Williams were the first African American family to move into Willingboro in 1960, benefitting from Rev. Willie James's lawsuit seeking to abolish Levitt and Sons' policy against sales to African Americans. Charles Williams quickly became active in the community. He was a founder of the Kinsmen, a black civic group, and vice president of the Willingboro Chamber of Commerce. Williams met with business managers at the Willingboro Plaza to get them to hire blacks and other minorities. He also worked toward the establishment of Burlington County College. In the 1990s, the township honored the Williamses with a plaque and trophy case in the municipal building. (Courtesy Willingboro Public Library.)

### James Cresswell Stuart

Few people in the Willingboro area are spoken of with such deep respect and affection as James Cresswell Stuart. The son of a veterinarian and a sought-after seamstress, Stuart grew up on the farm. Deeply religious, Stuart joined the Beverly Presbyterian Church at age 13 and was active with the YMCA (in 1918 he was a charter member of the Burlington County YMCA) and the American Youth Foundation Camp Conference. In 1930, he married Eleanor Hartman, a schoolteacher from Bordentown. They tried their hand at a flower business in Bordentown, but flowers were a luxury during the Depression and Stuart's father's failing health called the young couple back to the farm. The Stuarts had five children. Their son Jimmy tragically died at 22 from a staph infection, a condition that today could have been treated with antibiotics. While farm life was difficult, the couple did everything for the family. Eleanor taught fourth grade (at the school that would later be named for her husband) and volunteered for the PTA. James served on the state Farm Bureau and was president of the Beverly Cooperative Growers Association and New Jersey State Board of Agriculture. In 1984, he received the Distinguished Service Award in Agriculture. In the 1950s, most of the family holdings were sold to Levitt and Sons for the large-scale development that would transform Willingboro. But the Stuarts did not leave. James served on the Willingboro Board of Education from 1936 to 1963, and as chairman of the township planning board insisted to Levitt that residents have a say in the development of their community. He was chairman of the Municipal Utilities Authority, was elected to the Burlington County Board of Freeholders in 1958, and was a member of the county welfare board. He was a charter member of the Beverly and Willingboro Rotary clubs, was active in the Willingboro Heritage Commission and the Riverfront Historical Society, a trustee for Burlington County Memorial Hospital, a secretary for the Coopertown Cemetery Association, and a member of the Beverly Masonic Lodge. Eleanor Stuart passed away in 1980. James—indeed a man for all seasons—died in 1999 at age 95. (Courtesy *Burlington County Times*.)

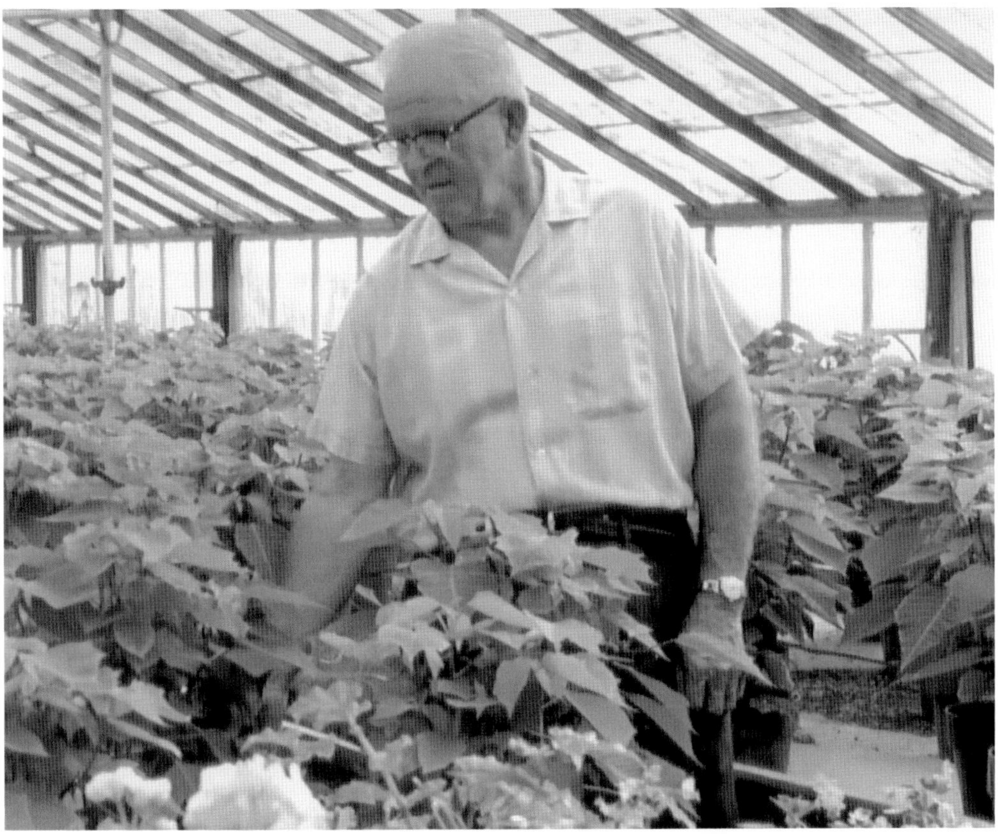

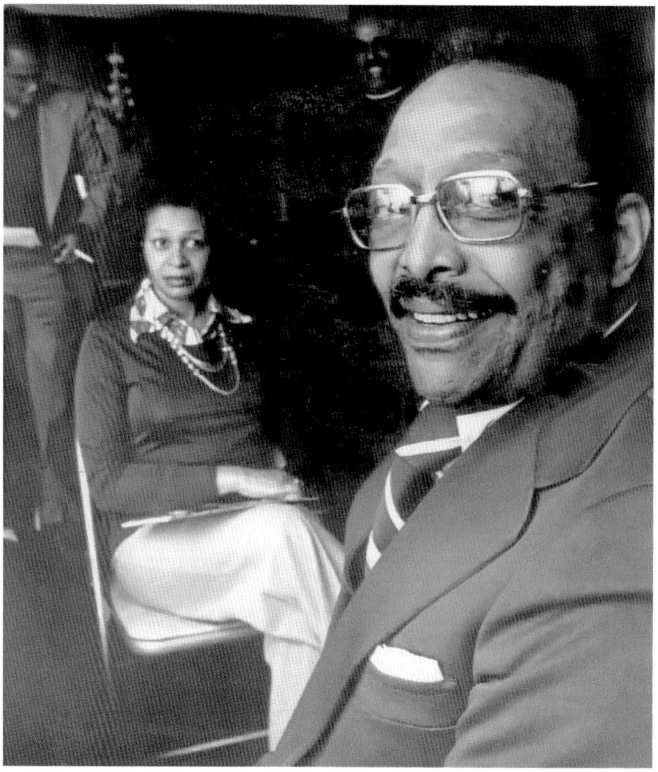

### Madison Thomas

Madison Thomas was the longtime executive director of the Kinsmen, an African American fraternal organization founded in 1960. Likely the first community organization established by African Americans in Willingboro, the Kinsmen were dedicated to self-help and community service. A retired US Civil Service employee who worked with youth in Philadelphia, Thomas led the Kinsmen as it supported school scholarships, the Willingboro Track Club, and the Miss Black America pageant, among others. (Courtesy Willingboro Public Library.)

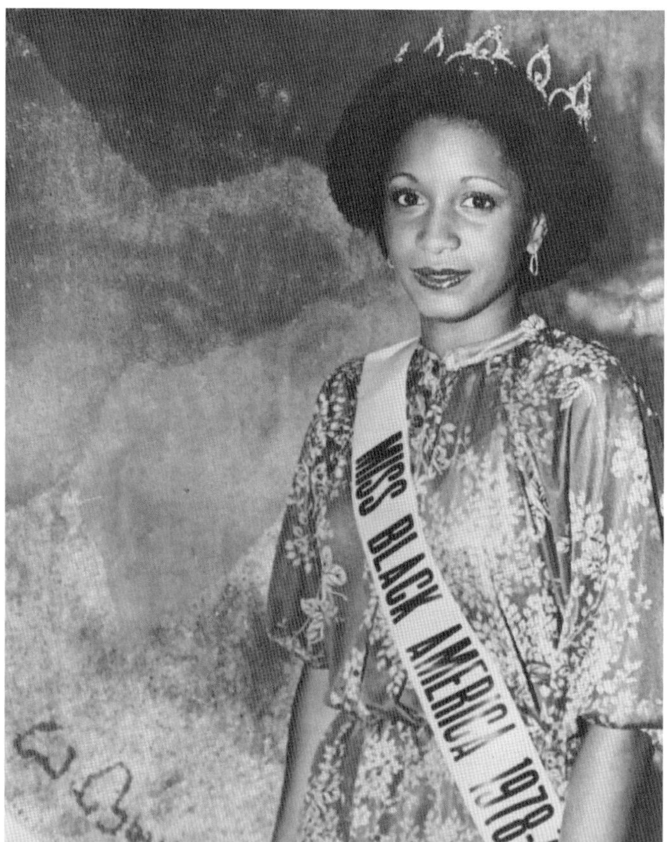


### Lydia Jackson

Lydia Jackson won the 1978 Miss Black America pageant, created to protest the lack of black women in the Miss America pageant. The event promoted the speech, talent, style, and poise of young African American women and often received nationwide press coverage. Jackson, a 19-year-old graduate of John F. Kennedy High School, captured the crown by singing an aria from the opera *The Barber of Seville*. (Courtesy Willingboro Public Library.)

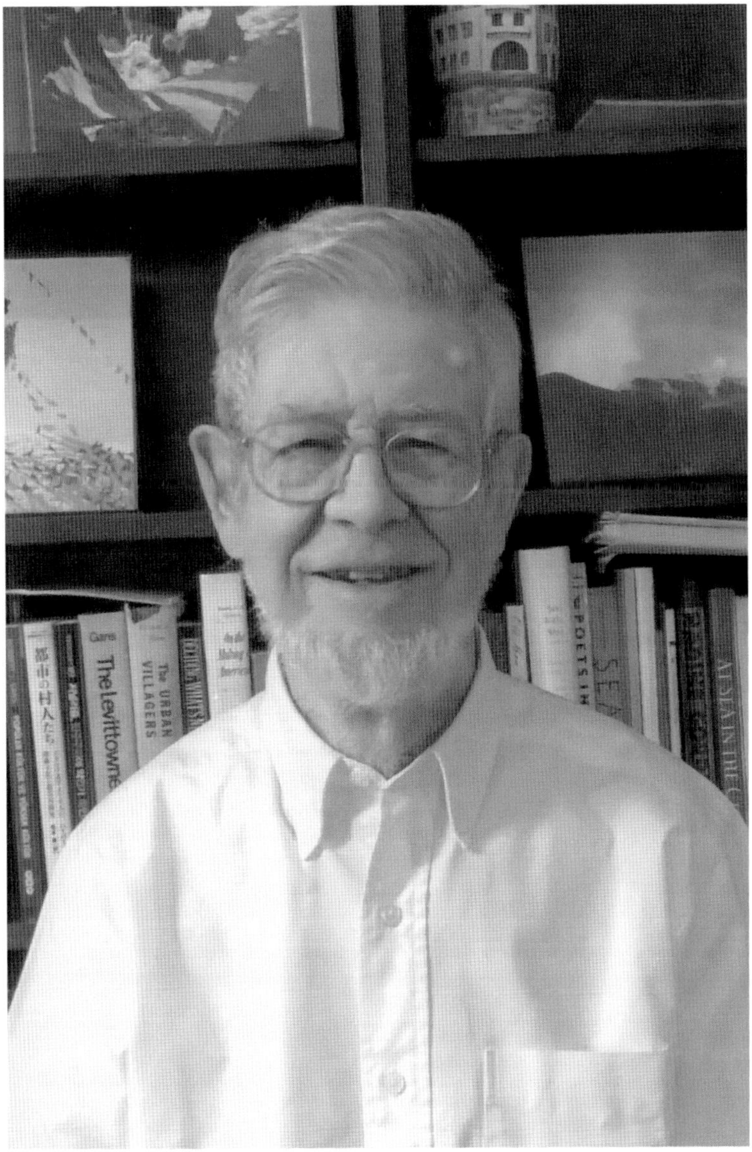

**Herbert J. Gans**

Born in Cologne in 1927, Herbert J. Gans left Nazi Germany in 1938, arriving in America in 1940. Earning degrees from the University of Chicago and University of Pennsylvania, Gans is one of the most influential sociologists and urban planners of his generation. In 1967, he published *The Levittowners: Ways of Life and Politics in a New Suburban Community* based on two years of participant-observation in the new Levitt-built suburb. In the book, Gans studies three major aspects of life in Willingboro: development and growth of the town through residents' involvement in community organizations, including politics; characteristics of life; and the effects that suburbia will have on its new inhabitants. According to Gans, the Levittowners are the archetypical American characters, sharing the same way of life, values, religion, beliefs, ethnicity, and living standards, representing the "American way of life." Yet the book refutes a popular depiction of the post-war suburbs as homogeneous and conformist, with residents' class and other differences structuring social and political life. Gans is a professor at Columbia University. (Courtesy Herbert Gans.)

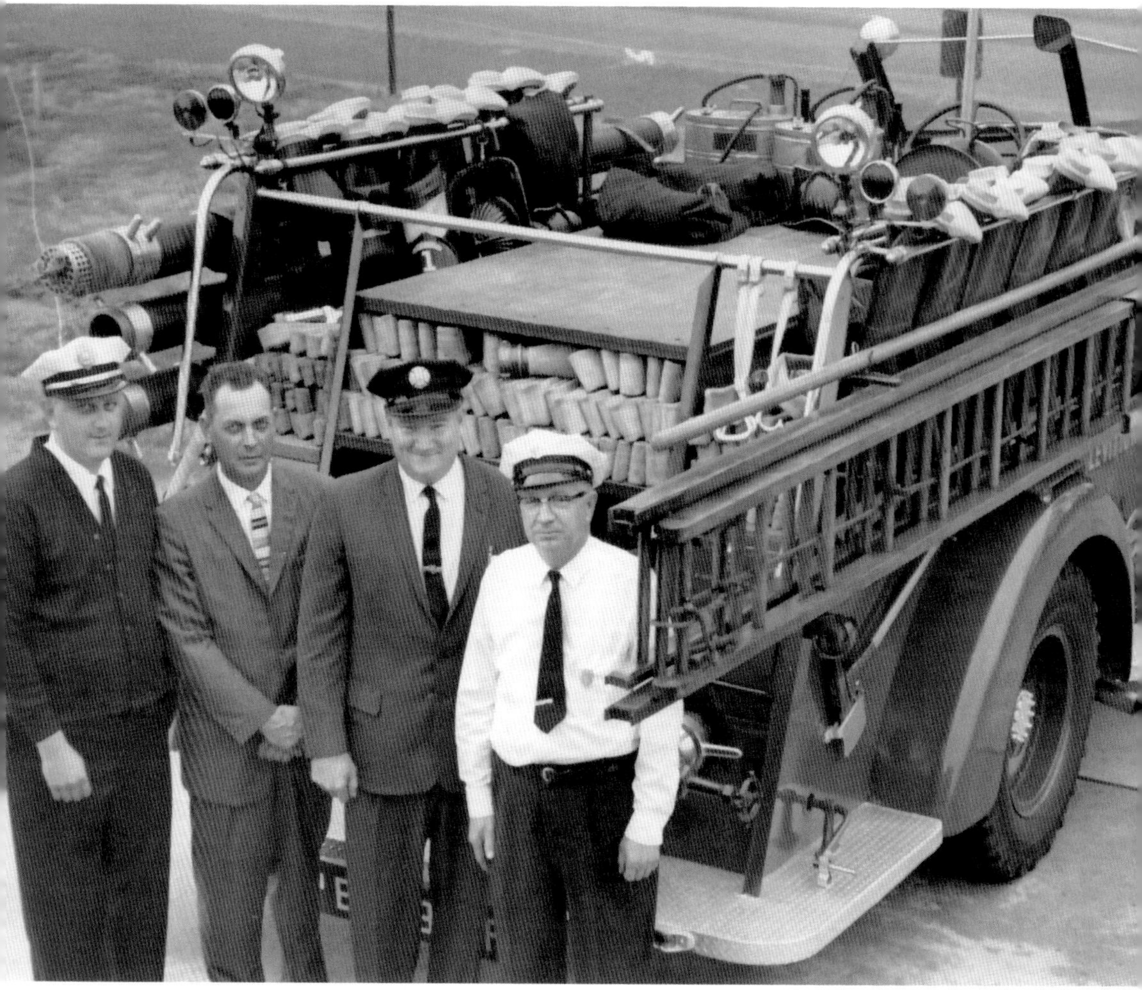

**Charles Van Sciver**

Charles Van Sciver (second from left, seen here with Willingboro Fire Department founders Woody Addis, Harry Jackson, and Larry Ruch) served as mayor of Levittown in 1960, and later as recreation department director. The town was renamed Levittown only a year earlier, and Levitt and Sons were busy building homes and the businesses such as the Fox Theater, which Van Sciver dedicated. A farmer, Van Sciver belonged to a family whose history in the area stretched back more than 300 years. The Dutch Van Scivers migrated from southern New York, joining the Quakers purchasing land from the Lenni-Lenape Indians. The Van Scivers farmed land on both sides of Route 130 and were active in the community: In the 1880s, Edwin Van Sciver served as constable, riding down country lanes aboard a white stallion, pistols at his side. One hundred years later, Richard Van Sciver served as police chief. Today, Van Sciver Parkway honors the family's contributions to the town. (Courtesy Willingboro Fire Department.)

### Jack McHugh

A native of the Bronx, Jack McHugh (on the right) guided Willingboro through some of its most expansive and challenging years as township manager from 1964 to 1974. Previously a municipal administrator in New England, McHugh had hardly begun his work in Willingboro when the former schoolhouse that housed town offices, the police station, and the library burned in a spectacular fire. McHugh spent the next three years overseeing the planning and construction of the new municipal complex on Salem Road. In 1969, the large Kimble tract on Beverly-Rancocas Road became the target of a Philadelphia developer who wanted to build apartments there. Hearing residents' opposition, McHugh and the township council worked to secure state and federal grants to acquire the land for a park. Their efforts set the standard for other towns wishing to buy land for parks. Mill Creek Park opened in 1974, with its large, man-made sledding hill dubbed "McHugh's Mountain." McHugh left later that year to become administrator of Middlesex County. He retired from that job in 1987 and became a management consultant. McHugh and his wife, Carmen, remained in Willingboro, with their seven daughters graduating from high school here. He volunteered for several groups, including the library. McHugh is remembered for being a strong and skillful manager, knowledgeable about complex issues affecting the town and creating a model of government efficiency. He now resides in Massachusetts. (Courtesy Willingboro Library.)

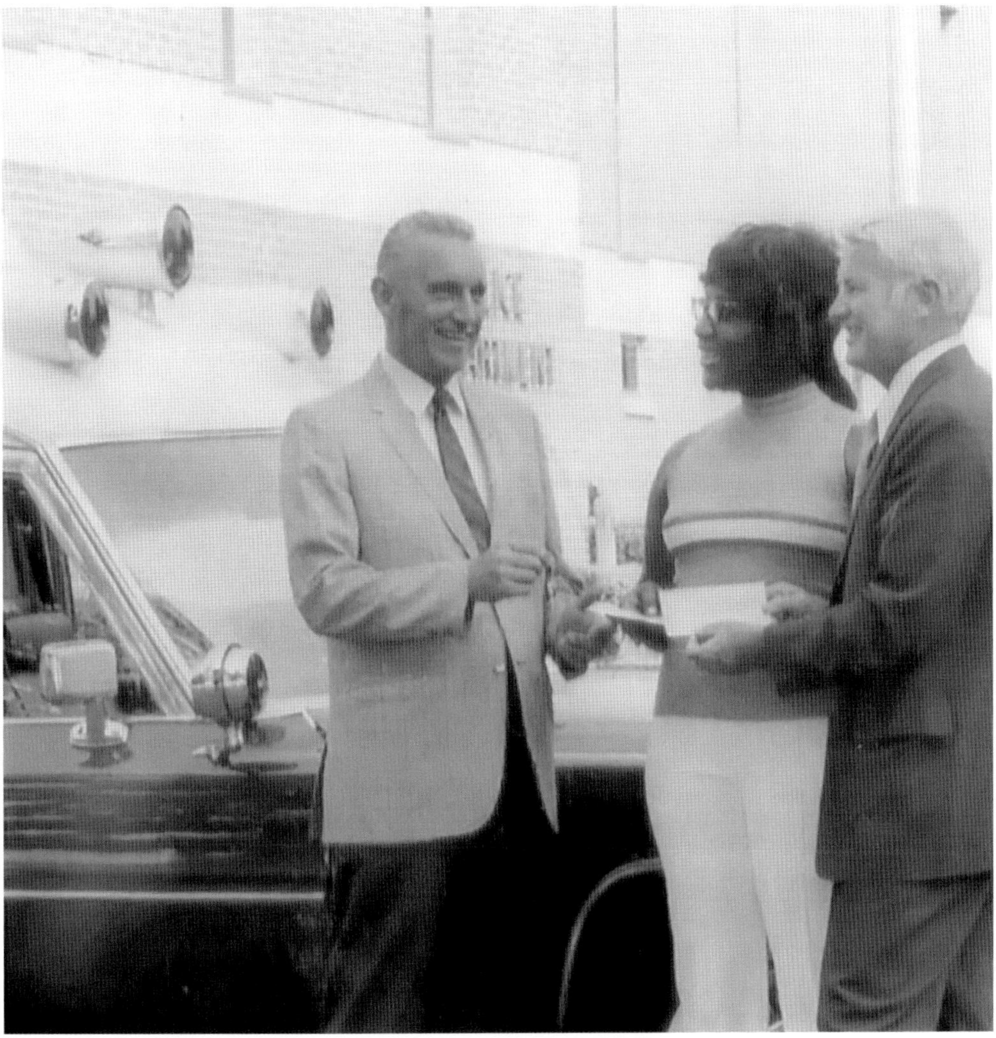

### Harry McFarland

Harry McFarland (at left with Philadelphia Phillies manager Pat Corrales) came from New England in 1968 to serve as recreation department director as Levitt and Sons was still developing the new town. Working with men such as Roy Paige and William Lewis, McFarland bolstered the recreational opportunities already offered by local youth groups. Working with Levitt, McFarland helped to develop Fairmount Park and Broido Park, whose band shell for years was home to the Willingboro Jazz Festival. "They never reneged on a promise," McFarland recalled of Levitt and Sons. "A number of things they did with a handshake." Among his greatest accomplishments were the creation of 180-acre Mill Creek Park (famous for its sledding hill, wooded trails, tennis courts, playing fields, and picnic areas) from the former Leonard Kimble farm and the renovation of the former John F. Kennedy High School into a community center. McFarland also led the township's public works department and served as interim township manager in 1974. He retired in 2007. (Courtesy Harry McFarland.)

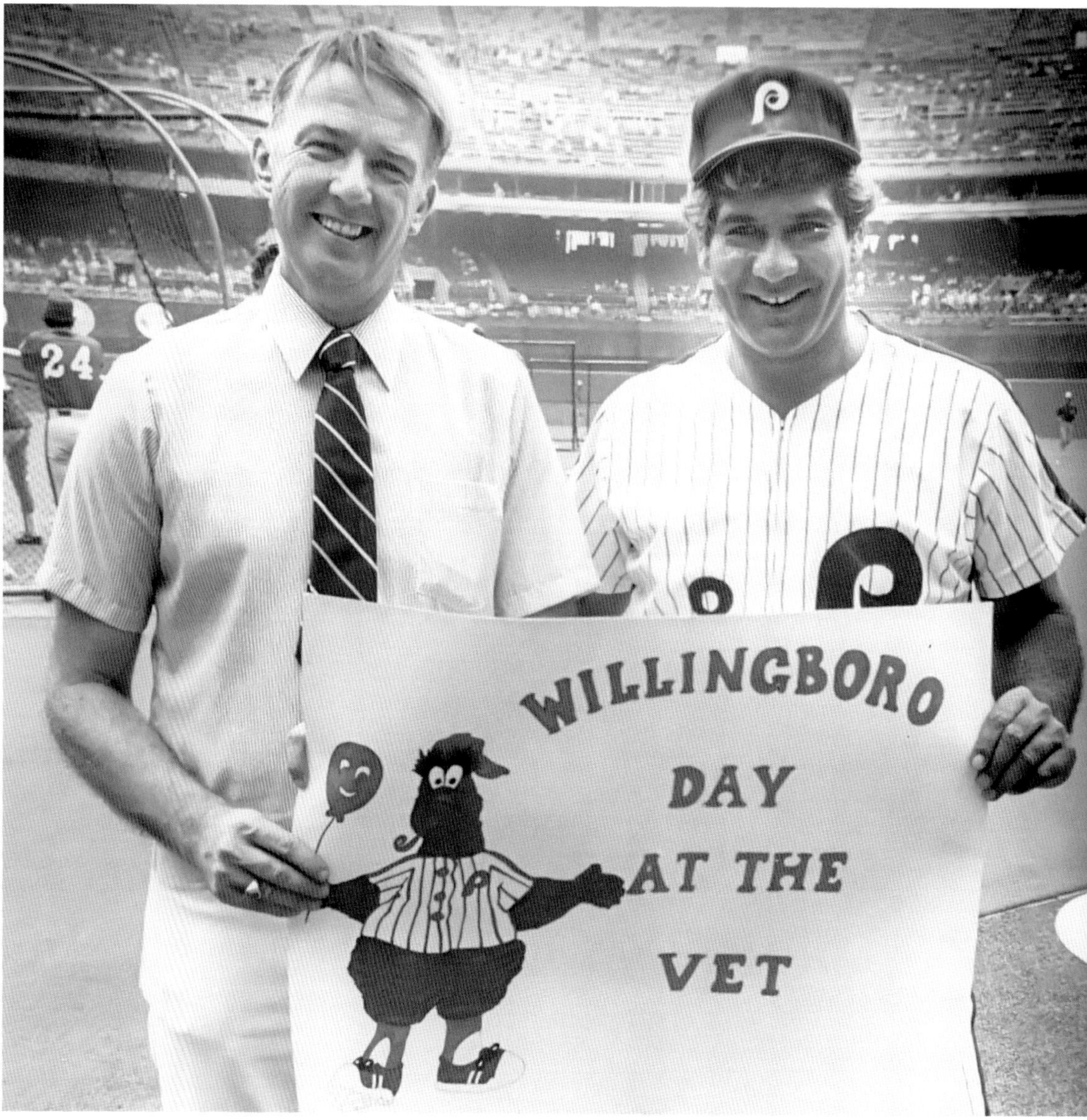

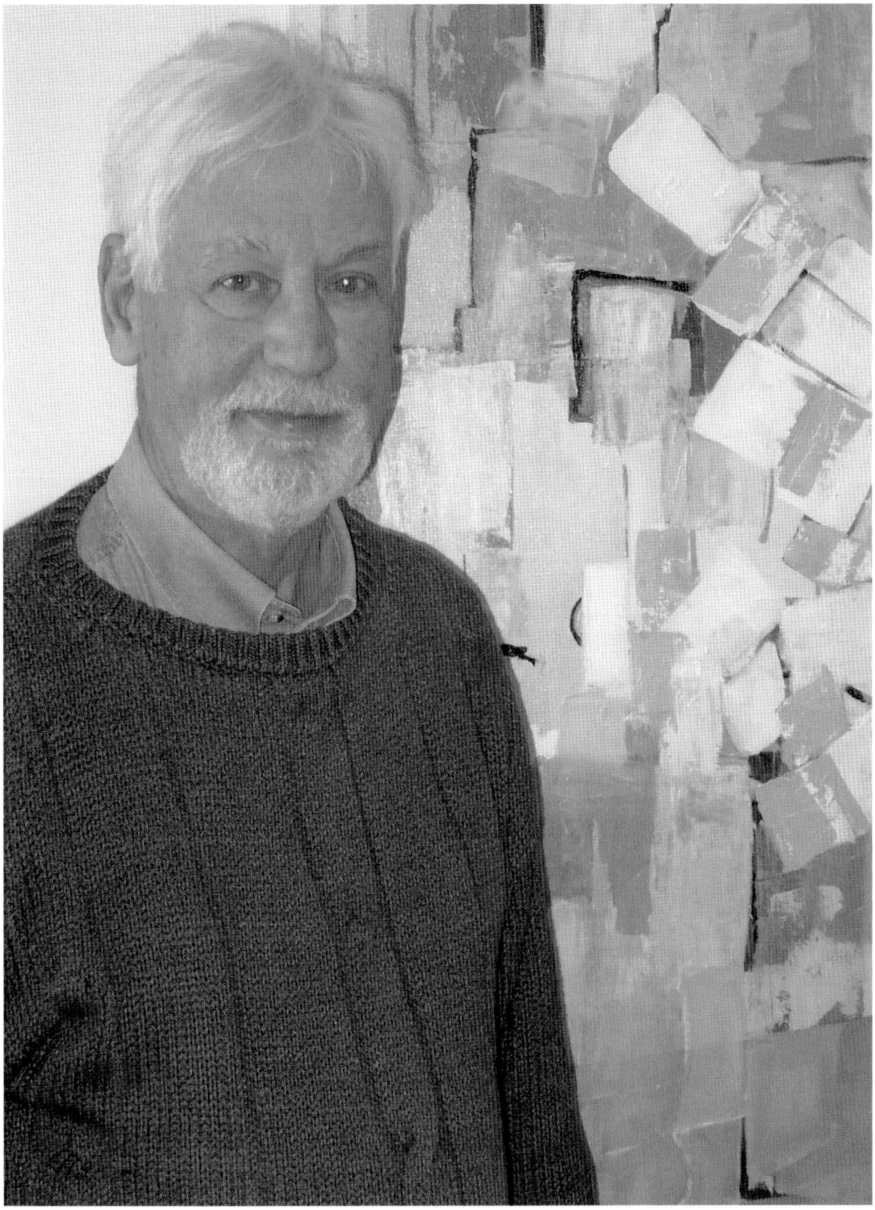

**John Tegley**

A native of Pennsylvania, John Tegley came to Willingboro from Easton, Massachusetts, in 1974 to serve as township manager (succeeding Jack McHugh). The town had grown to more than 40,000 inhabitants and was becoming more racially diverse. Tegley and township council worked to provide residents with access to government, services, jobs and organizations—Tegley recalls playing on a township-organized volleyball team with future Olympian Cindy Stinger. Seeing the need for a domestic abuse shelter, the township purchased a farmhouse from J. Cresswell Stuart and created Providence House. The shelter is operated by Catholic Charities of the Diocese of Trenton and is open to all county residents. Tegley resigned in 1986 to become chief operating officer for Zurbrugg Health System. He later also served as township manager in Mount Holly. A painter, Tegley and his wife, Janet, still reside in Willingboro.

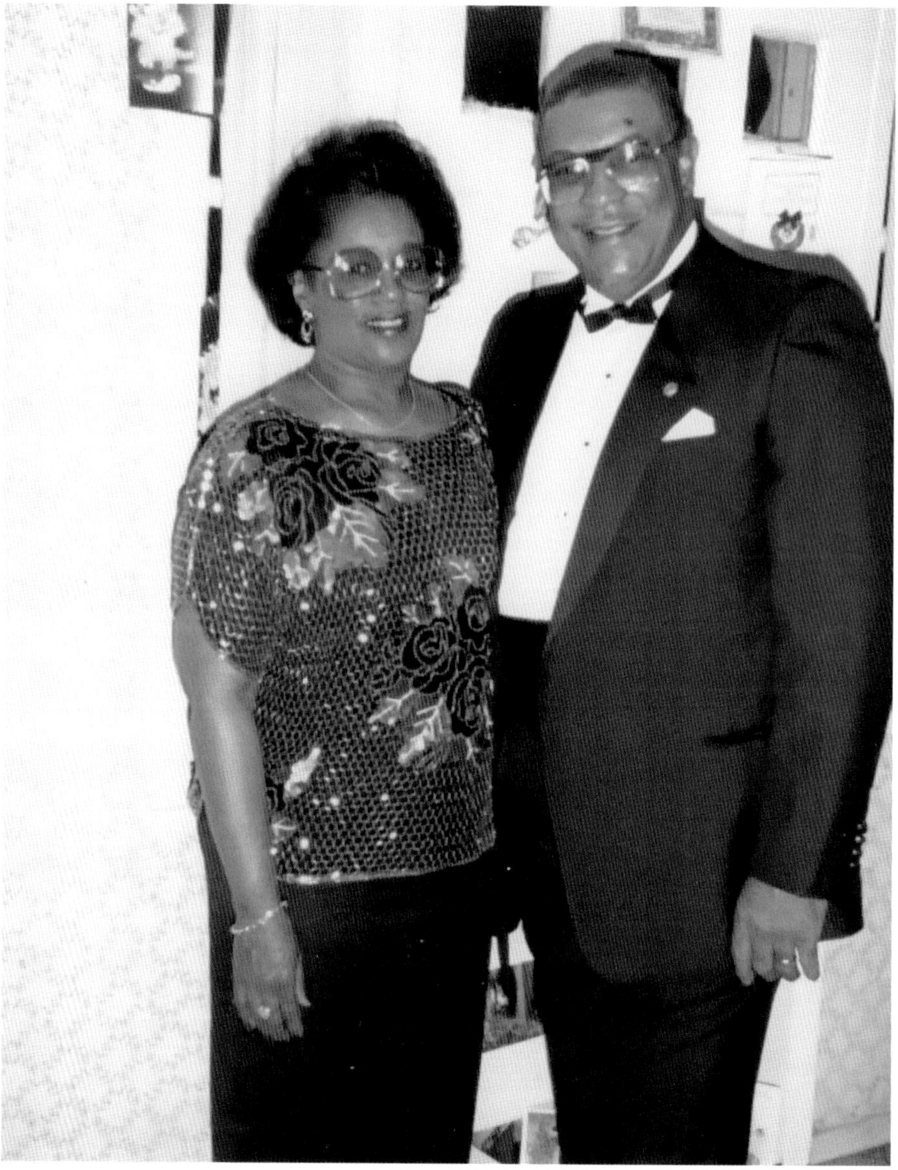

**Chester M. Whittaker**

A native of Tarboro, North Carolina, Chester Whittaker was a mentor to his children and neighborhood youth. Whittaker graduated from Virginia State's ROTC program and was commissioned an officer at Fort Dix. A special-education teacher and track coach, Whittaker later worked for the New Jersey Department of Education, overseeing youthful offenders; as director of minority affairs for the National School Boards Association; as special assistant to former governor Brendan Byrne; and as an assistant to the president of Burlington County College. Whittaker gave advice and helped black men and women get jobs and advance in their careers, a concept he called the "multiplication of power." Yet he did not miss the important events in his children's lives. As a boy picking tobacco, Whittaker and his brother used to have preaching contests, and before his death in 1997, Whittaker "answered the call" and became a Baptist minister. In 2009, Whittaker's daughter Celeste documented her father's life in the book *The Epitome of Fatherhood.* (Courtesy Celeste Whittaker.)

 22

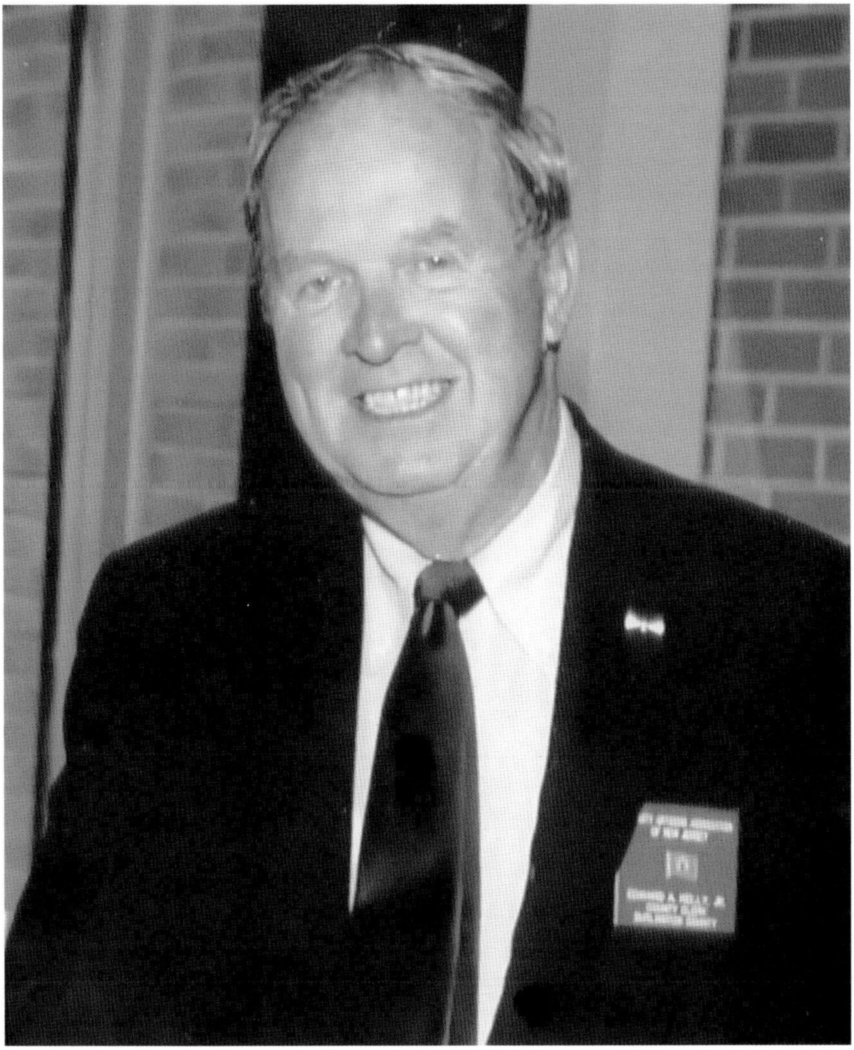

**Edward Kelly**

Affable and ever-smiling, Edward Kelly earned the unofficial title "Mr. Willingboro." Born in 1927 in Philadelphia to Irish immigrant parents, Kelly played basketball and football growing up. During World War II, Kelly served in the North Atlantic and in the Pacific, and spent 22 years in the US Army Reserve. Kelly got involved in the community shortly after he and his wife, Millie, moved into Willingboro in 1958. Named "Outstanding Young Man of the Year" by the Jaycees in 1960, Kelly served on the school board from 1961 to 1964. In 1966, he was elected to township council as a Republican and served as mayor in 1970. In 1969, Kelly was elected Burlington County clerk, a position he held until 1994. Active in more than 70 organizations, including Corpus Christi Roman Catholic Church, the Rotary, the American Red Cross, Knights of Columbus, Chamber of Commerce, and Boy Scouts, Kelly has spent countless hours advocating for the military and veterans. A leader of the Burlington County Military Affairs Committee, he supported Fort Dix and McGuire Air Force Base when both installations faced closure, and he is a lifetime member of the Veterans of Foreign Wars, the American Legion, and the Burlington County Detachment of the Marine Corps League. As the *Burlington County Times* once put it, "From the wearing of the green to waving the Stars and Stripes, [Kelly] has a gleam in his eye and urbanity hard to match. A man for all occasions, he gets things done." (Courtesy Willingboro Public Library.)

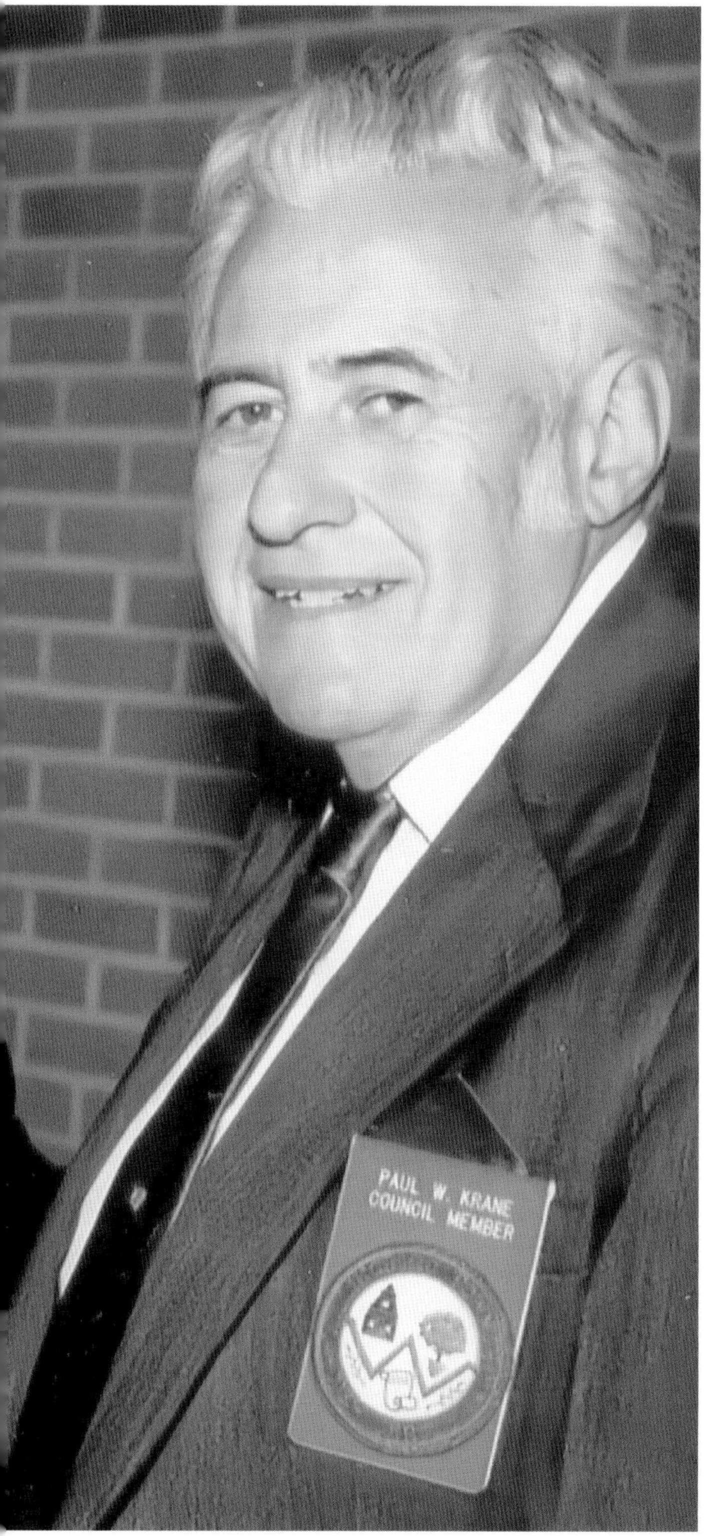


**Paul Krane**

Often called Willingboro's elder statesman, Paul Krane served on township council for more than two decades. He is an illustration of a true American success story. As German troops invaded his native Romania in 1940, Krane and 13 other Jewish families fled Europe for Palestine. Lacking proper documents, the French in Syria sent them to Iraq. Caught in an uprising against the British, the group managed to get to India, and eventually Cuba. But they arrived just before the Japanese bombed Pearl Harbor, and they were forced to wait out the war in Cuba. Krane attended the University of Havana, even though he spoke neither English nor Spanish. In 1945, the family settled in New York, with Krane working in a knitted goods business. He went to school at night, earning bachelor's and master's degrees. In the late 1950s, Krane and his wife Lillian, now living in Philadelphia, heard about the new Levittown. They moved into the first section, Somerset Park, in November 1958. Murray Zidel, who was elected mayor in 1962, encouraged Krane to become active in community affairs. He worked on voter registration and the zoning board before being elected to township council in 1967. Quiet and dignified, Krane was known as a voice of reason and was respected in and out of Willingboro. During one of his terms as mayor, he led a delegation to Wellingborough, England, Willingboro's sister city. He retired from the New Jersey Department of Commerce in 1991. In 2000, Krane was named to the New Jersey State League of Municipalities Elected Officials Hall of Fame. Krane died in 2010. (Courtesy Willingboro Public Library.)

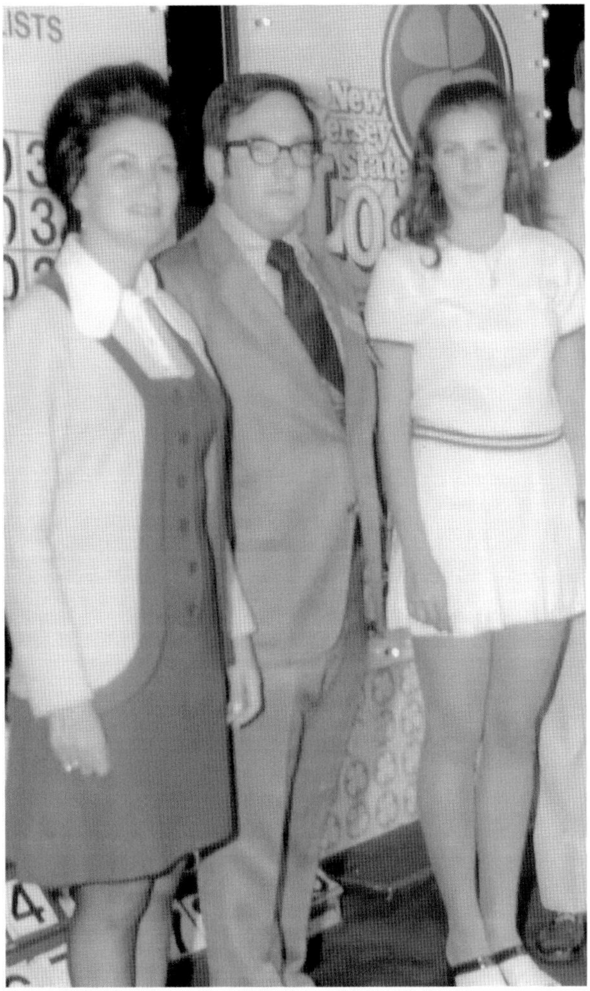

**William J. Kearns Jr.**
Perhaps no one knows more about Willingboro government and municipal law than William J. Kearns Jr. Kearns (center) earned his undergraduate degree from Saint Peter's College and his law degree from the Rutgers University School of Law. He was admitted to practice before the New Jersey Supreme Court and US District Court in 1965, and later to the US Supreme Court, US Tax Court, and the US Court of Appeals. Kearns was elected to three terms on township council, serving twice as mayor, as well as sitting on the planning board and local assistance board. During his time on council, Kearns was instrumental in the founding of a domestic violence abuse shelter in town and advocated open government. Senior partner in the law firm Kearns, Reale & Kearns, he served as Willingboro township solicitor for nearly 20 years, and now serves as attorney for several municipalities. A frequent lecturer on local government and government ethics, Kearns is general counsel for the New Jersey State League of Municipalities. He is a past president of the International Municipal Lawyers Association (IMLA) and the Burlington County Bar Association, and is a permanent trustee of the New Jersey Institute of Local Government Attorneys (ILGA). He holds the diplomat designation from the ILGA and is one of the original IMLA Fellows. He is a recipient of the Michael A. Pane Award for Ethics in Municipal Government and was a member of the Governor's Task Force on the Local Government Ethics Law. In 2011, he was named a "Super Lawyer" by *NJ Monthly* magazine. Kearns also has been active in the United Way, Family Service, Knights of Columbus, Jaycees, and Rotary. He writes about wine and classical music. (Courtesy *Burlington County Times*.)

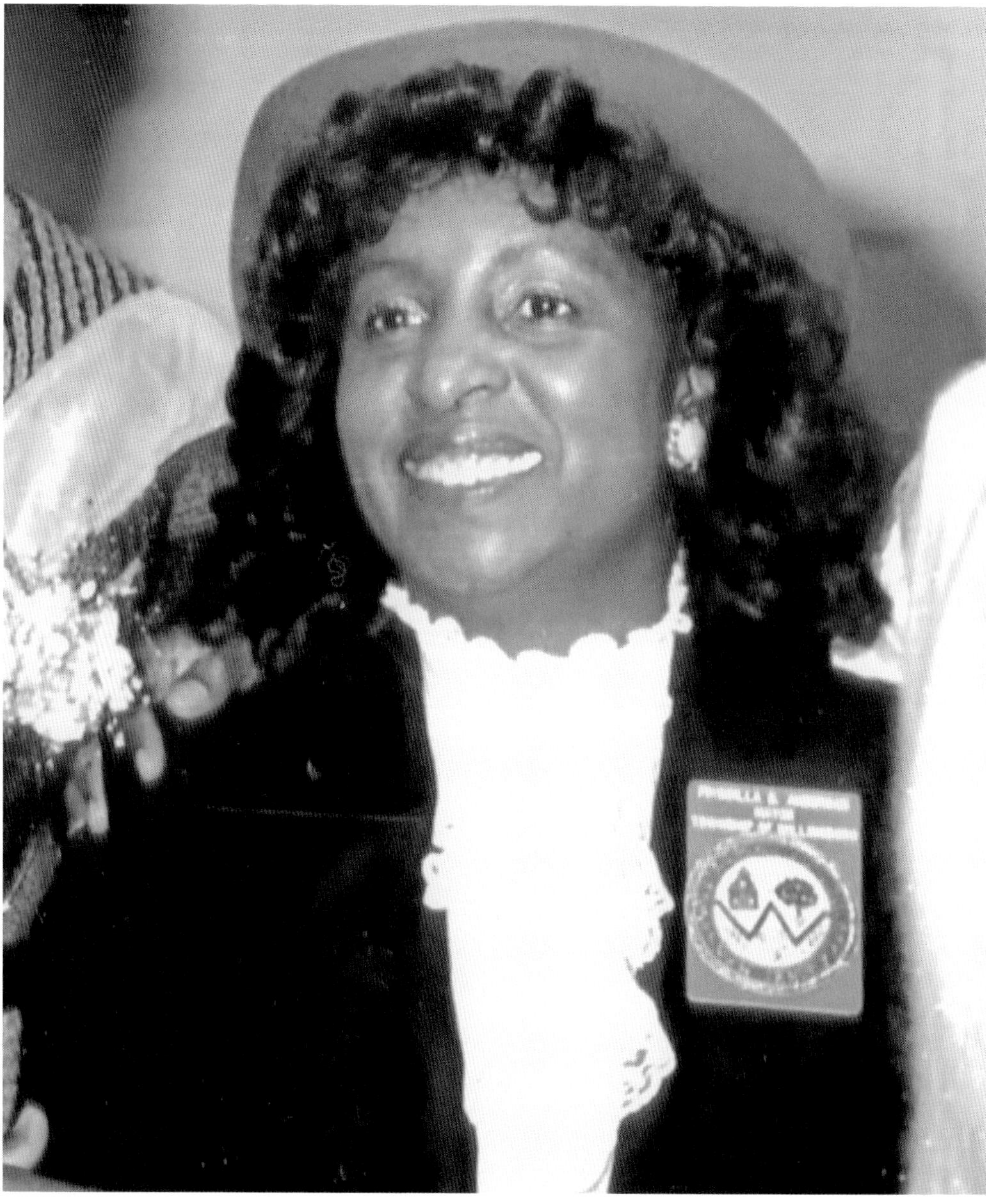

**Priscilla Anderson**

A teacher and guidance counselor with bachelor's and master's degrees in education, Priscilla Anderson was elected to township council in 1981, 1985, and 1989, holding the mayor's post in 1984 and 1991. Anderson had a special interest in young people and established the Willingboro Youth Achievement Awards to recognize their service to the community. Twice a visiting fellow at Princeton University, in 1988 Anderson published *The History and Contributions of Black Americans to the Development of Willingboro*; the treatise has become a resource for historians and sociologists. In 1991, Anderson switched from the Democratic to the Republican party and became the first black legislator from Burlington County to serve in the state assembly. She served until 1993. Anderson later served as Burlington County Bridge Commission vice chairwoman. In 2012, she was honored as a Notable Woman of New Jersey. (Courtesy *Burlington County Times*.)

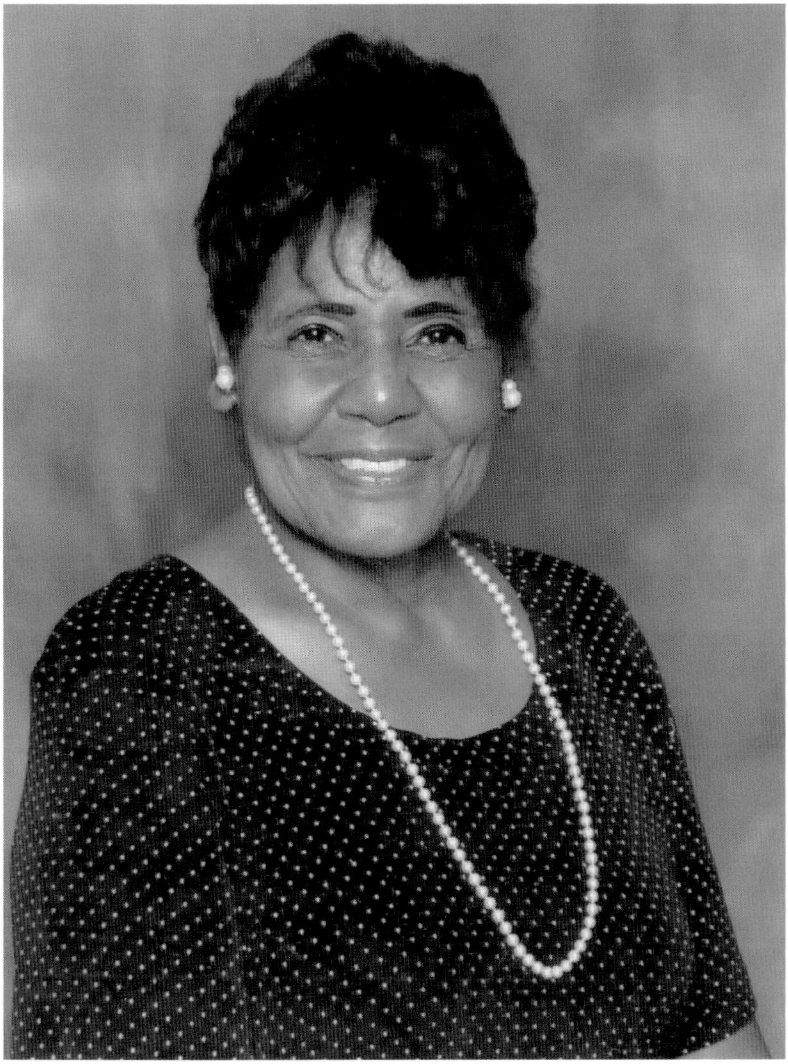

**Marie White Bell**

Marie White Bell is a trailblazer in every sense of the word, with her life and career serving as an inspiration to African American women and legions of others. A native of York, Pennsylvania, Bell became a research chemist with Hoffmann-LaRoche in Piscataway. But some volunteer work at her church got her interested in the law, and after she and her husband, Dr. Conrad Bell, moved to Willingboro, she attended Seton Hall University at night, graduating in 1973. Bell found her way into law and politics, working on the campaign of Gov. Brendan Byrne. She became the first African American woman elected to Willingboro Township Council, and in 1980, its first black female mayor. In 1981, she was elevated to the bench, becoming the first black female municipal judge in Burlington and Camden Counties. And when she was appointed to the New Jersey Superior Court in 1997, there was yet another milestone: the first black woman to serve in that capacity in Burlington County (she was the first African American female to be a law clerk there as well). Bell officially retired in 2006, but continues to hear cases.

"I always tried to be fair to all," Bell told the *Burlington County Times*. "I thought that I understood African American culture, which gave me, perhaps, a more expansive view of society. But I treated everyone the same, whether the issues were female-oriented or male-oriented." (Courtesy Willingboro Library.)

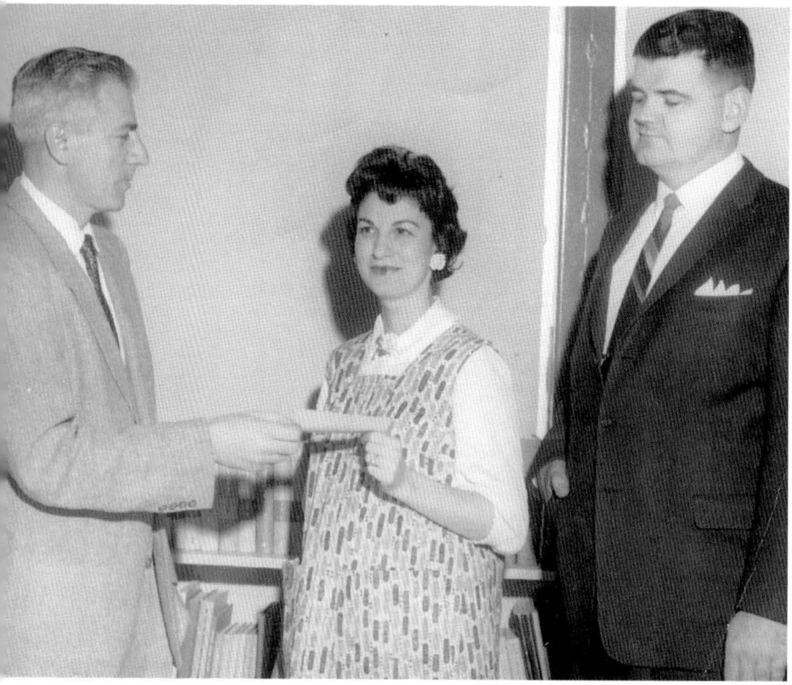

**Catherine Costa**
A mother of three, Catherine Costa (center) moved to Willingboro in the late 1950s and was instrumental in the creation of the township library. Costa was inspired to enter politics when presidential candidate John F. Kennedy visited Willingboro in October 1960. In 1971, she became the first woman elected to the Burlington County Board of Freeholders. She later served in the state assembly and senate, and was head of the New Jersey Alcoholic Beverage Control Board. (Courtesy Willingboro Public Library.)

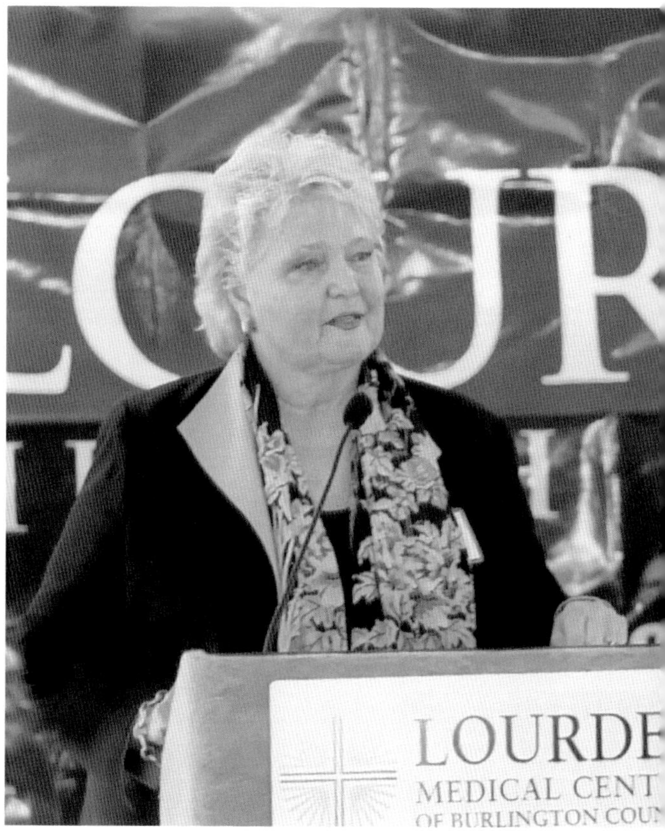


**Diane Allen**
A longtime friend of Willingboro, Diane Allen has represented township residents in the New Jersey Legislature since 1996, first in the assembly and currently in the senate. A graduate of Moorestown High School and Bucknell University—where she founded the swimming team and competed on the rifle team—Allen began a broadcasting career at WJJZ Radio in Mount Holly. She went on to New Jersey Network and then KYW-TV in Philadelphia. She left television in 1994 and today is president of VidComm, Inc. During her time in the media, she won eight Emmy Awards. In the state senate, Allen has served as deputy minority leader and majority whip, and has focused on education, health, senior, and historic-preservation issues. (Courtesy Lourdes Health System.)

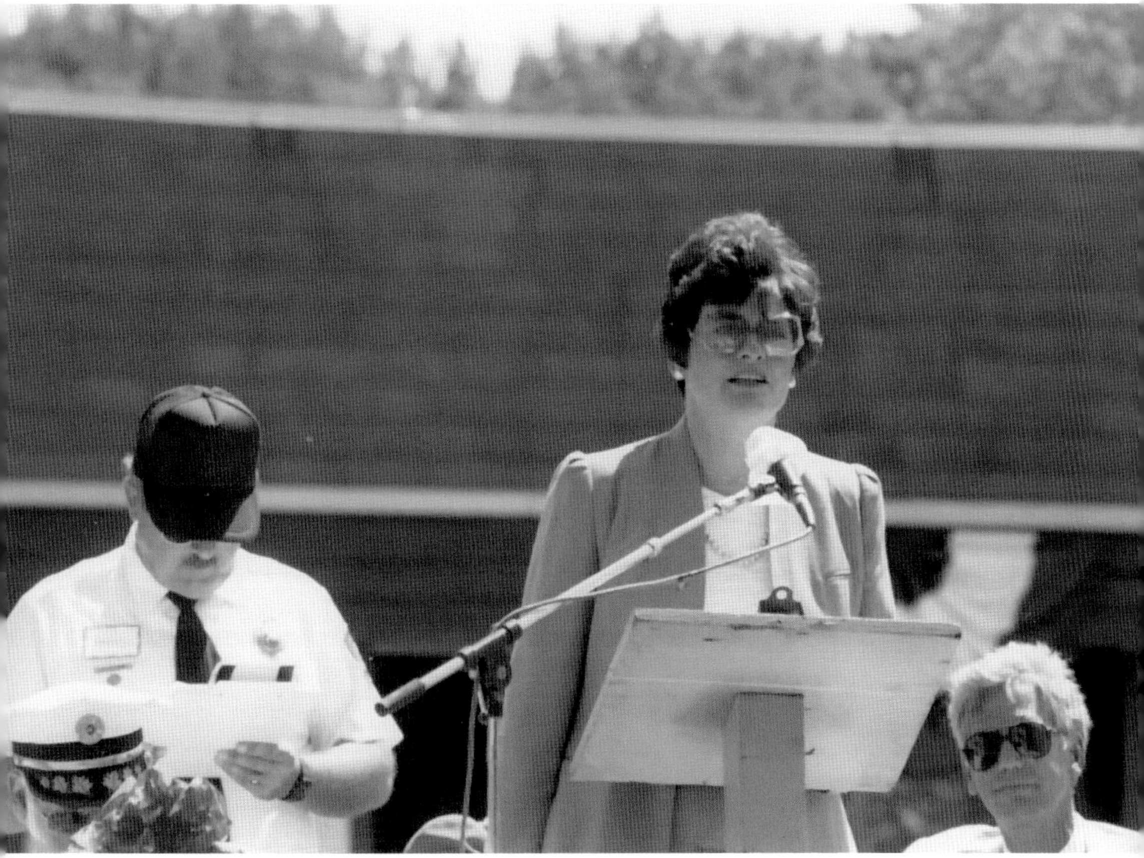

**Barbara Kalik**

Barbara Kalik served on township council from 1972 to 1978, becoming Willingboro's first female mayor in 1974. She served as mayor again in 1977. Outspoken and independent, Kalik served in the New Jersey General Assembly from 1977 to 1991 and chaired or co-chaired the Revenue and Finance Committee and the Joint Appropriations Committee, among others. Her legislative interests resulted in laws addressing workers' right to know about toxic substances in the workplace, child support, tax reform, workers' compensation, and casino regulation. Over the years she received many honors, including from Rotary, the Veterans of Foreign Wars, and the Willingboro Women's Club. (Courtesy Willingboro Fire Department.)

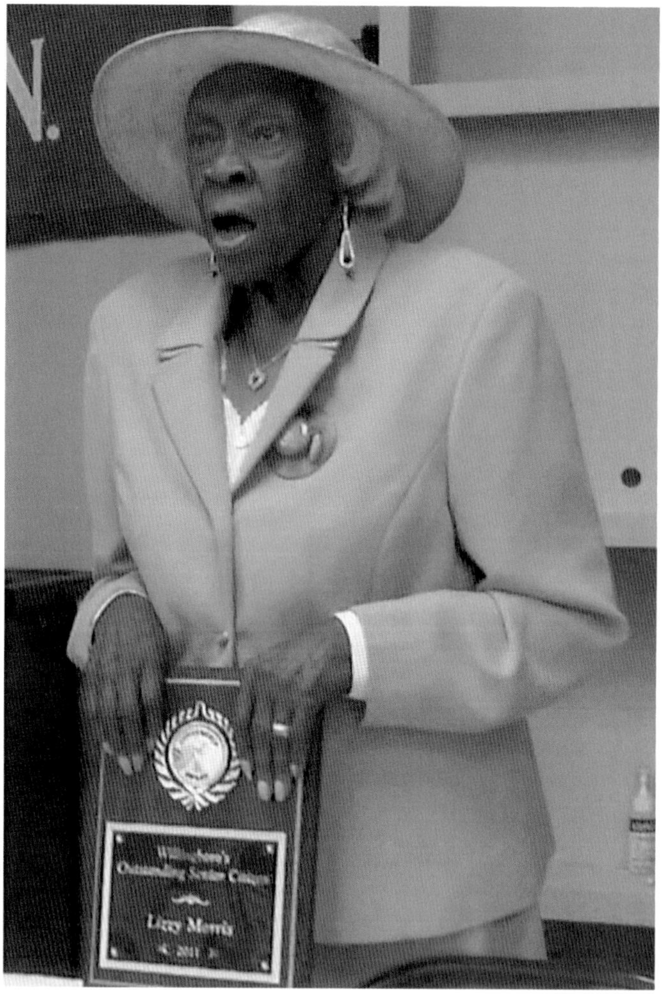

**Lizzie Morris**

A native of West Virginia, Lizzie Morris worked as a seamstress in New York before moving with her husband, Wesley, a merchant marine, to Willingboro in 1966. Lizzie earned the title "town matriarch," known for getting things done and making sure others did their part to help the community. She helped establish the Willingboro Police Athletic League and was active with the Order of the Eastern Star and the Red Hat Society. She was vice chairman of the Willingboro Democratic Committee and president of the Willingboro Democratic Club, worked every Election Day, and was present at every party event. Yet Morris was just as known for her cooking. Before Wesley died in 1993, they prepared lunch on Mother's Day Saturday for Willingboro firefighters, emergency squad members, and police, and donated proceeds to a scholarship fund. She continued the Wesley Morris Memorial Luncheon until her death. Morris also cooked for the squad's monthly meetings, made pies for Rotary—who named her its first Person of the Year—and delivered desserts to Democratic governors, scheduled appointment or not. She also fed families in need, personally collecting food from local stores to fill 30 to 50 baskets, which the police would deliver on Thanksgiving and Christmas. A member of the Willingboro Environmental Commission, Morris annually took hundreds of plain grocery bags to schools for students to decorate, which ShopRite then used to bag food on Earth Day. She also served on the zoning board, youth achievement committee, and parade committee. Before her passing in April 2010 at age 93, she received the Willingboro Lifetime Pillar Award and the Willingboro Education Association Lifetime Achievement Award. (Courtesy Lavonne Johnson.)

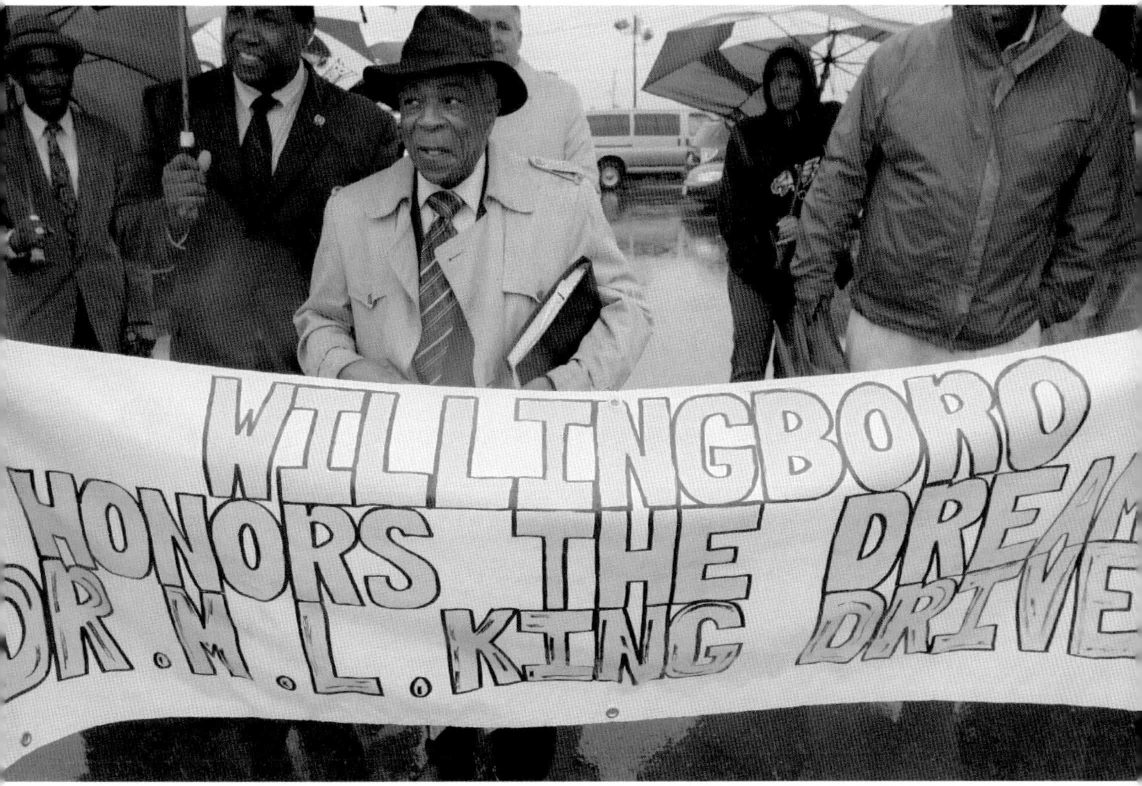


**Jesse Epps**

Jesse Epps (center) has participated in the struggle for civil rights for nearly five decades, including serving as an advisor to Rev. Dr. Martin Luther King Jr. and Pres. Lyndon Johnson. Born in Dublin, Mississippi, during the height of depression and segregation, Epps was trained in labor relations at Syracuse, Rutgers, and Cornell universities. He first worked for the International Union of Electrical Workers in Syracuse, serving as chief steward and an executive board member on its education and civil rights committees. From 1960 to 1972, Epps served as assistant to the international president of the American Federation of State, County, and Municipal Employees, helping to direct field operations in Georgia, Maryland, Ohio, New York, Tennessee, Florida, and Louisiana. In spring 1968, he was hand-picked to go to Memphis to assist in settling the sanitation workers strike there. Epps is credited with inviting Dr. King to Memphis to organize the striking workers. Epps was with Dr. King when he was assassinated on April 4, 1968. Epps later advised President Johnson on matters relating to the participation of youth, students, and minorities in the Democratic Party and in government. Epps founded Neighbors Uniting American Families (NUAF), a grassroots nonprofit organization that seeks to overcome differences in culture, race, religion, and politics. (Courtesy the Associated Press/Julio Cortez.)

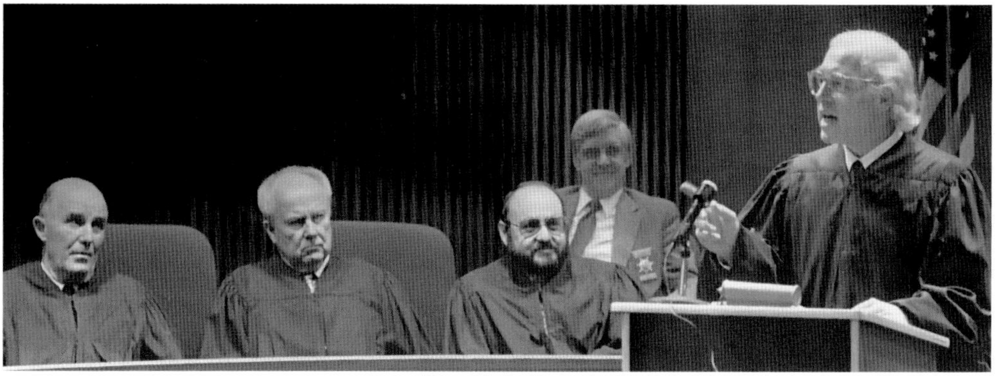

**Victor Friedman**

With long, silver hair curling nearly to his shoulders, Victor Friedman (right) has been described as appearing more like an English magistrate than a Superior Court judge in Burlington County. Raised on a North Jersey chicken farm, Friedman, with his wife, Sally, was one of Willingboro's early residents. Friedman worked for and later partnered with Sidney W. Bookbinder, who served simultaneously as solicitor for the township committee, board of education, planning board, and municipal utilities authority. Friedman later established his own law firm and gained notice as a defense lawyer when he was retained by the state public defender's office to defend a North Jersey mobster. He obtained a plea bargain of six years in prison for four murders, earning him a reputation as a tough negotiator. In 1978, after 18 years of private law practice, Friedman was appointed a Superior Court judge, serving 11 years in the civil division and 11 in the criminal division. Rated the best judge in Burlington County in a statewide survey, Friedman had the reputation of being a tough, demanding jurist who took a defendant's presumption of innocence seriously. Judge Friedman also gained attention when he ordered the state attorney general to turn over records to 18 defendants who accused the New Jersey State Police of practicing racial profiling on the New Jersey Turnpike. Away from the bench, Friedman is known for his warmth, wit, and service to Burlington County College, the Willingboro Chamber of Commerce, and other organizations. (Courtesy Sally and Victor Friedman.)

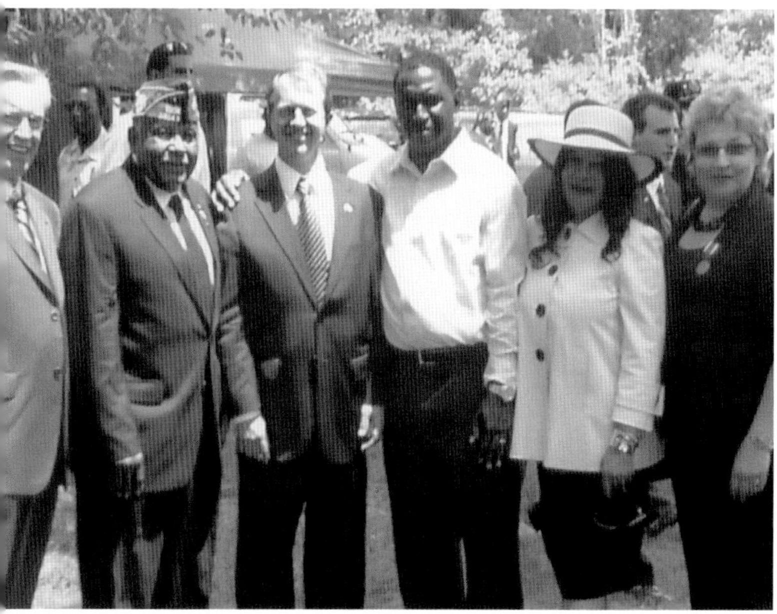

**Eddie Campbell Jr.**

Eddie Campbell Jr. (second from left) was appointed to township council after the death of his wife, Doreatha, in 1998. A retired US Marine, Campbell has served as mayor and deputy mayor. He has helped to shepherd many improvements in town in recent years, including redeveloping the Willingboro Plaza into a modern, multi-use shopping center and renovating the municipal building and Kennedy recreation center. (Courtesy Lavonne Johnson.)

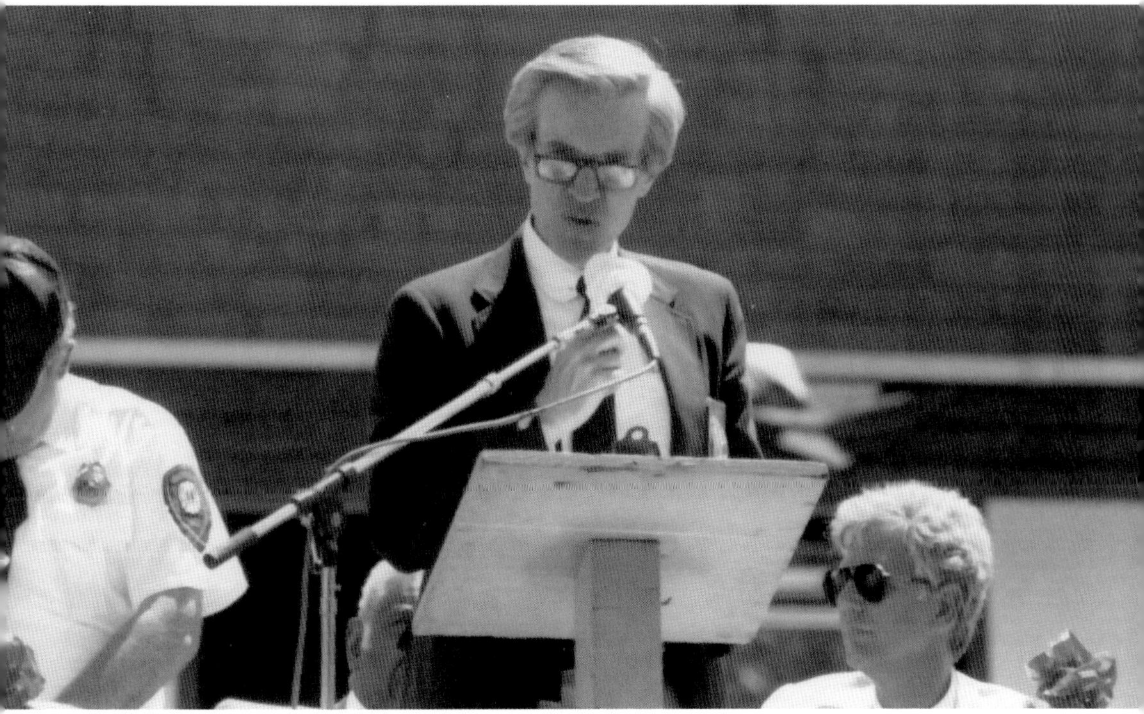

**James Ayrer**
Willingboro's longest-serving public servant, James Ayrer has been on the Willingboro Township Council for more than 30 years. First elected in 1980, the retired director of research for the Philadelphia Public School District has served as mayor and deputy mayor and has focused on providing residents good government while keeping taxes low. Ayrer holds a doctorate in educational psychology with an emphasis on measurement and statistics. He has been a deacon at Corpus Christi Roman Catholic Church for two decades. (Courtesy Willingboro Emergency Squad.)

**Lavonne Johnson**
Lavonne Johnson (center) served on the Willingboro Board of Education from 1989 to 1991 and on Willingboro Township Council from 1996 to 2003. Her accomplishments include working with developers to revitalize the former Willingboro Plaza, renovating the former John F. Kennedy High School into the Kennedy recreation center, and opening the Doreatha Campbell senior housing complex. (Courtesy Willingboro Public Library.)

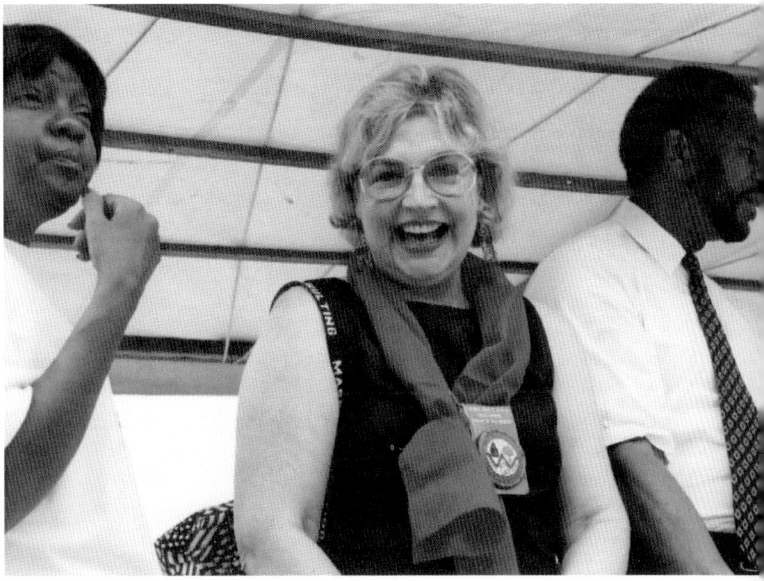

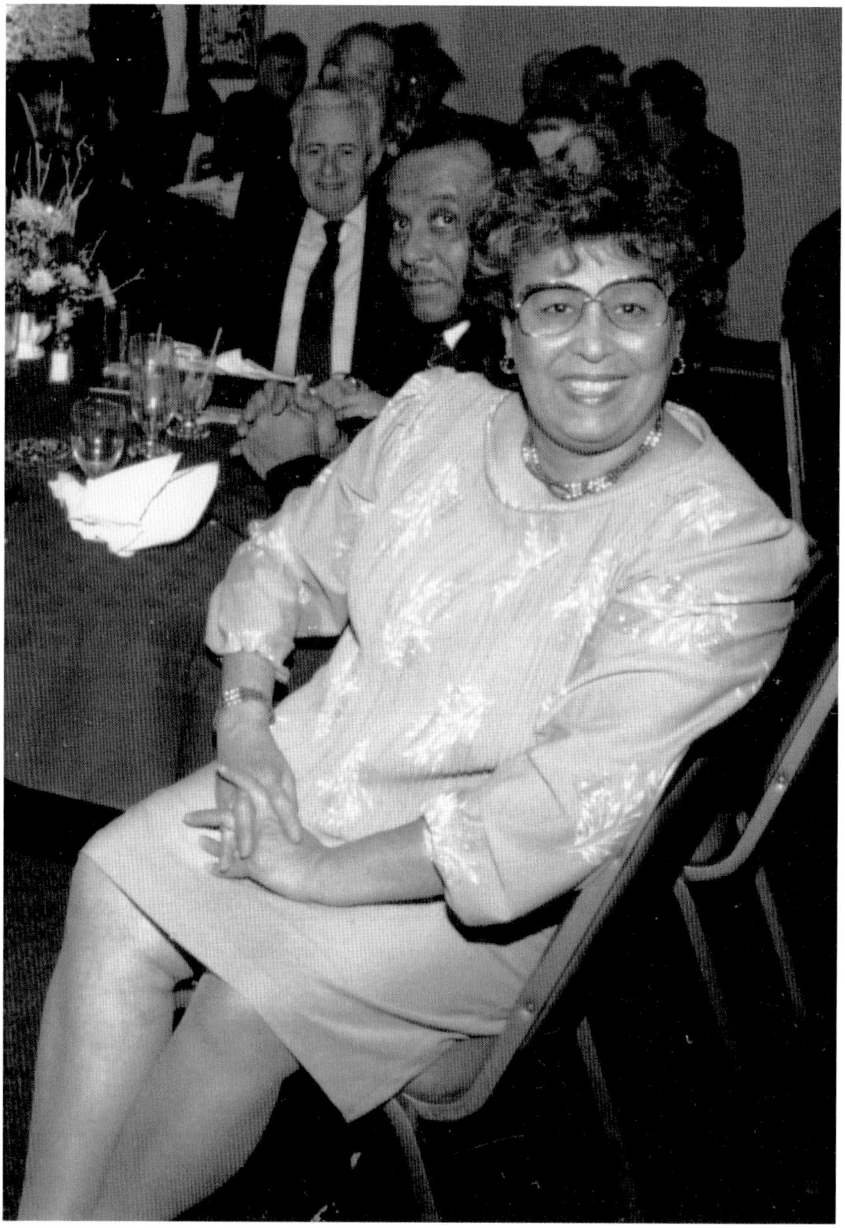

**Doreatha Campbell**

A tireless advocate for education and known for helping anyone in need, Doreatha Campbell served on the Willingboro Township Council from 1983 until her death in November 1998. She served as mayor four times during her 15-year tenure. Campbell was a member of the Willingboro Planning Board, Youth Advisory Board, and Affirmative Action Committee, as well as third vice president of the New Jersey State League of Municipalities. Campbell was active in Tabernacle Baptist Church and served as president of its nurses unit auxiliary for 12 years. In 2000, a five-story senior housing complex, the tallest building in town, was named in her honor. A few years later, a main thoroughfare in the new Willingboro Town Center was named Campbell Drive. Campbell's husband of 47 years, Eddie, was appointed to complete her term. He remains on the Willingboro Township Council today. (Courtesy Willingboro Fire Department.)

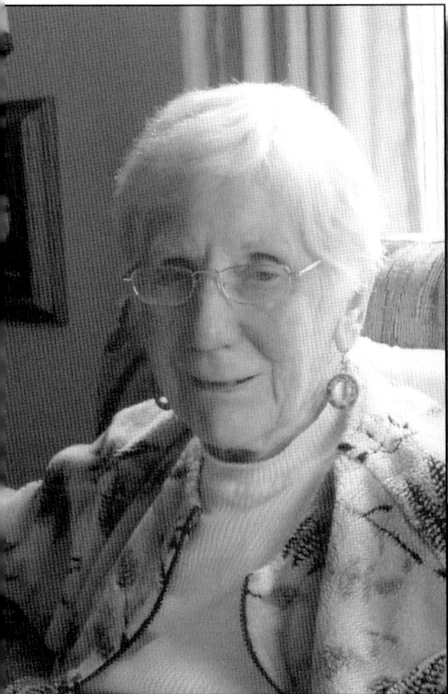

**Marion Huddleston**
Marion Huddleston moved with her family from Chicago to Willingboro in 1960. Huddleston worked in Willingboro public schools for 23 years, first as an elementary school teacher at Buckingham Park School, and then as Language Development Title I coordinator. Her last position was teaching math at Twin Hills Elementary. Huddleston co-founded Literacy Volunteers of Burlington County and served as its first director. She helped establish Friends of the Willingboro Library, and serves on the Willingboro Environmental Commission. (Courtesy Suzanne Woodward.)

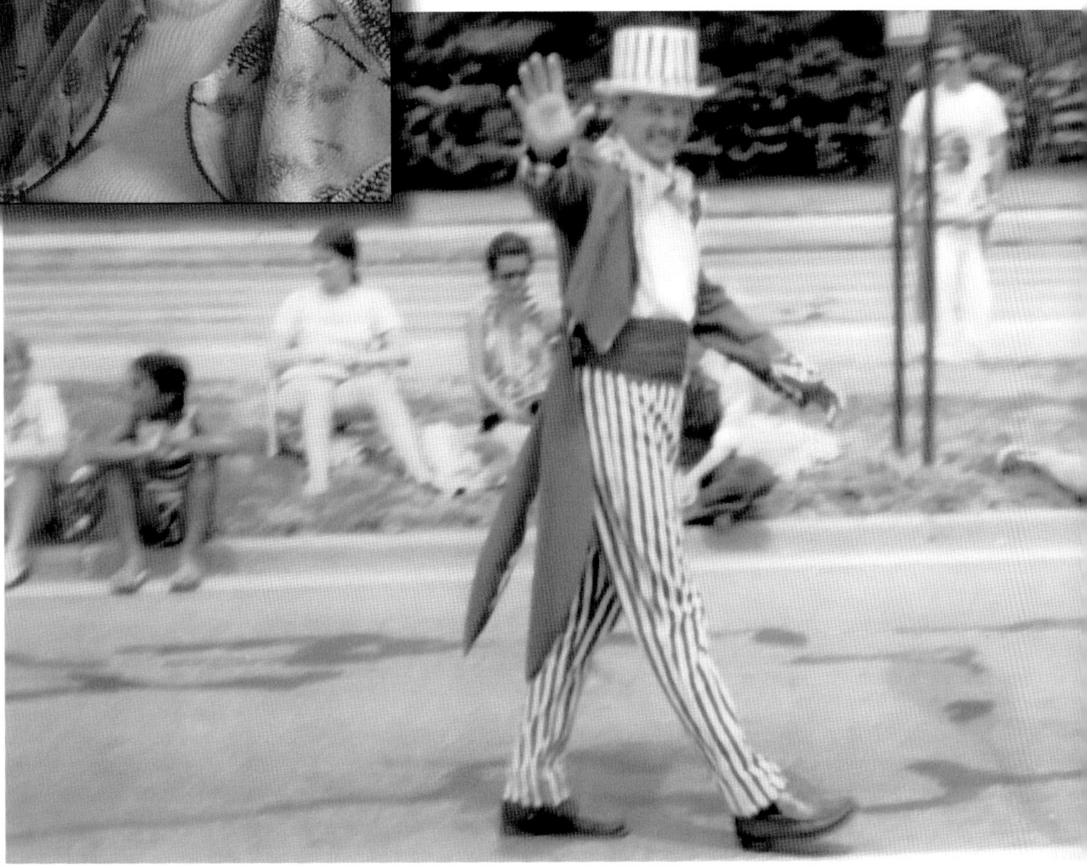

**William McGrath**
A history teacher at Willingboro High School, William McGrath was a member of the Willingboro Township Council and served as mayor in the bicentennial year of 1976. For the Independence Day parade, McGrath led the festivities dressed as Uncle Sam. Serving alongside McGrath that year were William Kearns, Lenore Stern, and Barbara Kalik. (Courtesy William McGrath.)

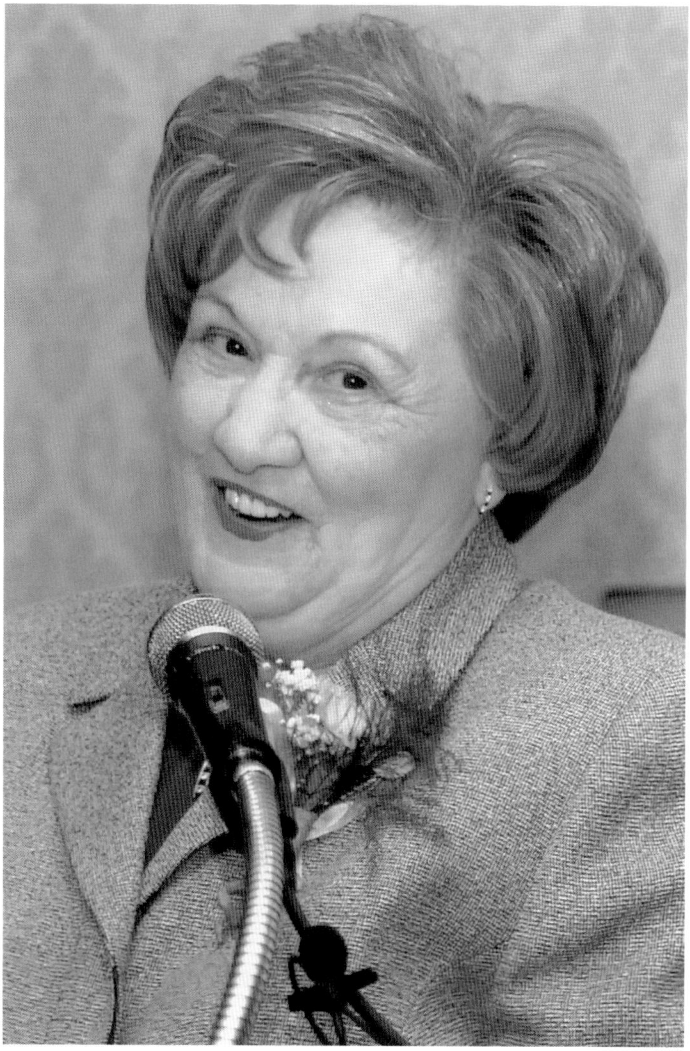

### Millie Gama

Millie Gama came to Willingboro almost by accident. She and her husband, David, were driving from Rochester, New York, looking for a new home. A friendly waitress at Ponzio's Diner in Cherry Hill recommended the growing town of Willingboro. It was a relationship that lasted more than 30 years and benefited both Gama and Burlington County greatly. In 1975, Gama landed the job of executive director of the Willingboro Chamber of Commerce. Under her leadership, the chamber grew from 100 members to more than 400 and changed its name to the Burlington County Chamber of Commerce to reflect its mission as a regional organization seeking to increase visibility of the business community. Gama was on the forefront of redevelopment efforts of Route 130, and she led the chamber until her retirement in 2003. She volunteered for scores of other organizations, including Boy and Girl Scouts, Willingboro Fun Day in the Park, the American Red Cross, the Federal Prison Advisory Committee at Fort Dix, and the Burlington County College Foundation board, where she served as a trustee. Gama received countless awards, including a 2001 Outstanding Woman of Burlington County, the Burlington County Volunteer Center Community Service Award, the YMCA Outstanding Woman Achievement Award, and the Willingboro Rotary's Service Above Self Award. Gama died after a long battle with cancer in 2010. (Courtesy Burlington County College.)

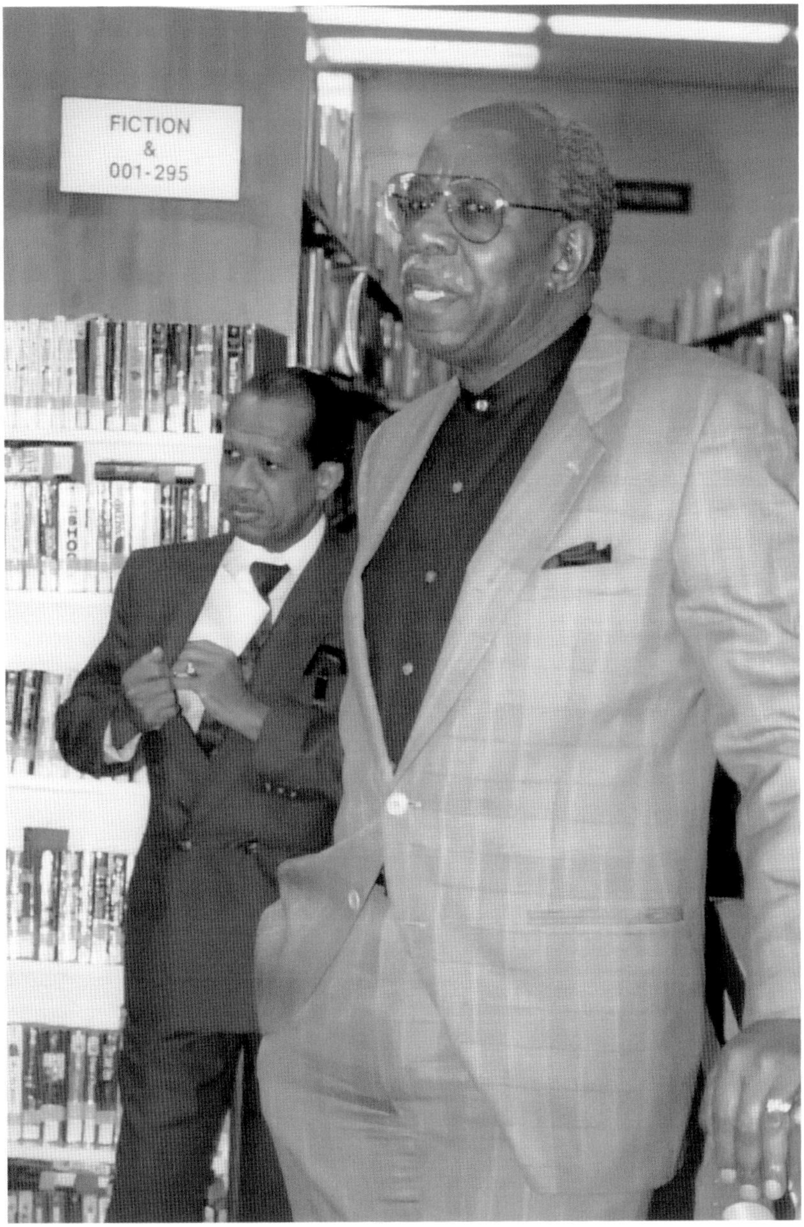


**Delbert Payne**

A native of Philadelphia, Delbert Payne served one term on the school board in the late 1970s and was a long-time trustee of the Willingboro Library. Payne earned a bachelor's degree in chemistry from North Carolina A&T University and a master's degree in organic chemistry from the University of Pennsylvania. He attended the US Army's Civilian Schooling Program and retired as a lieutenant colonel. Payne served as commanding officer of the nuclear, biological, and chemical test division at Fort Greeley, Alaska. He also served as director of human relations and manager of the corporate equal opportunity and corporate social investment programs at Rohm and Haas Company in Bristol, Pennsylvania. Payne was a fan of track and field, and a five-kilometer race is held in his honor each year to benefit the library. (Courtesy Willingboro Library.)

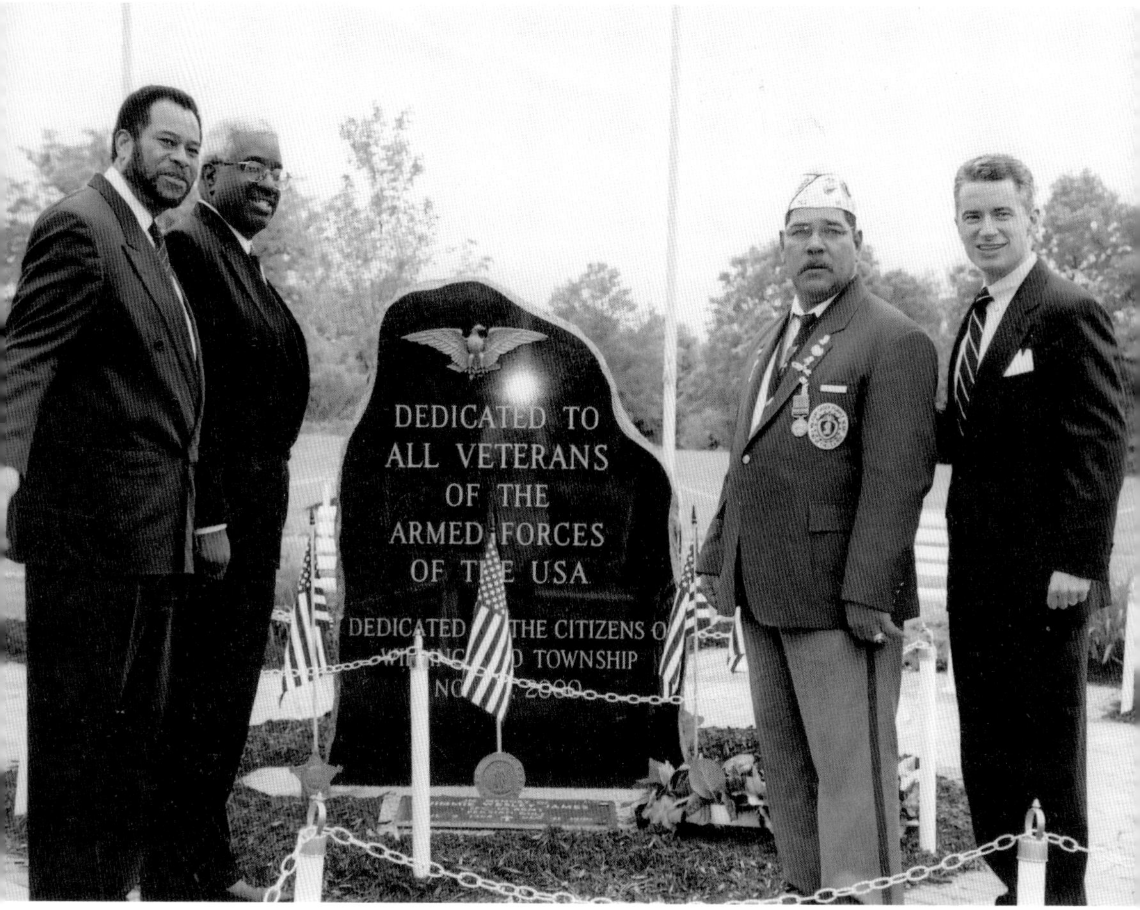


**Ron Dash**

If there's a community event, chances are Ron Dash (second from right) will be there helping out. The oldest of 13 children from Brooklyn, Dash became accustomed to his father bringing home needy people to have dinner with them. Dashed joined the US Marine Corps and was seriously injured, receiving the Purple Heart. He later served in the US Army Reserve and Army National Guard, retiring as a staff sergeant and working for New York City Transit. Dash is a staunch advocate for veterans. He is commander of the Military Order of the Purple Heart Chapter 26 and a member of other military groups, is an adviser to Willingboro Township Council on veterans' issues, and is on Congressman Jon Runyan's Military Academy Advisory Committee. A father of eight, including three in the military, he also prepares meal baskets and organizes a dinner for needy residents during the holidays. (Courtesy Ann Marie Stephenson.)

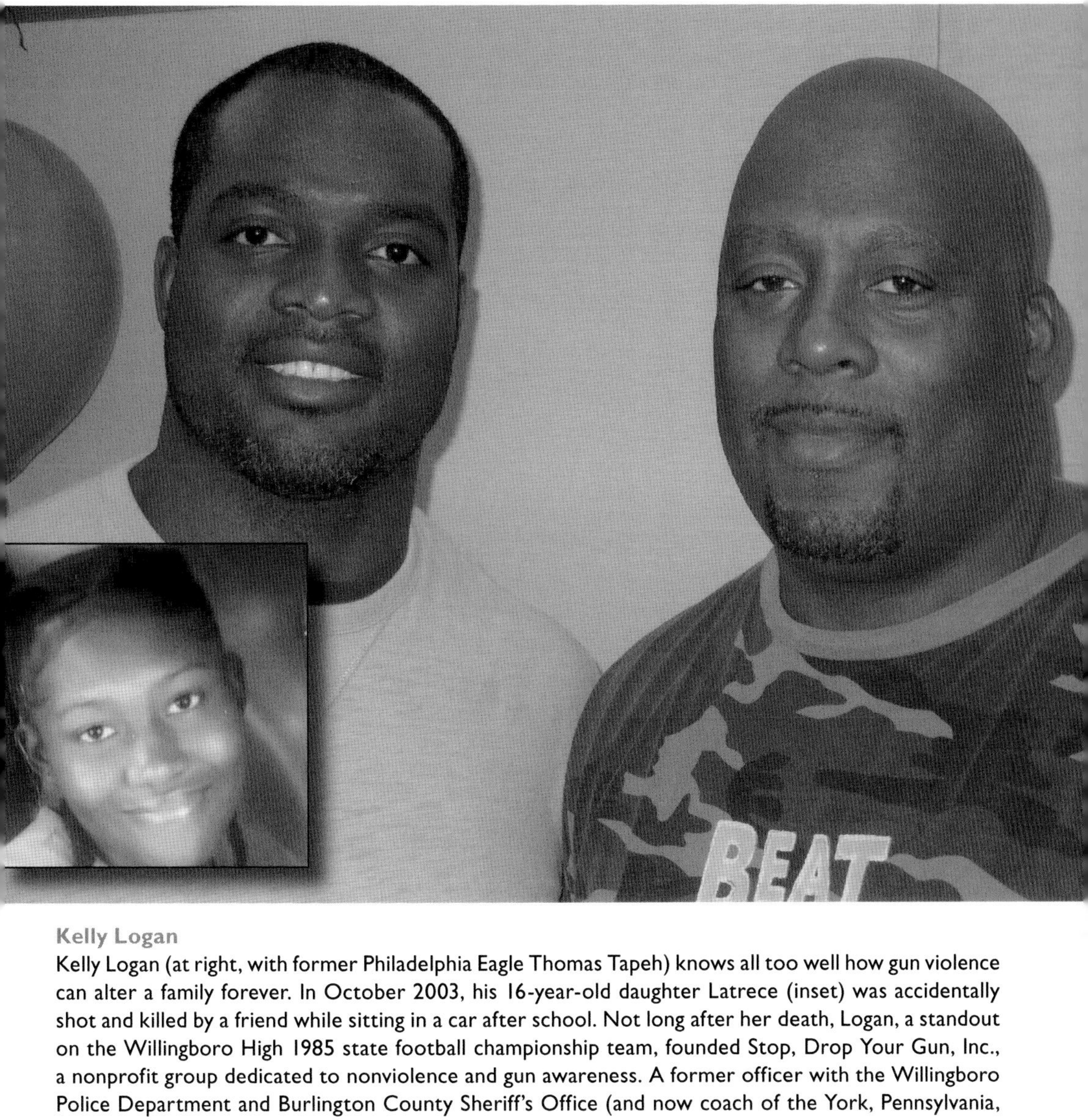


**Kelly Logan**

Kelly Logan (at right, with former Philadelphia Eagle Thomas Tapeh) knows all too well how gun violence can alter a family forever. In October 2003, his 16-year-old daughter Latrece (inset) was accidentally shot and killed by a friend while sitting in a car after school. Not long after her death, Logan, a standout on the Willingboro High 1985 state football championship team, founded Stop, Drop Your Gun, Inc., a nonprofit group dedicated to nonviolence and gun awareness. A former officer with the Willingboro Police Department and Burlington County Sheriff's Office (and now coach of the York, Pennsylvania, Capitals arena football team), Logan spreads his message at schools, churches, and other organizations across the region. He gets young people comfortable talking with their parents and law enforcement about violence, guns, gangs, and bullying to help prevent future tragedies. The group also operates a mentoring program for young people and a support group for fathers who have lost children to violence.

### Marilyn Marshall

As a teacher in Willingboro, Burlington Township, and Waterford, Camden County, Marilyn Marshall recognized that some students need assistance to succeed, from notebooks and pencils to just someone to talk to. As many parents did not have the financial means to buy school supplies, Marshall often paid for the supplies herself. Still seeing a need when she retired in 2006, Marshall joined other educators to establish the Hold On To Education Foundation, which provides scholarships, school supplies, and workshops for youth in the community. A jazz musician, Marshall reached out to some of her music contacts, including former members of the Temptations and Delfonics, to perform at fundraising events. "The best part is the joy I see in the young people's eyes when they've accomplished something," she said. (Courtesy TKM Productions.)

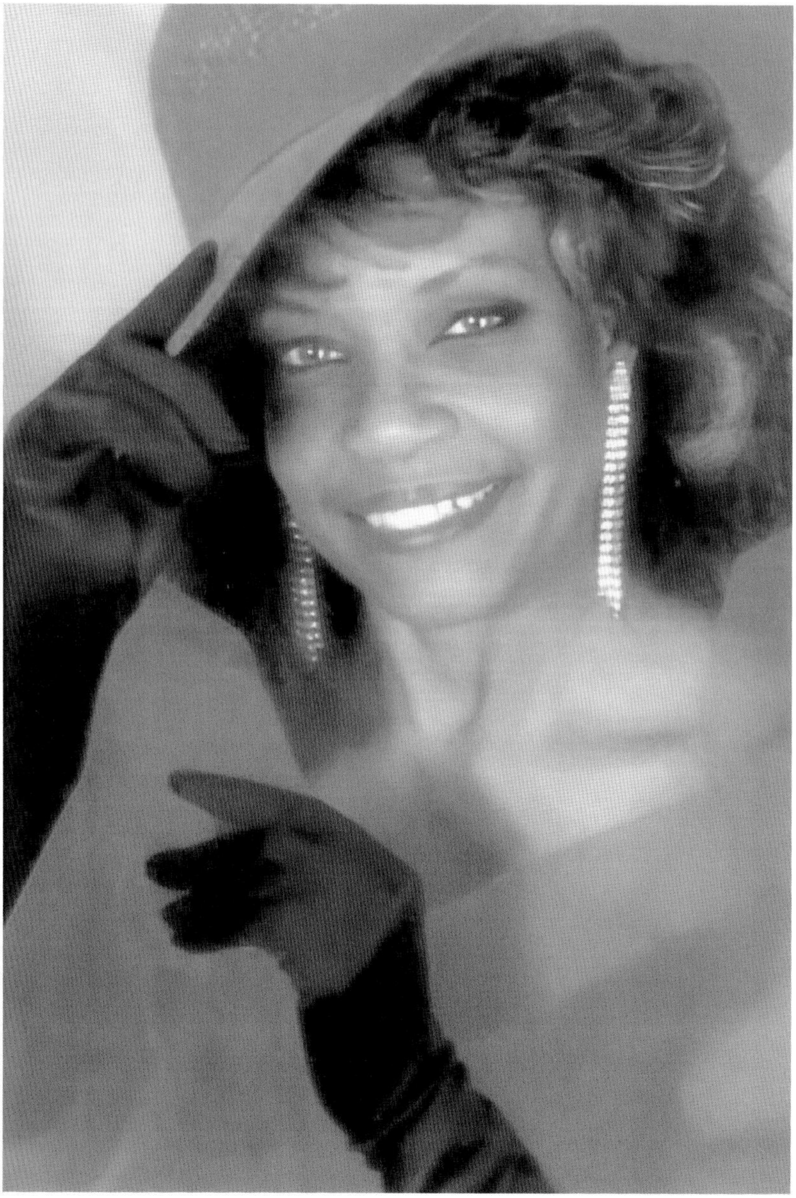

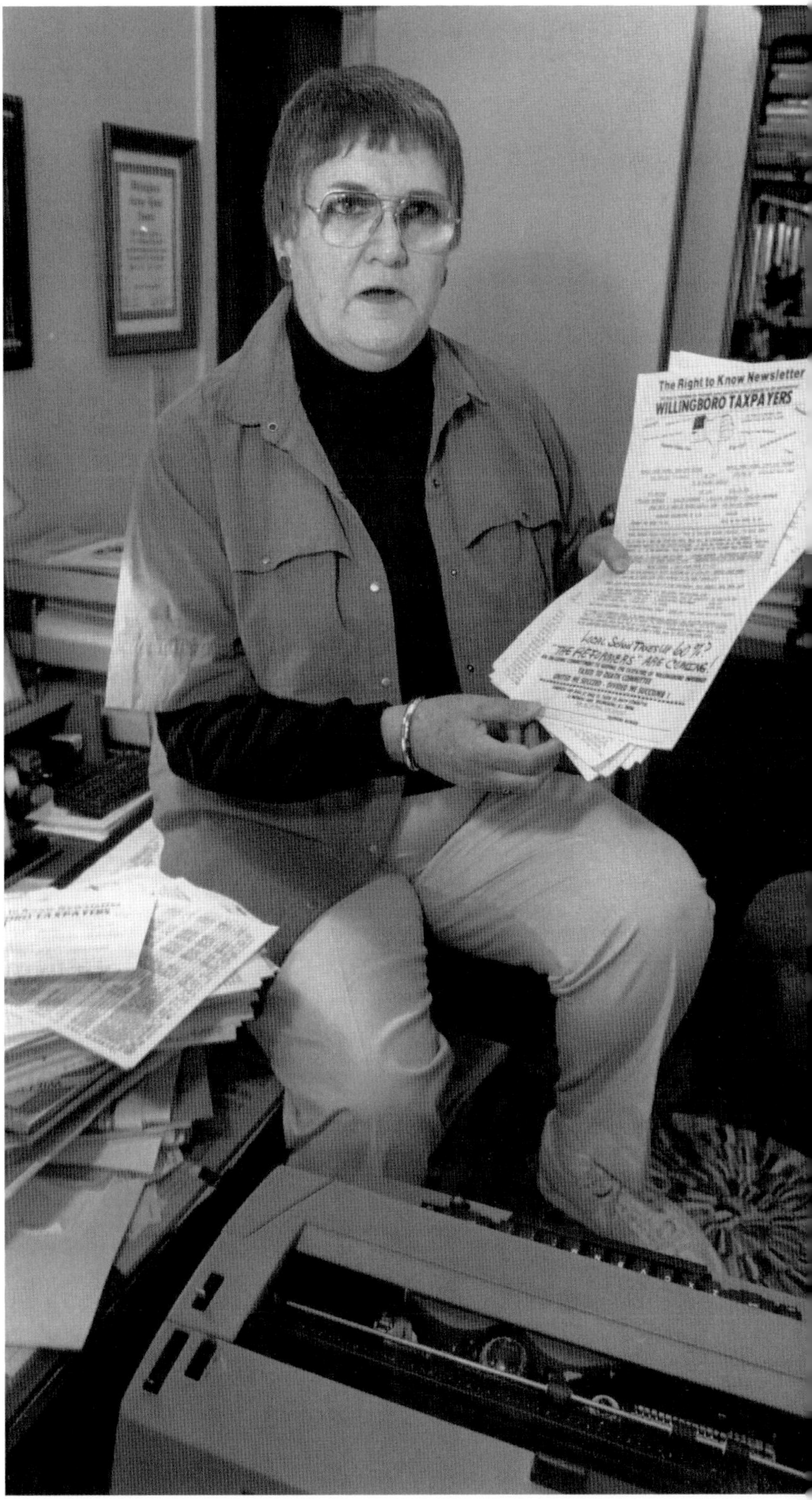


**Margaret Reynolds**
Margaret Reynolds was first elected to the Willingboro Board of Education in 1978, and served on and off for more than two decades, including as president and vice president. A self-described fiscal conservative, Reynolds vocally pressed to keep school spending down. She founded the Taxed to Death Committee, and hammered her points at board and Willingboro Township Council meetings, through letters to the editor, and through her own newsletters. She kept meticulous records and often could be found making copies of years-old board actions and articles for colleagues, the public, and newspaper reporters. Reynolds often clashed with fellow board members and the teachers union, who accused her of not being interested in education. Failing health eventually forced Reynolds to step down from the board and leave the area. (Courtesy the *Philadelphia Inquirer.*)

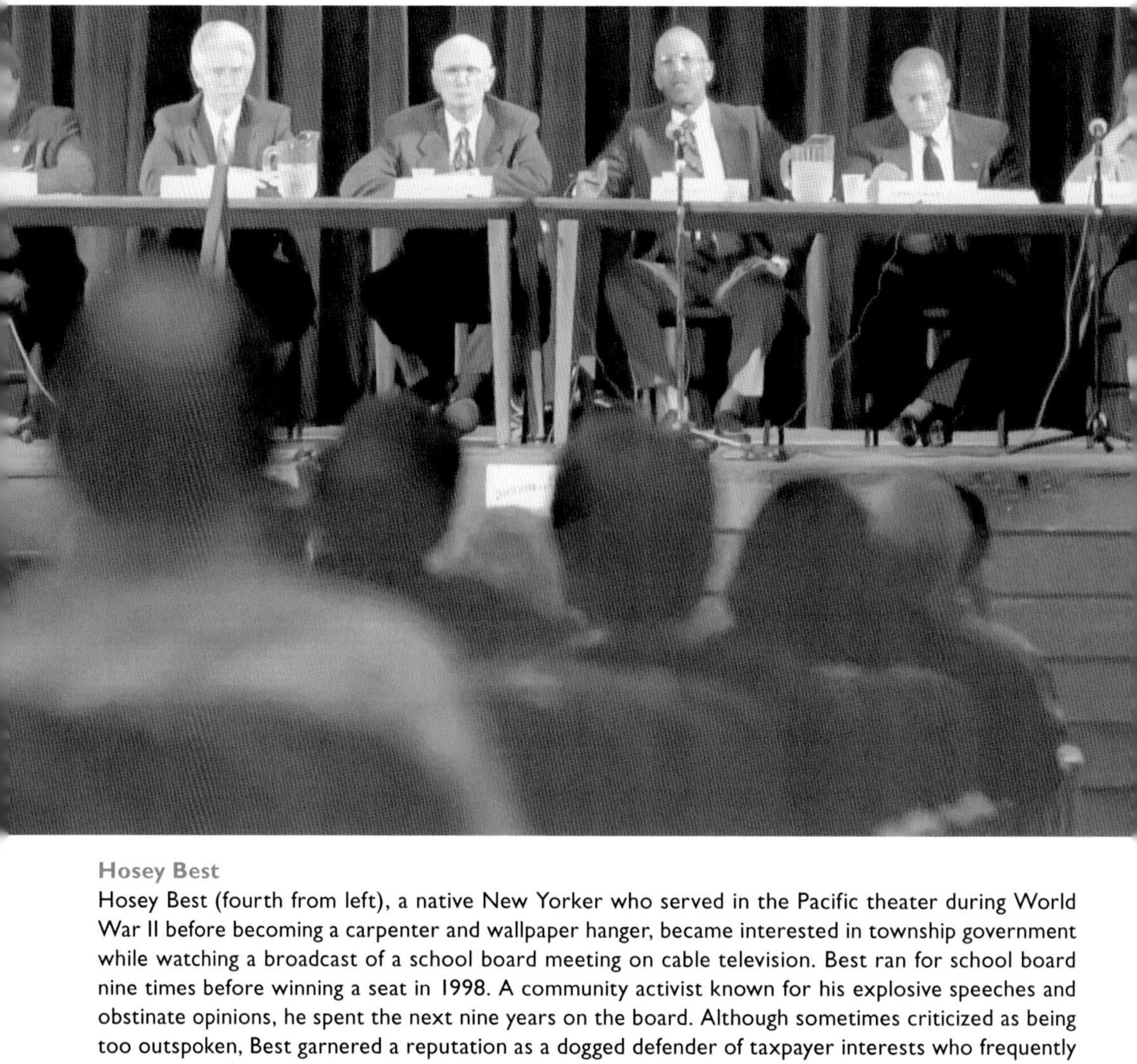

**Hosey Best**

Hosey Best (fourth from left), a native New Yorker who served in the Pacific theater during World War II before becoming a carpenter and wallpaper hanger, became interested in township government while watching a broadcast of a school board meeting on cable television. Best ran for school board nine times before winning a seat in 1998. A community activist known for his explosive speeches and obstinate opinions, he spent the next nine years on the board. Although sometimes criticized as being too outspoken, Best garnered a reputation as a dogged defender of taxpayer interests who frequently criticized teacher contracts and salaries, once performing his own school roof inspection as the board prepared to spend millions on repairs. Best published his own newsletter, *Hosey Best Reports for You*, questioning government spending. Best also ran unsuccessfully for Burlington County freeholder and state assembly. He died in March 2011 at age 86. (Courtesy the *Philadelphia Inquirer.*)

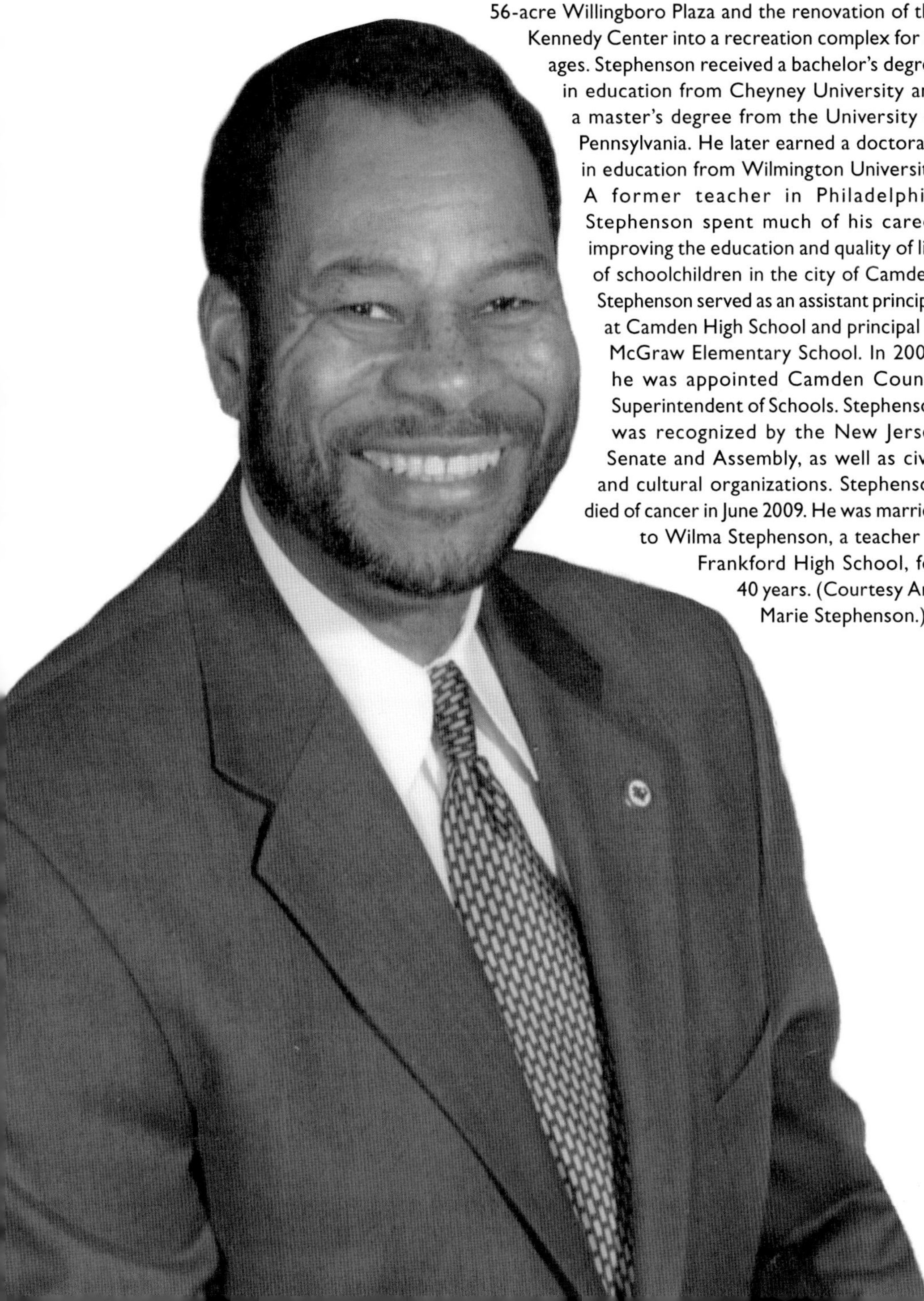

**Paul Stephenson**

Paul Stephenson spent much of his career improving the lives of children and his community. A five-term member of Willingboro Township Council, including stints as mayor and deputy mayor, Stephenson helped to lead the redevelopment of the former 56-acre Willingboro Plaza and the renovation of the Kennedy Center into a recreation complex for all ages. Stephenson received a bachelor's degree in education from Cheyney University and a master's degree from the University of Pennsylvania. He later earned a doctorate in education from Wilmington University. A former teacher in Philadelphia, Stephenson spent much of his career improving the education and quality of life of schoolchildren in the city of Camden. Stephenson served as an assistant principal at Camden High School and principal of McGraw Elementary School. In 2004, he was appointed Camden County Superintendent of Schools. Stephenson was recognized by the New Jersey Senate and Assembly, as well as civic and cultural organizations. Stephenson died of cancer in June 2009. He was married to Wilma Stephenson, a teacher at Frankford High School, for 40 years. (Courtesy Ann Marie Stephenson.)

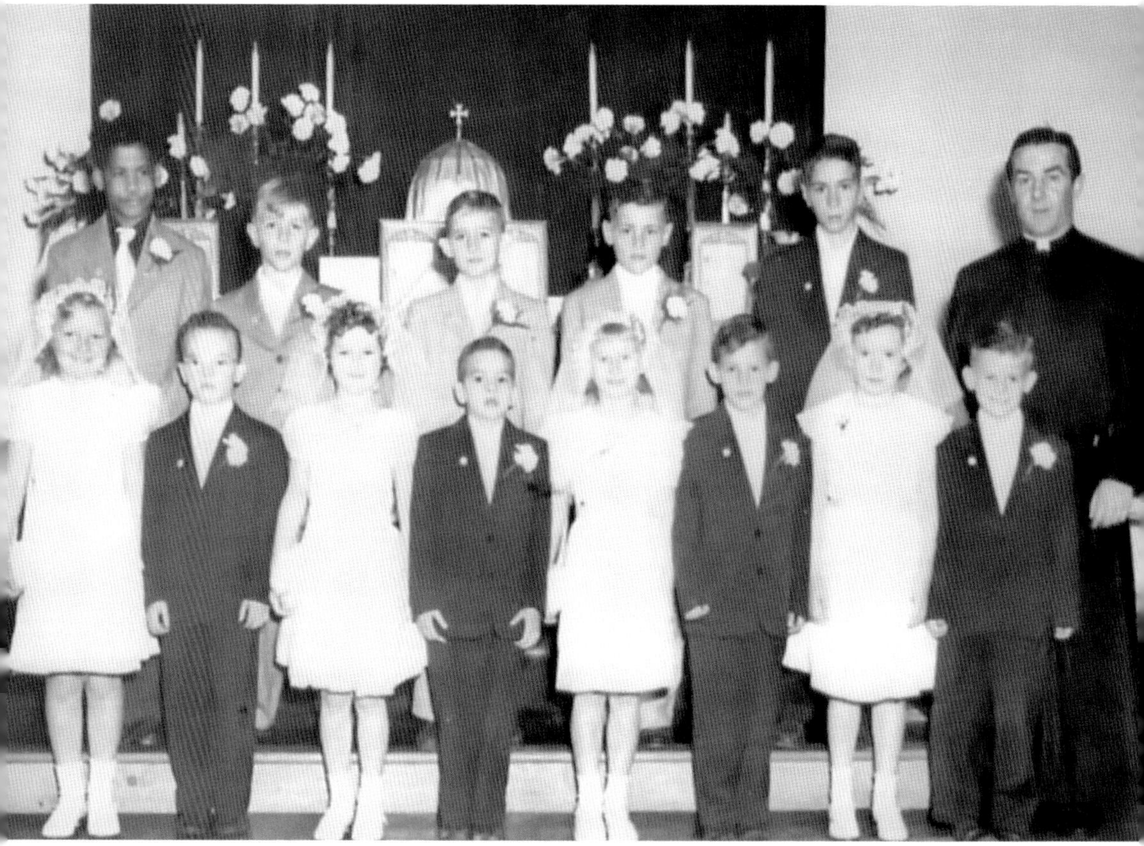

**Father Francis P.J. Coan**

Born in South Amboy, Francis P.J. Coan was ordained to the priesthood in June 1941. In 1959, he was assigned to be the founding pastor of Corpus Christi, a new Roman Catholic Church opening in Levittown. Father Coan celebrated his first mass and first baptism at Corpus Christi on May 3, 1959. He officiated at the church's first wedding, of Lois Trautmann and Roger Whalen, on July 9, 1960. Father Coan (pictured with children celebrating their First Communion in 1959) oversaw the initial growth of the parish, breaking ground on a new school in November 1959—the school opened in September 1960 to 400 students—and a new convent in March 1964. After five years at Corpus Christi, Father Coan was transferred to a parish in Far Hills. He died in 1985. (Courtesy Corpus Christi Roman Catholic Church.)

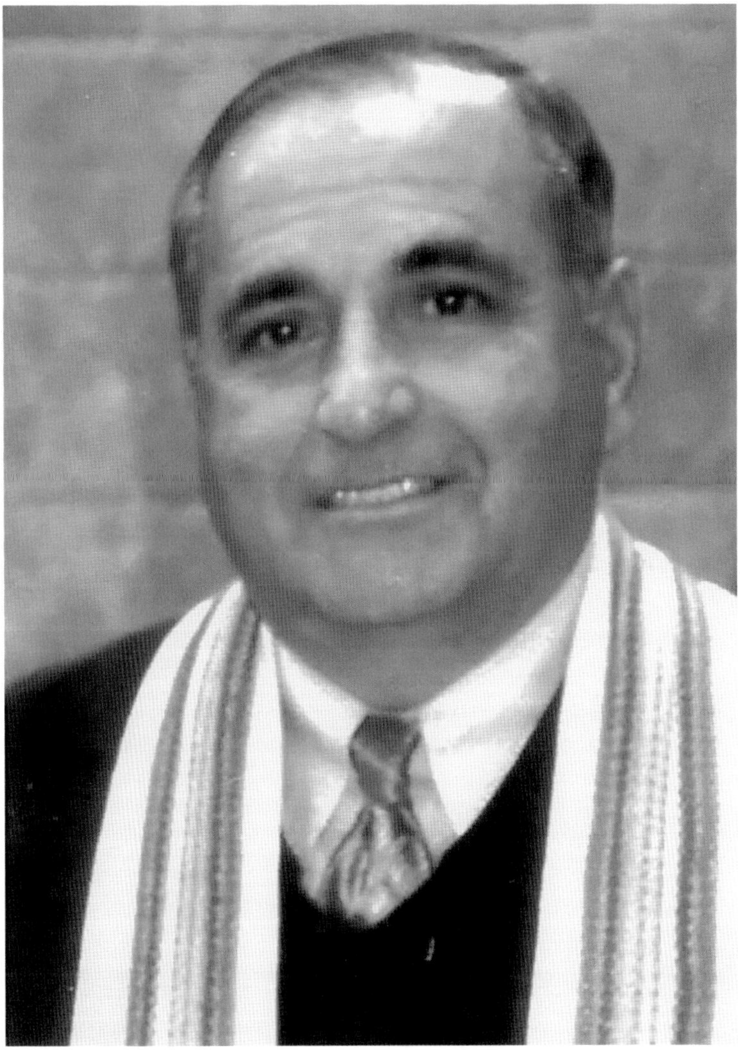

**Rabbi Richard A. Levine**
As Willingboro grew, the new residents were eager to establish houses of worship. Two synagogues were founded, Temple Emanu-El (now Adath Emanu-El) and Beth Torah. Emanu-El was born in January 1959 when five families met to discuss forming the first Jewish Reform congregation in Burlington County. The first services were led by student rabbis in a house on Pinafore Lane. Richard A. Levine was installed as the congregation's first full-time rabbi the same weekend in 1964 that its new home opened on John F. Kennedy Way. A native of Brooklyn, Rabbi Levine graduated from the Wharton School of the University of Pennsylvania, with a bachelor's degree in economics. He later received his rabbinical ordination from the Hebrew Union College-Jewish Institute of Religion in New York City in 1964, having won a number of academic awards. He received an honorary Doctor of Divinity in 1989. A father of nine and grandfather of 12, Rabbi Levine was the first New Jersey rabbi to serve as president of the Greater Philadelphia Board of Rabbis. He also was president of the Delaware Valley Association of Reform Rabbis and president of the Tri-County Board of Rabbis. He also served on many other boards and organizations. As Willingboro's demographics changed, Rabbi Levine led the congregation's move to a new building in Mount Laurel in 1997. Rabbi Levine retired in June 2005 and serves as Emanu-El's rabbi emeritus. (Courtesy Temple Adath Emanu-El.)

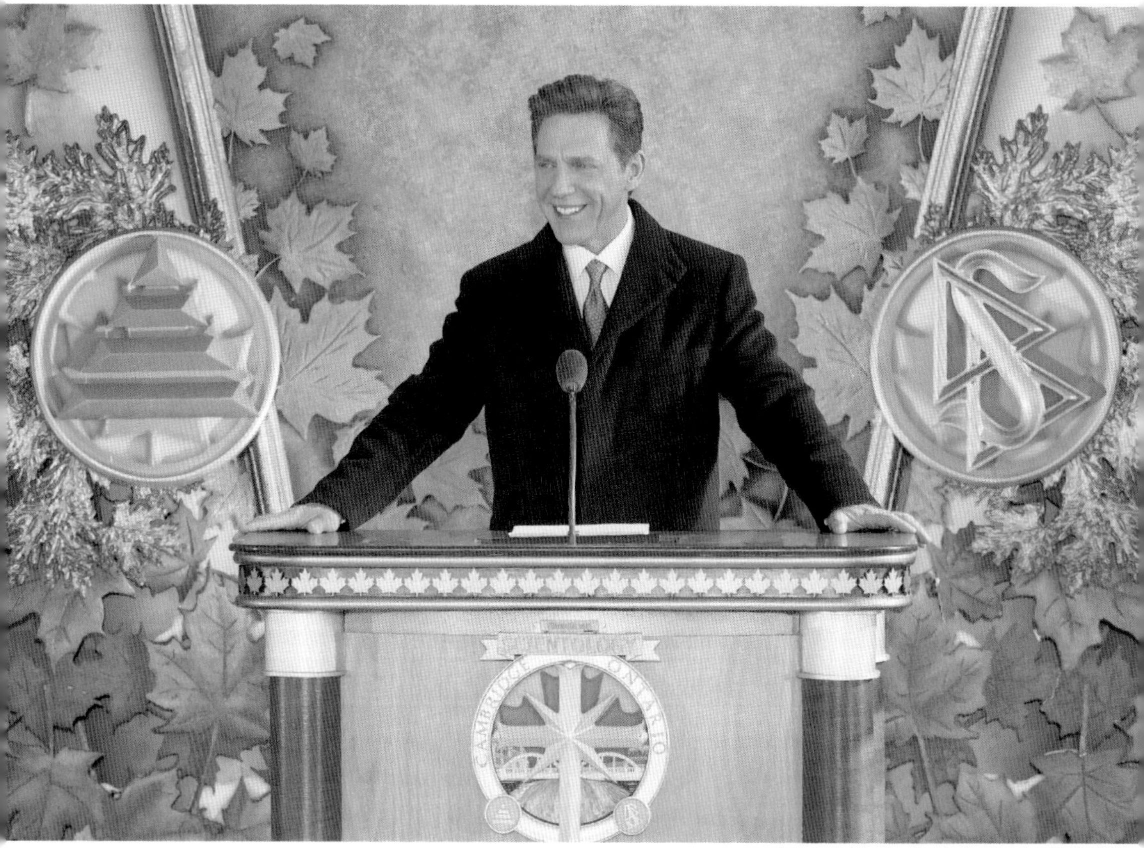

**David Miscavige**

David Miscavige, the ecclesiastical leader of the Scientology religion and chairman of the board of its Religious Technology Center, spent the first 12 years of his life in Willingboro. It was while living in Willingboro that he discovered the teachings of L. Ron Hubbard. According to a January 2012 article in the *Philadelphia Inquirer*, Miscavige was born in nearby Bucks County in 1960 and lived in a two-story Colonial on Peartree Lane. He attended Pennypacker Park Elementary School, played baseball and, like his older brother Ronnie, suited up for the Pennypacker Park Patriots football team. They spent summers at the Jersey Shore, where his sisters Lori and Denise performed on *Tony Grant's Stars of Tomorrow* show on the Steel Pier. Former neighbors said his asthma and bouts of wheezing cut his days short. After many doctor visits and trips to the emergency room, Ronald Miscavige Sr. took his son to see a man who practiced the teachings that Hubbard espoused in his book *Dianetics*. The visit supposedly cured the boy's asthma. The family studied Scientology in South Jersey briefly, and in 1972, abruptly sold their Willingboro house and moved to England to delve more deeply into the religion. The family eventually resettled in Broomall, Delaware County, though at age 16, Miscavige moved to Florida to work for the church. Today, the church spans the globe, with 10,000 churches in 167 countries. (Courtesy The Church of Scientology.)

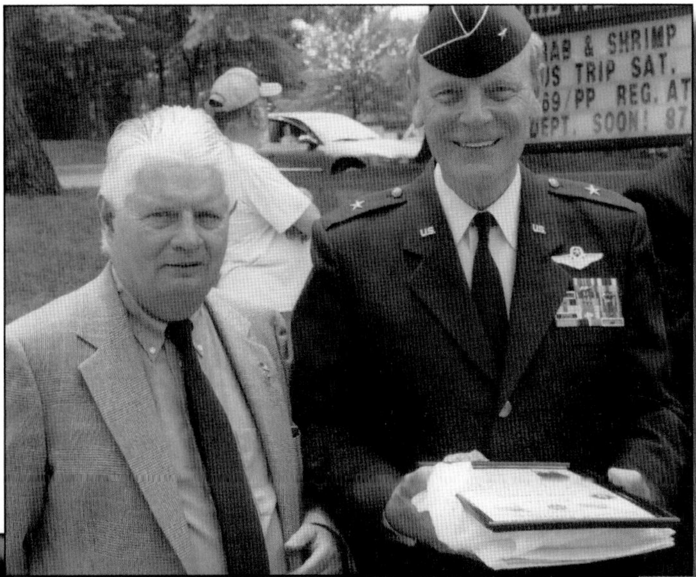

**Jim Gray**
A graduate of John F. Kennedy High School, Jim Gray (left) was the township's longtime special events coordinator, organizing the Independence Day and Memorial Day parades, fireworks displays, and other events. Thousands of people would line the streets as marching bands, floats, fire trucks, and youth groups paraded past. In 2009, he was appointed to fill an unexpired term on the Willingboro Township Council. (Courtesy Jim Gray/Willingboro Public Library.)

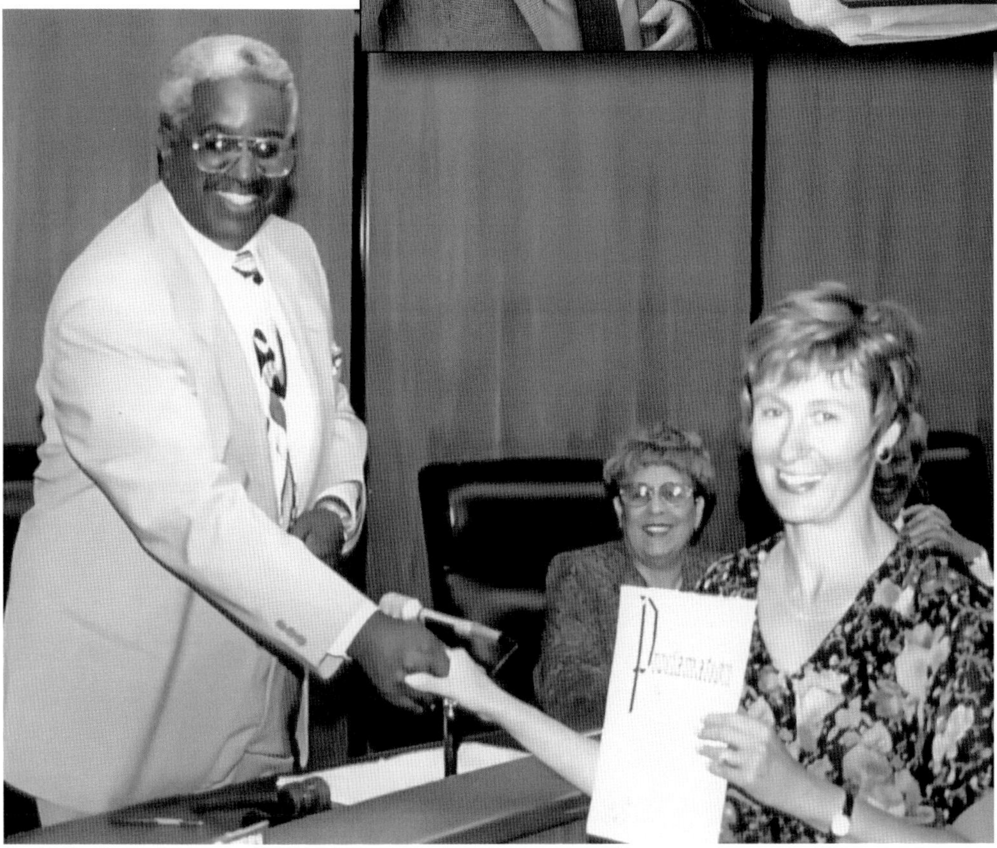

**Jeffrey Ramsey**
A lawyer by training, Jeffrey Ramsey served on Willingboro Township Council for 15 years, including stints as mayor and deputy mayor. During his time in office, council dealt with issues such as revitalizing the former Willingboro Plaza and John F. Kennedy High School and a referendum on liquor sales. He stepped down to take a job with the state parole board. (Courtesy Willingboro Library.)

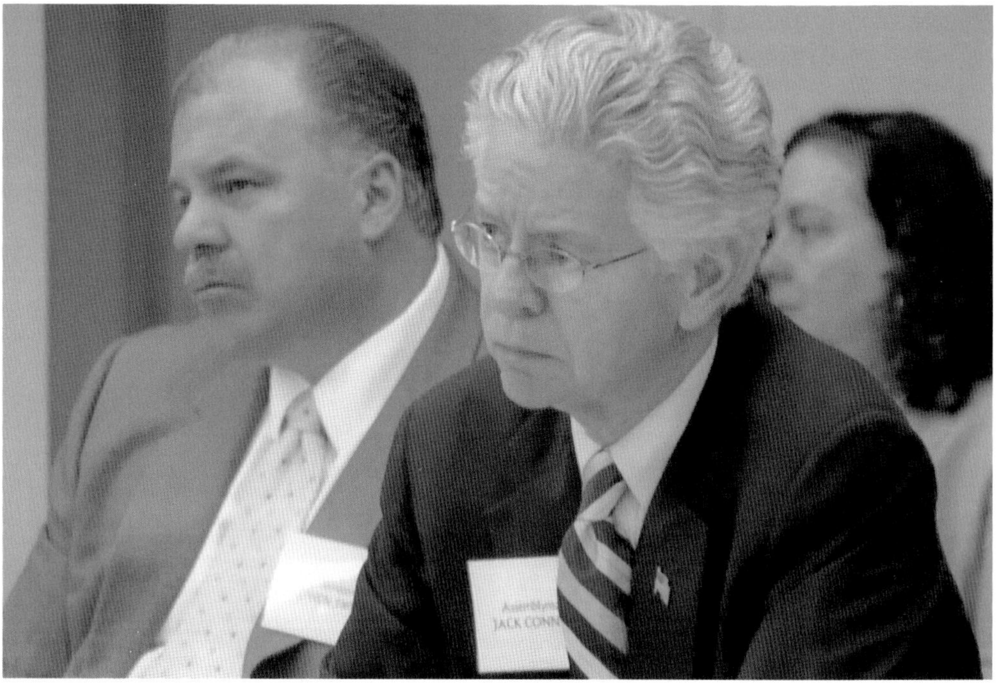

**Jack Conners**

An early resident of Willingboro, Jack Conners (at right) is known as New Jersey's champion of military veterans and their families. A veteran of the US Army National Guard and Army Reserves, Conners was a member of the state assembly from 1998 to 2011. As a representative of the Seventh District (which includes Willingboro), Conners served as deputy speaker and chairman of the Military and Veterans' Affairs Committee. In 2011, Conners was appointed Camden County director of veterans affairs. (Courtesy Lourdes Health System.)

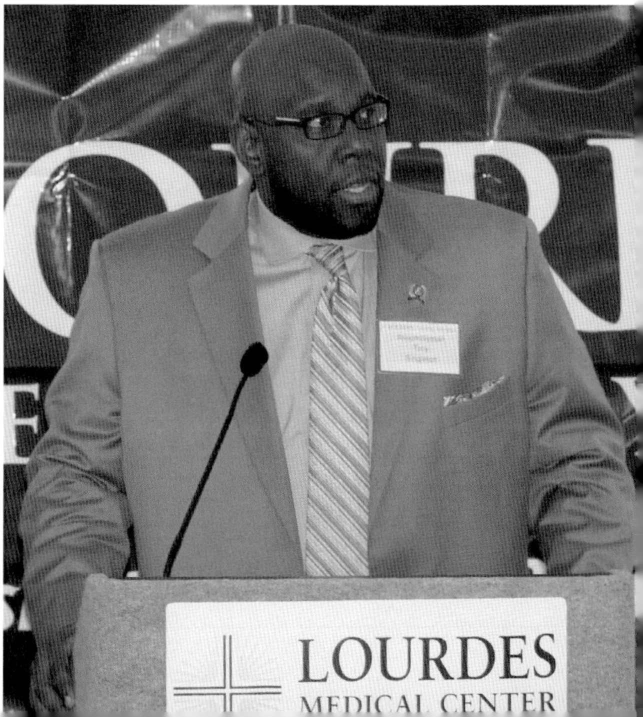


**Troy Singleton**

A graduate of Willingboro High School, Troy Singleton has devoted most of his adult life to serving New Jersey residents in legislative, government affairs, political, and policy posts. Singleton began his career as legislative director for Seventh District New Jersey Assemblymen Herb Conaway and Jack Conners. He later was named deputy executive director of the New Jersey Democratic State Committee and the New Jersey General Assembly Majority Office, as well as chief of staff for the assembly speaker. In August 2011, he was selected to fill Conners's unexpired term. That November, Singleton was elected to his first full term in the assembly. (Courtesy Lourdes Health System.)

# CHAPTER TWO

# On the Ball

## Athletes and Sports Heroes

There must be something in the water.

That was then state senator Jack Casey's theory as the town honored Olympian Lamont Smith following his gold medal–winning performance on the US men's 1,600-meter relay team. Smith was just the latest Willingboro native to achieve greatness in the Olympics, including nine-time gold medalist and "athlete of the century" Carl Lewis and his sister, champion long jumper Carol Lewis.

For a town of its size and relatively short modern history, Willingboro has had an extraordinary number of star athletes and coaches. An extensive recreation program and organizations such as the Willingboro Track Club have provided township youngsters with ample opportunities to excel and have a good time. Success can be found in many sports.

Coached by Tyrone Belford and Nelson Hayspell, football players Kareem McKenzie, Shaun Phillips, and Dezman Moses have enjoyed successful careers in the National Football League. Willingboro High graduate Josh Meekins was briefly on the Chicago Bears before injury cut his playing days short.

On the hard court, Crystal Langhorne has become the cornerstone of the WNBA Washington Mystics. The all-time leading scorer and rebounder for the Maryland Terrapins, Langhorne led the team to the NCAA Championship, as well as helped the US National Team to gold. Fellow Willingboro High basketball star Tiffany Crews starred for Northeastern University and recently started a mobile sneaker business.

On the soccer pitch, Charles Duccilli coached John F. Kennedy High School to nine championships. The Temple University standout played for the Philadelphia Spartans and Philadelphia Atoms, leading the latter to its only league title. Willingboro native Peter Vermes has played at the highest levels here and abroad, representing the United States in the 1988 Olympics and playing a vital role in the resurgence of American soccer. Today, Vermes is the manager of Major League Soccer's Sporting Kansas City. And Cleveland Lewis, older brother of Carl and Carol Lewis, was an All-American soccer player at Brandeis University. As the Brandeis all-time scoring leader, he led the team to the first national championship in university history.

A gentle giant, Robert Marella, better known by his ring name "Gorilla Monsoon," was just one of several people associated with professional wrestling to reside in Willingboro. During a career that lasted four decades, Marella went from being a singing Italian, to a bearded monster, to a fan favorite. Most famously, when Muhammad Ali rushed into the ring following a 1976 match, Marella hoisted the boxing heavyweight champion into an airplane spin and slammed him to the mat. Marella later became a beloved broadcaster, known for his hyperbole and expressions like, "Pandemonium is running wild, you can cut it with a knife!"

There may not be anything special in the water, but the athletic prowess of the individuals in these pages and others have become an important source of community pride.

**Crystal Langhorne** (BELOW AND OPPOSITE PAGE)
Education was always the first concern in the Langhorne household, and from an early age Crystal exhibited a fierce work ethic, finishing her homework and taking care of chores. She brought that same passion to the basketball court, playing at Memorial Junior High School and on AAU teams. Once her father said she could miss church for basketball, the rest, they say, is history. Langhorne led Willingboro High to the girls Group 3 state title her sophomore year, was named the New Jersey Gatorade Player of the Year in 2003 and 2004, and became the school's all-time leading scorer. She won the under-16 AAU national championship and was named tournament MVP. At the University of Maryland, she led the Terrapins to the 2006 NCAA national title. She finished her college career as the school's leading scorer and rebounder—the only Terp man or woman to record 2,000 points and 1,000 rebounds. She also became the first Maryland player to have her jersey raised to the rafters while still active. The Washington Mystics selected Langhorne with the sixth overall pick in the 2008 WNBA draft. She had a difficult rookie year, but the power forward has come to be the cornerstone of the team, leading the Mystics in scoring in 2011 and 2012 with 18.2 and 14.7 points per game, respectively. (Both, courtesy NBA Photos.)

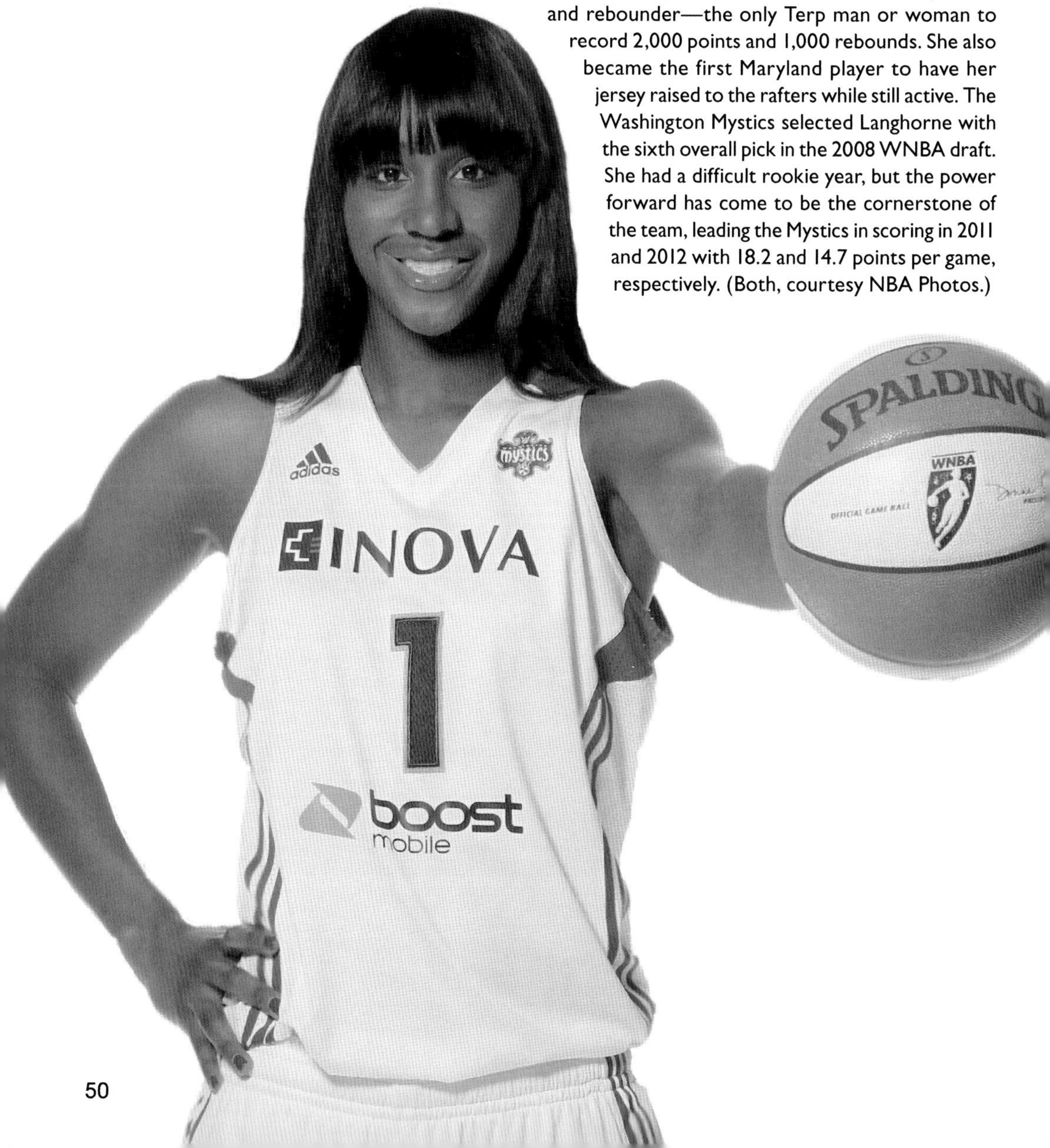

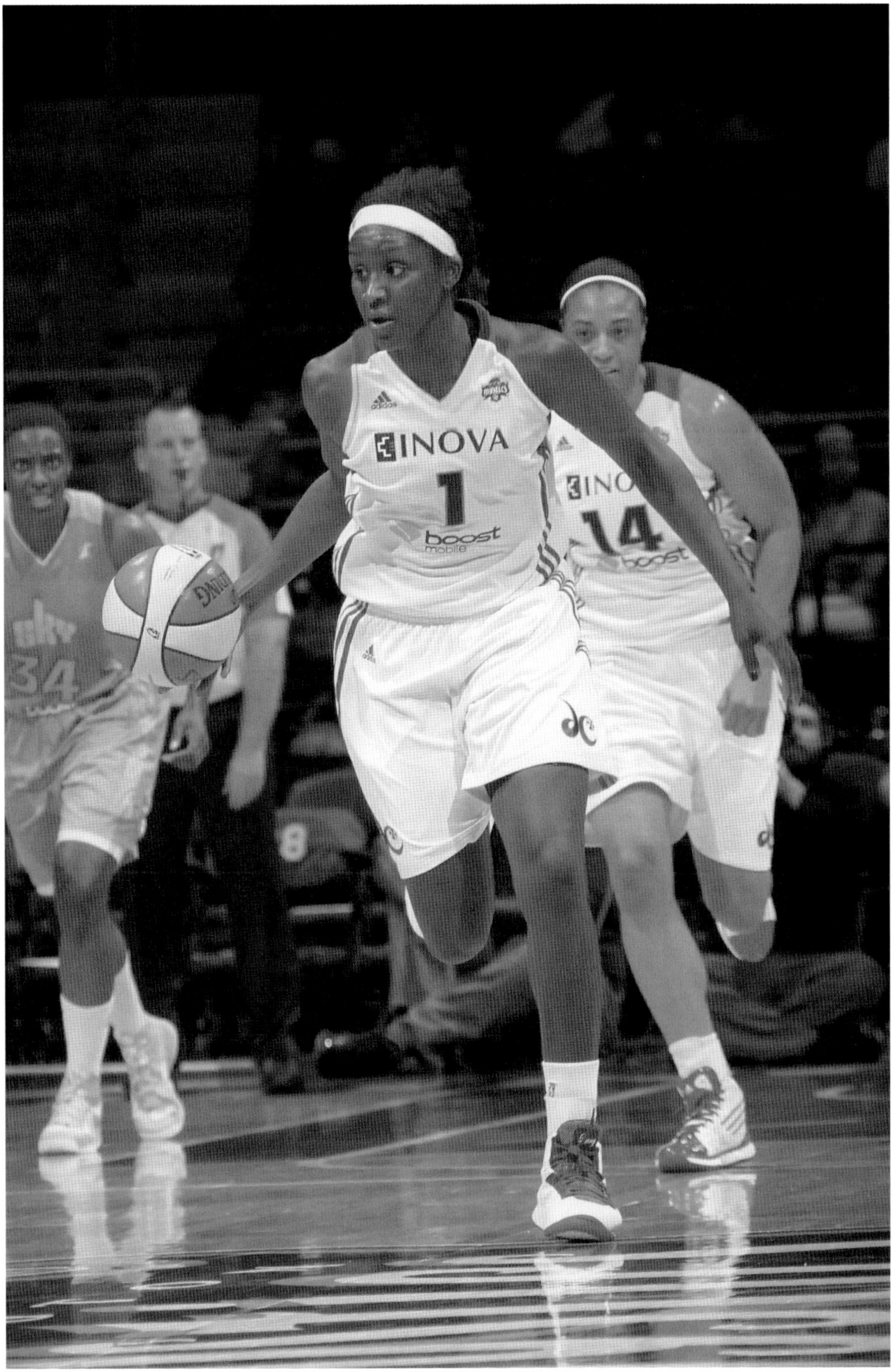
INOVA
1
boost
mobile
INOVA
14
boost
sky
34

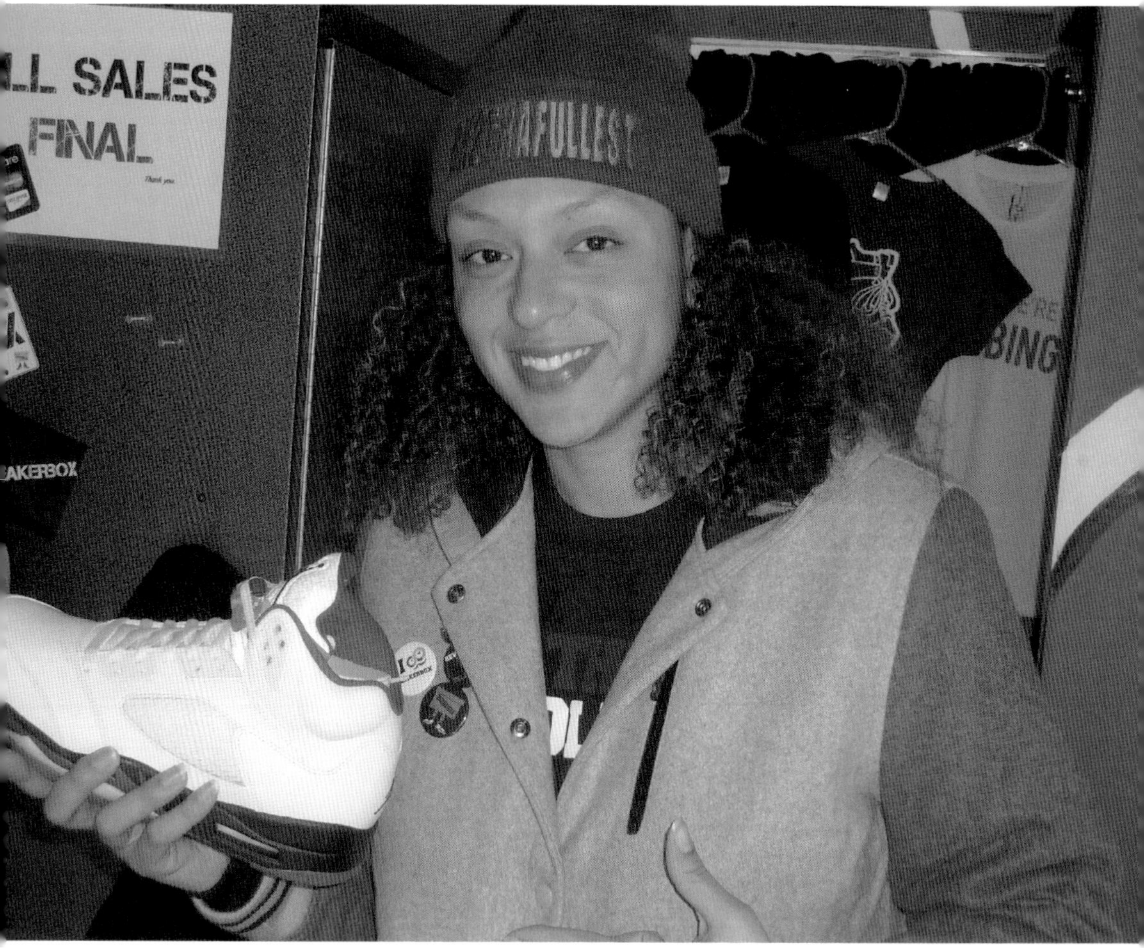


**Tiffany Crews**

Tiffany Crews is best known for her prowess on the basketball court. But this former Willingboro High and Northeastern University star is taking her skills to the streets. In 2012, Crews and business partner Angela Schipano launched Sneakerbox, selling fashionable athletic shoes, t-shirts, and sports-related items from the back of a specially outfitted van. Crews, who graduated from Northeastern in 2011 with a degree in sociology and international affairs, and Schipano came up with the idea for a sneaker truck while working at the Nike store in Boston. They noticed the plethora of food trucks on city streets and thought a mobile sneaker store would be a good venture. The winter of 2013, Crews—who averaged 17.6 points per game her senior season at Willingboro—and Schipano embarked on a cross-country tour, attracting crowds at each stop anxious to experience the sneaker store on wheels. So far, the partners are enjoying themselves and hope to expand their business.

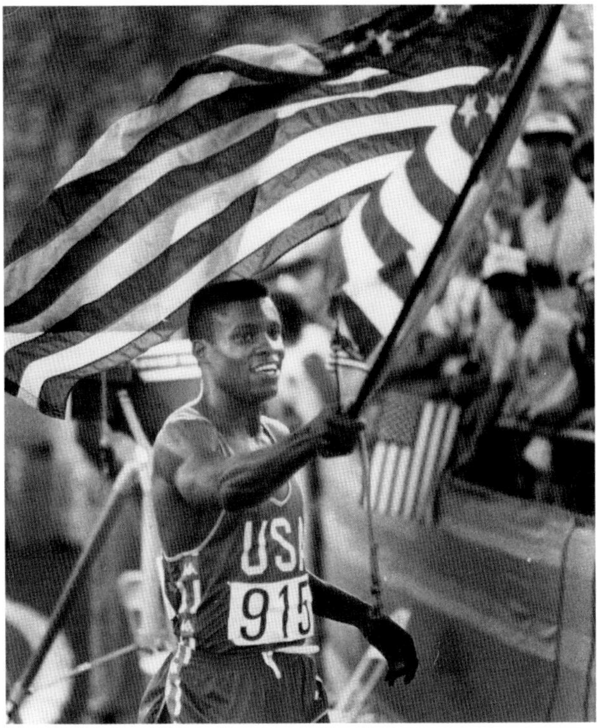


**Carl Lewis**

Perhaps no other person is more associated with Willingboro than Carl Lewis. Born in Alabama and raised in Willingboro, Lewis was long the world's dominant sprinter and long jumper. His 10 Olympic medals (9 gold), 10 World Championship medals (8 gold), and numerous world records earned Lewis titles of "Sportsman of the Century" by the International Olympic Committee and "Olympian of the Century" by *Sports Illustrated* magazine. Coached by his parents, William and Evelyn Lewis, Lewis emerged as a promising athlete first at John F. Kennedy High School and then at Willingboro High. By his senior year, Lewis had become one of the top long jumpers in the world and days after graduating broke the high school long jump record. Lewis enrolled at the University of Houston and qualified for the 1980 Olympic Games in the long jump and 4-by-100 meter relay team, but the United States boycotted the event in Moscow. By 1981, Lewis was not only the top long jumper but the fastest 100-meter sprinter in the world. Lewis's success in both track and field events prompted comparisons to Jesse Owens, who dominated the sport in the 1930s and was a friend of William Lewis. Track and field remained a relatively low-profile sport, but with the 1984 Olympic Games in Los Angeles, Lewis became a household name, winning four gold medals. That year, Lewis was drafted in the 10th round of the NBA draft by the Chicago Bulls, but he never played. He also was drafted by the Dallas Cowboys as a wide receiver but was not signed. Although challenged by Ben Johnson and other athletes in the coming years, in the 1988 Olympics in Seoul, Lewis won two golds in the 100-meter and long jump and a silver in 200-meters. At the 1991 World Championships at age 30, he ran what he called the greatest race of his career, setting a new world record of 9.86 seconds in the 100-meter dash against two of the fastest men in the world (the record would stand for three years). Success continued at the Olympics in 1992, winning three gold medals. Lewis's last Olympic gold came in Atlanta in 1996, where he won the long jump. Lewis retired in 1997, having won 22 gold medals, 3 silver medals, and 3 bronze medals in international competition. After sports, Lewis attempted an acting career, with limited success. In 2011, Lewis returned from California and filed petitions to run as a Democrat for New Jersey Senate. After a court battle, he was disqualified for not meeting residency requirements. Over the years, Lewis would return to his hometown to talk to youth and coach in the Willingboro High stadium that bears his name. (Courtesy the *Philadelphia Inquirer.*)

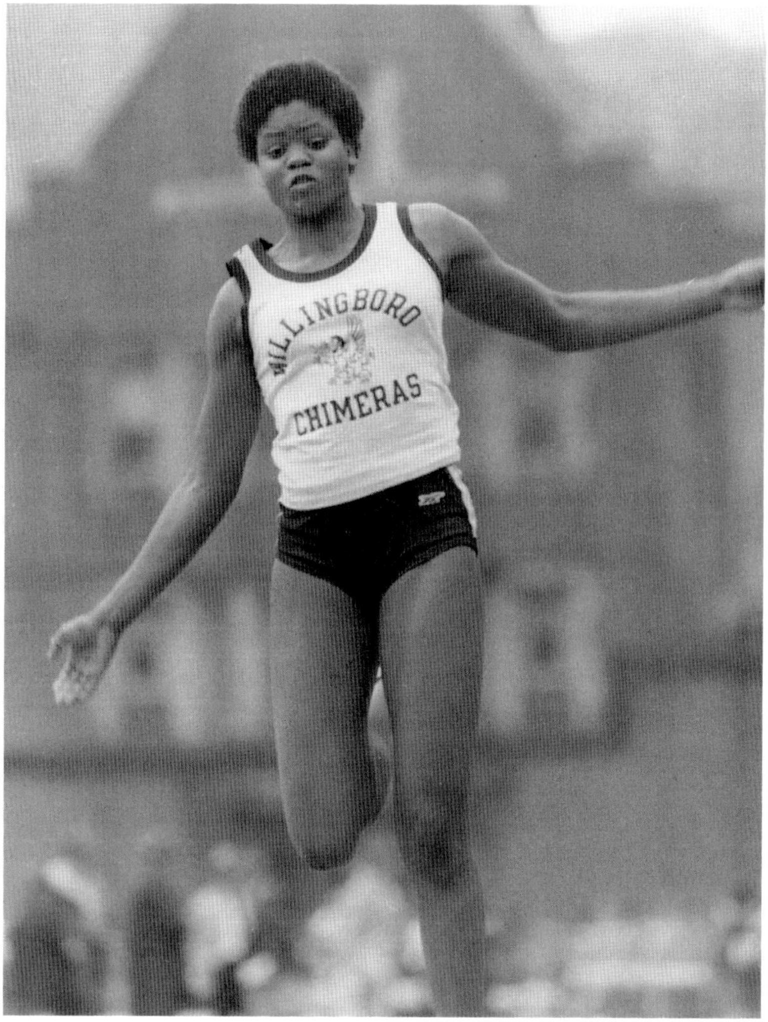


**Carol Lewis**

While often overshadowed by older brother Carl Lewis, Carol Lewis was one of America's top female long jumpers. A product of the Willingboro Track Club coached by her parents, Lewis came to prominence at Willingboro High School. Like her brother, Lewis qualified for the 1980 Olympic Games but did not compete because of the US boycott. However, at the Liberty Bell Classic, held in Philadelphia by countries not attending the Olympics, she won the silver medal in the long jump and received the Dial Award for the best female scholar-athlete of the year. Lewis, who set the high school indoor long jump record, followed her brother to the University of Houston and the Santa Monica Track Club. In 1982, she won the USA Outdoor Track and Field Championships, the first of many national titles (her jump from that event remains the American junior outdoor record). The next year, Lewis won the NCAA Outdoor Championships and a bronze medal at the World Championships in Athletics. Lewis won the 1984 Olympic trials and at the Summer Games in Los Angeles finished in ninth place in the long jump. In 1985, she won the NCAA Outdoor title again and a bronze at the World Cup. In August 1985, Lewis reached her peak, setting a personal best and twice breaking the American record. Her record stood for two years. In 1988, Lewis once again made the Olympic team but failed to qualify for the long jump finals. Following her retirement from track, Lewis worked as a commentator for NBC Sports, attending the 1996, 2000, and 2008 Olympics. (Courtesy the *Philadelphia Inquirer.*)

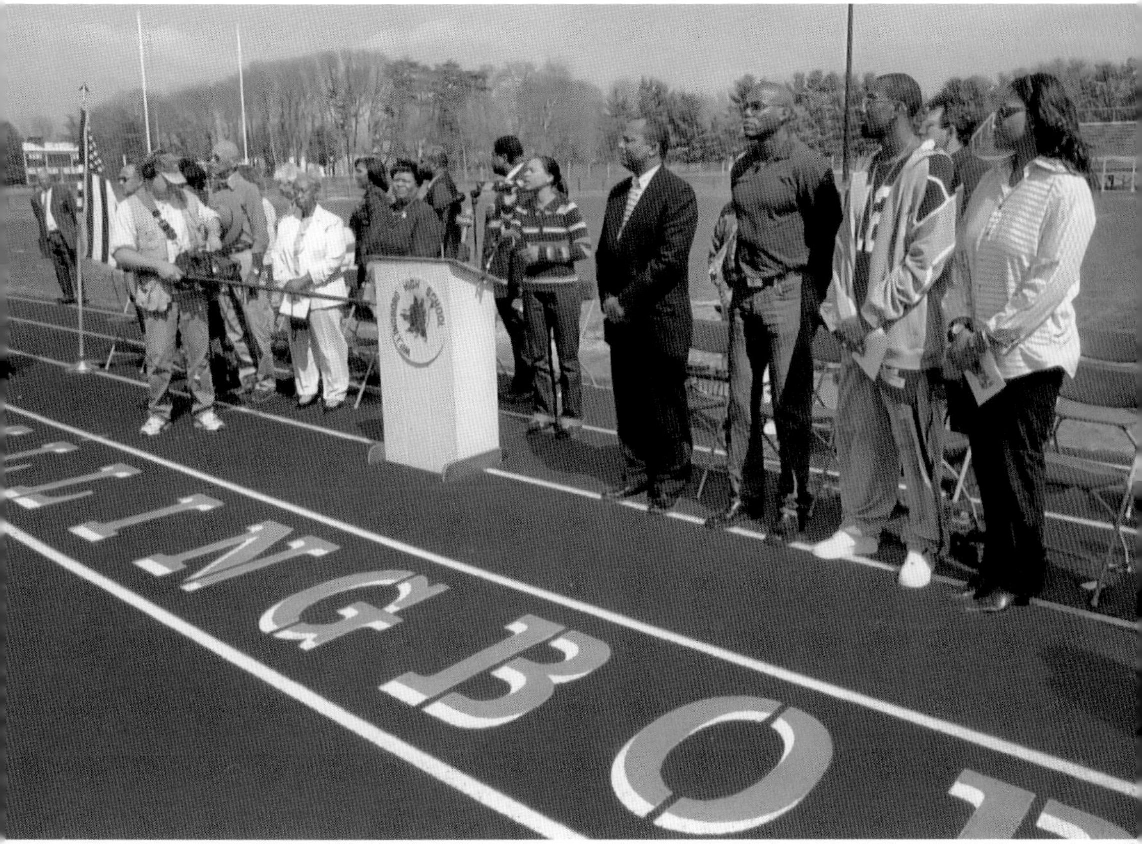


**Lamont Smith**
"Dominant" is thrown around a lot today to describe an outstanding athlete. In the case of Olympic gold-medalist Lamont Smith (second from right), there's never been a truer accolade. A 1991 graduate of Willingboro High School, Smith won six county and nine state championships over a two-year period. His high school personal best of 46.34 seconds in the 400-meter still stands as a Burlington County record. He also won three New Jersey all-group championships in 1991, the indoor all-group Meet of Champions state title, and in outdoor track, the all-group Meet of Champions crown in 1990 and 1991. The year he graduated, Smith was named to the US Junior National Team for the 400 meters. Smith continued his track and field career at Blinn College in Brenham, Texas. As a freshman, he was a member of the NJCAA National Championship 4-by-1,600 meter relay and earned All-American honors. In 1993, Smith won both indoor and outdoor NJCAA National Championships in the 400-meter. He went on to compete for the Santa Monica Track Club from 1994 to 2004. In 1996, at the Summer Olympic Games in Atlanta, Smith won a gold medal running the lead-off leg in the 4-by-1,600 meter relay. Smith currently lives in Dallas, Texas, and returns to Willingboro to support his alma mater. (Courtesy the *Philadelphia Inquirer.*)

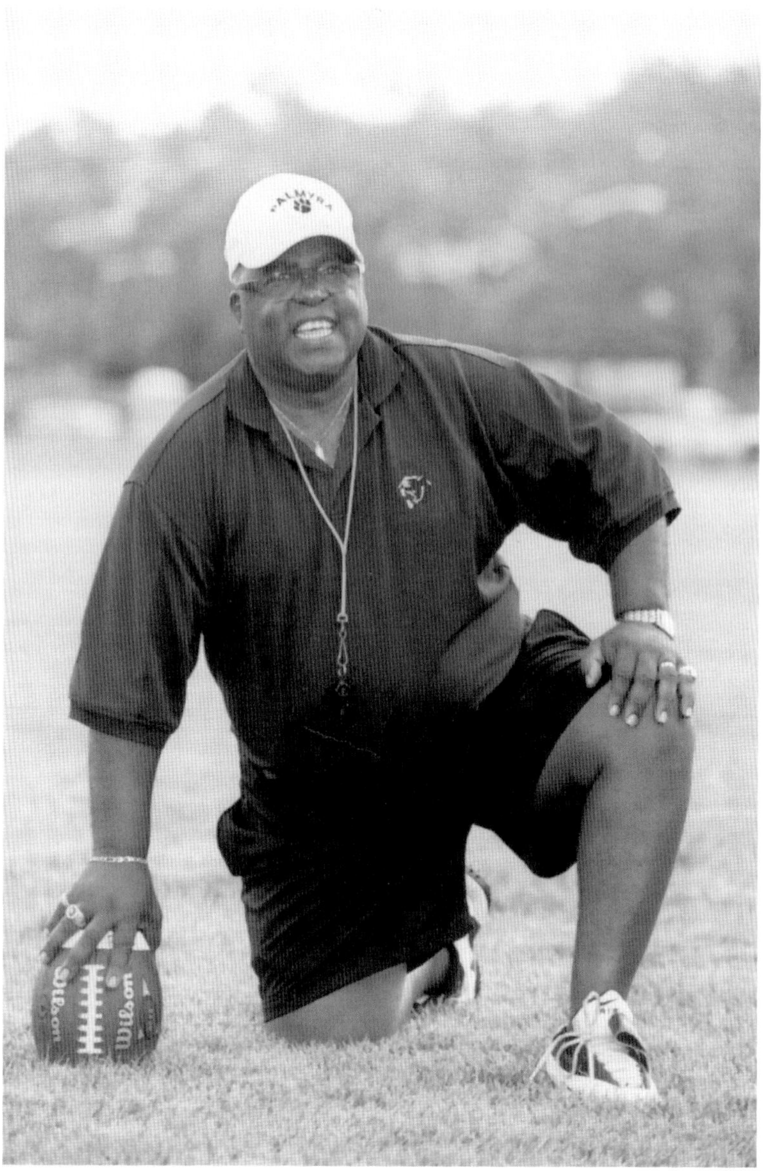

**Tyrone Belford**

For more than 40 years, Tyrone Belford has been a trailblazer, educating and inspiring thousands of young people as a teacher and football coach at John F. Kennedy, Willingboro, and Palmyra High Schools. Teaching at a time of social change—on his first day on the job at Kennedy High School in September 1970, riot police had to quell a fight between black and white students—Belford was one of the first minority football coaches in South Jersey. On the field, Belford amassed more than 150 wins, won championships, and sent 110 players to play football in college, with several going on to the NFL. He was inducted into South Jersey and state halls of fame and named coach of the year three times by area newspapers. Off the field, Belford established and taught the African American history course at Kennedy and Willingboro and was a founder of the Afro-American Club. Belford retired from Willingboro in 2006 and returned to Palmyra High School, where he started his career in 1967. He retired from Palmyra in 2013. (Courtesy Tyrone Belford.)

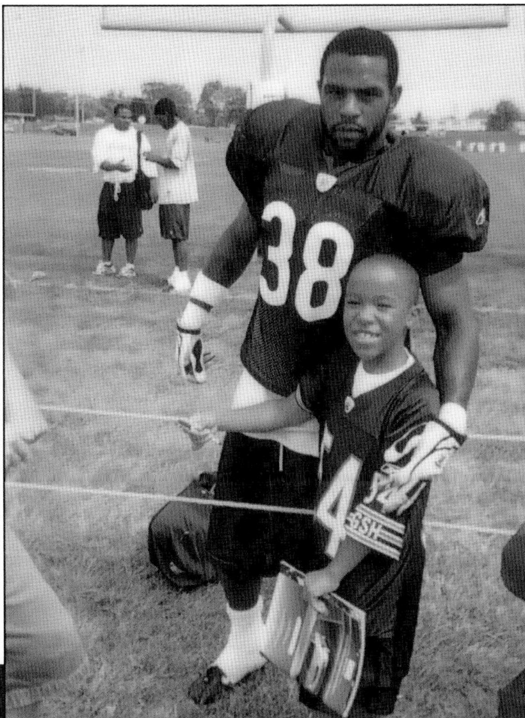


**Josh Minkins**
A gifted all-around athlete, Josh Minkins wrestled, ran hurdles, and played both sides of the ball for the Willingboro High School football team. His senior year, he ran for 1,003 yards, scored 25 touchdowns, had five sacks, and five interceptions. As a cornerback at the University of Louisville, Minkins was noted for his experience, speed and strength. In 2004, Minkins signed as an undrafted free agent with the Chicago Bears and had a brief career. (Courtesy Tyrone Belford.)

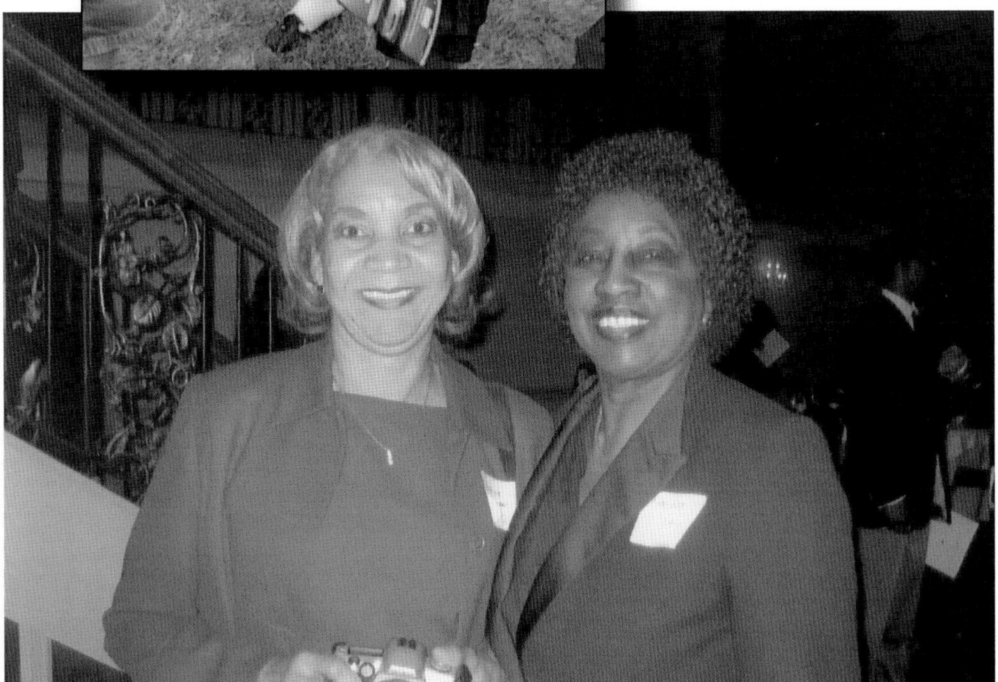

**Freddie George**
Freddie George helped to educate and inspire the children of Willingboro as a teacher for more than 35 years. A member of the Lewis family, George (right, with former Willingboro Track Club President Marion Coleman) supported the township's track and athletic programs. George teaches aerobics and fitness at the Kennedy Center. (Courtesy Lavonne Johnson.)

**Shaun Phillips** (BELOW AND OPPOSITE PAGE)
A linebacker with the Denver Broncos, Shaun Phillips moved from Philadelphia to Willingboro following eighth grade and graduated from Willingboro High School, starring in football, basketball, and track. He attended Purdue University on a football scholarship and graduated with a degree in hotel and restaurant management. He was picked by the San Diego Chargers in the fourth round of the NFL draft. One of the most energetic and exciting players in the NFL, Phillips was invited to the Pro Bowl in 2010 after helping the Chargers lead the NFL in total defense. The team's defensive player of the year in 2010, he is among the leaders in team history in quarterback sacks. After nine years with the Chargers, in 2013 he was signed by the Broncos. Phillips is one of the league's most recognized celebrities. He is a top fund-raiser for the After-School All-Stars, a nonprofit that provides programs for inner-city youth, and Free Wheelchair Mission, a foundation that donates wheelchairs to children in third-world countries. Off the field, Phillips interned at the New York Stock Exchange and completed an NFL business program at Northwestern University. He is a managing partner in a San Diego restaurant. In recognition of his achievements, in 2011 Phillips was invited to deliver the keynote address at the Willingboro High graduation. (Both, courtesy San Diego Chargers.)

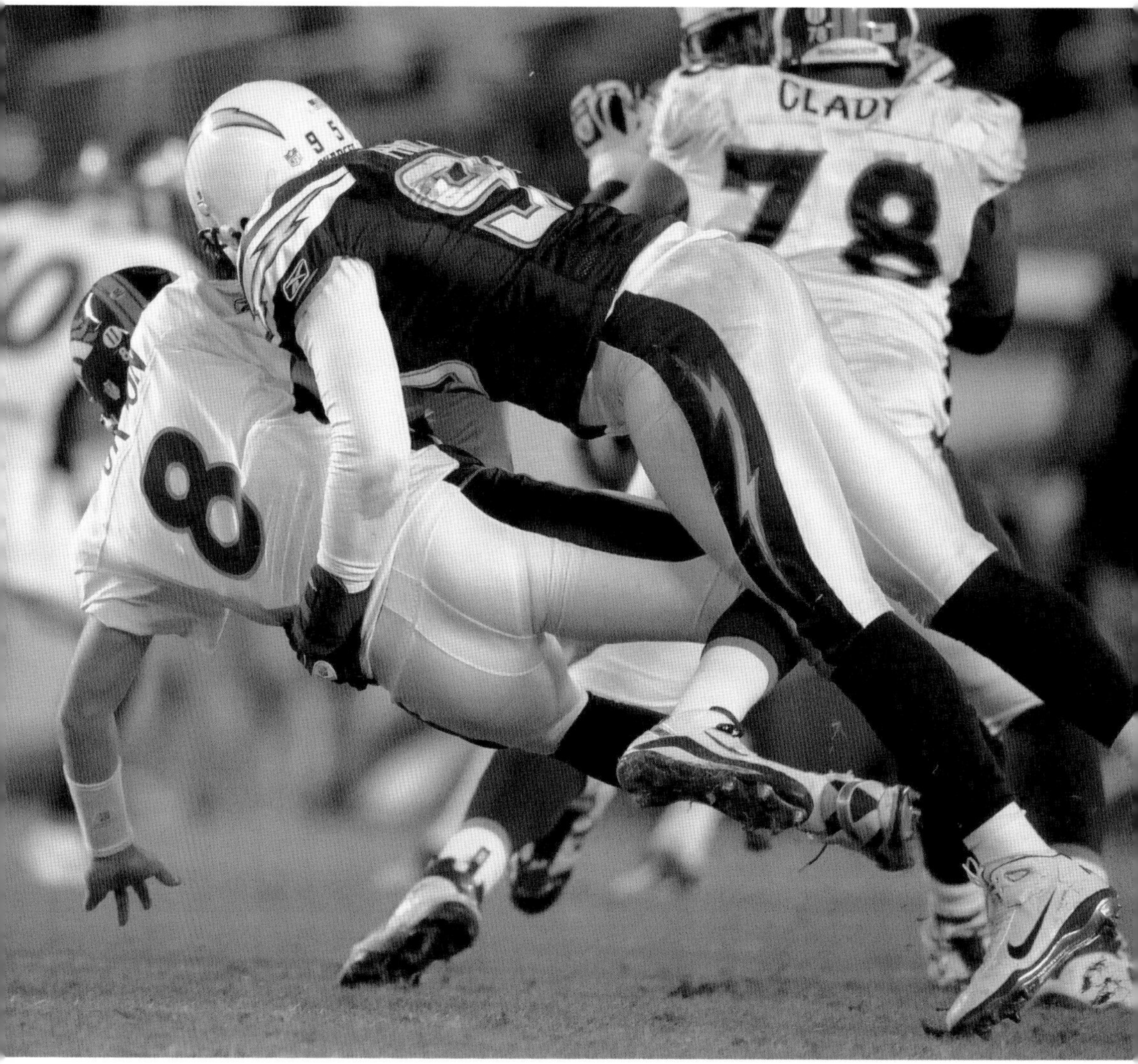

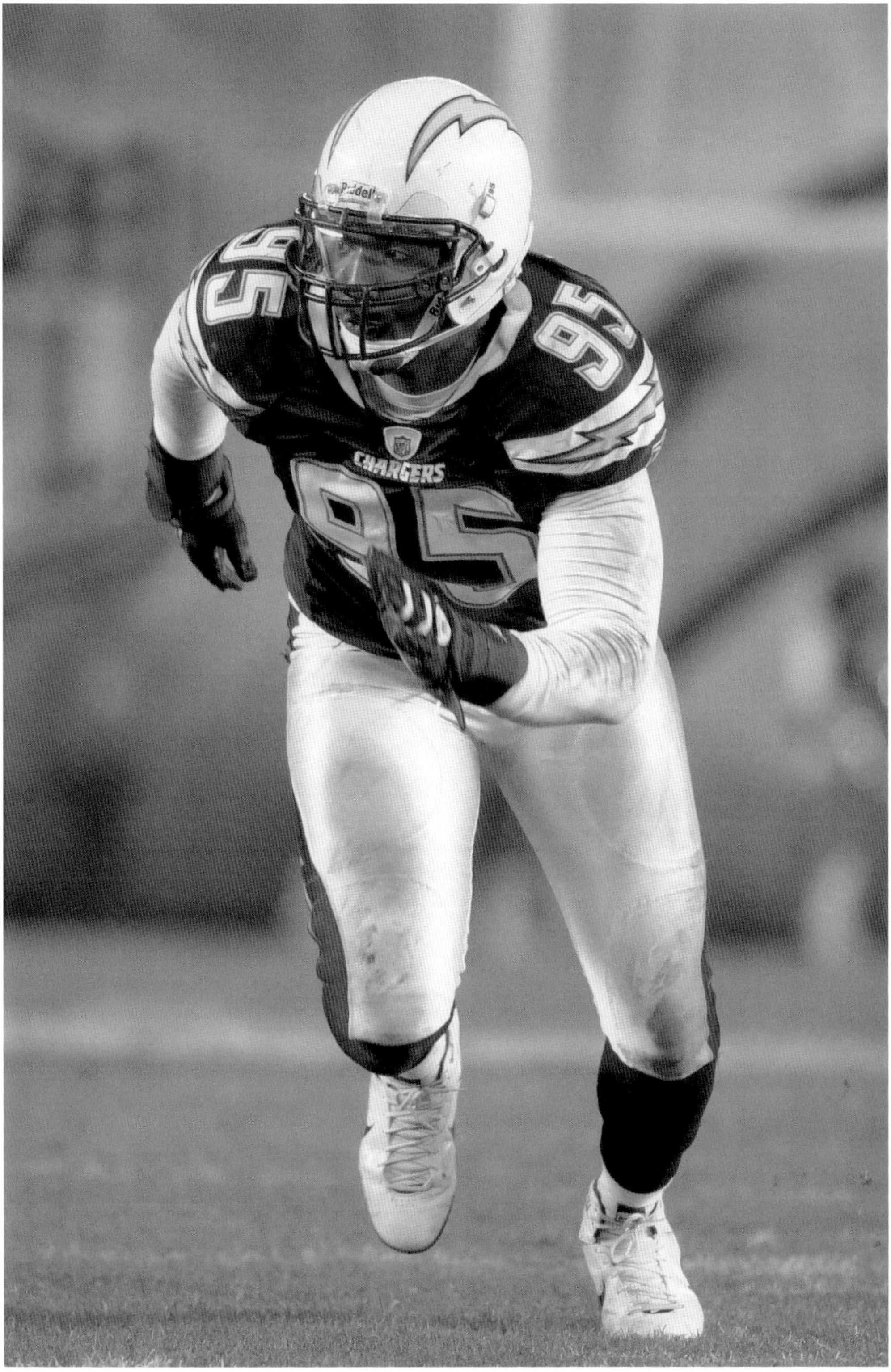
CHARGERS
95

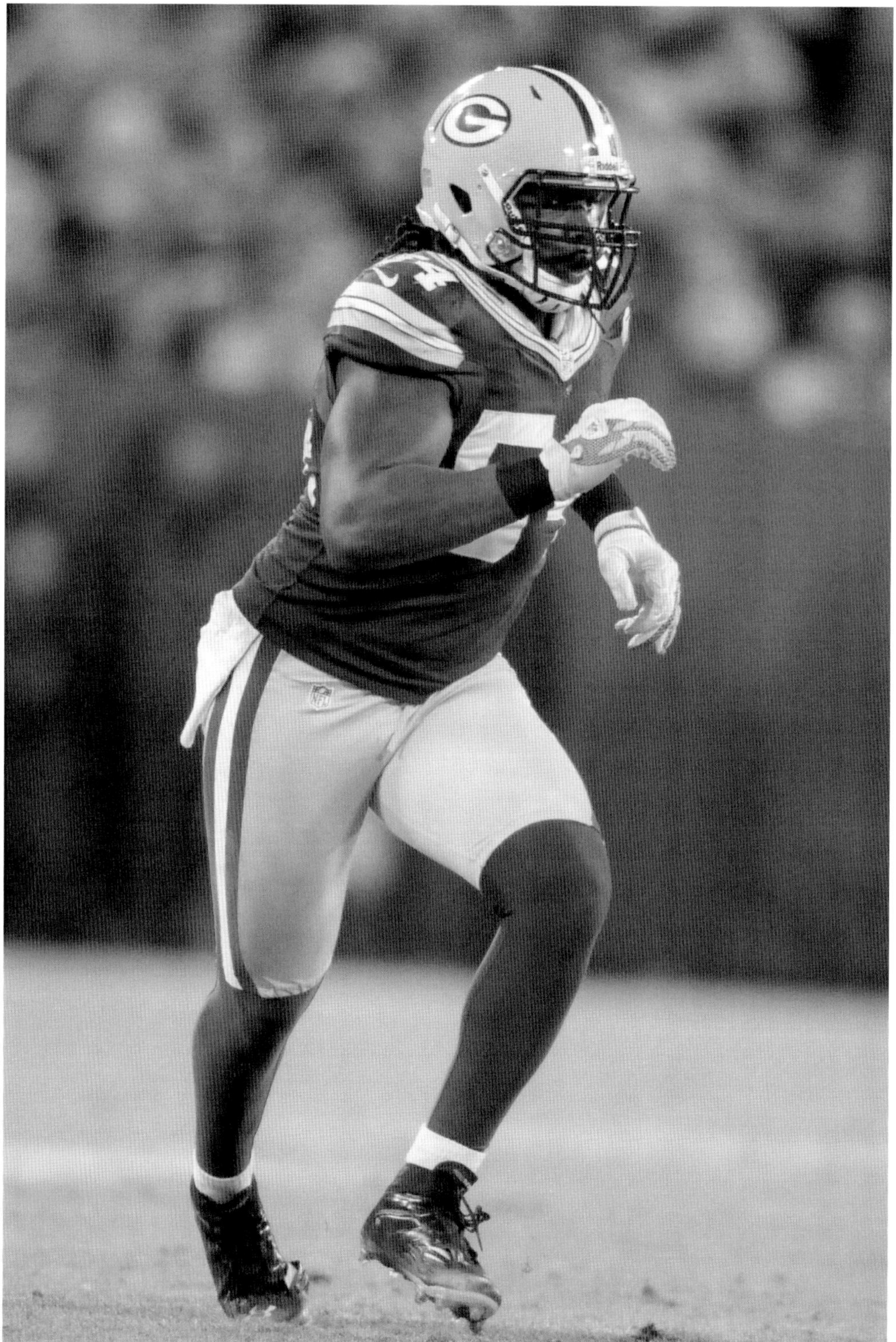

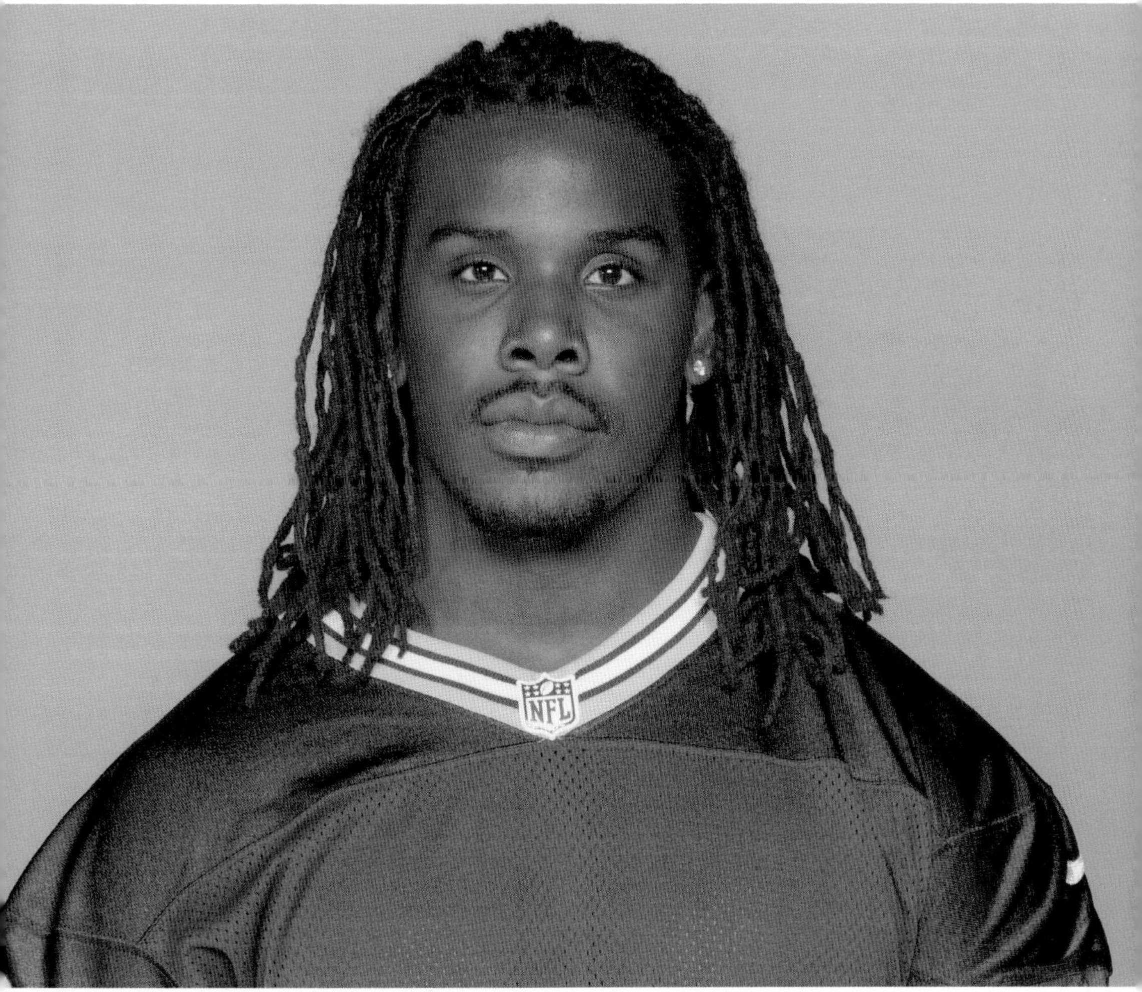

Dezman Moses (ABOVE AND OPPOSITE PAGE)
A three-sport standout at Willingboro High School, Dezman Moses excelled as a football wide receiver and linebacker. A *Burlington County Times* paperboy, he often was featured in the issues he delivered. During his senior season, he earned first-team all-county, all-conference, and all–South Jersey honors for recording 87 tackles and five interceptions and catching 35 passes for 596 yards and 10 touchdowns. Moses began his collegiate career at the University of Iowa. He transferred to Tulane and played two years there, ranking fifth in school history for sacks. Moses made the Green Bay Packers roster as an undrafted free agent in 2012. On October 28, 2012, Moses, a linebacker, scored his first career touchdown by returning a blocked punt. In 2013, Moses joined the Kansas City Chiefs. (Both, courtesy Green Bay Packers.)

## Kareem McKenzie

Kareem McKenzie played only two years of football at Willingboro High School before moving on to play in college at Penn State and then 11 years in the National Football League, winning two Super Bowls. McKenzie was selected in the third round of the 2001 NFL draft by the New York Jets and as a right tackle established himself as a top-flight run blocker. He joined the New York Giants in 2005, and was an integral part of the team winning Super Bowl XLII and XLVI. Nicknamed "Big Bear," he retired following the 2011–2012 season after being released by the Giants. Rather than enter into coaching or broadcasting, McKenzie was applying to doctorate programs in clinical psychology, with the hope of someday opening his own practice to counsel current and former NFL players on the pressures of playing and then transitioning to regular life. (Courtesy Tyrone Belford.)

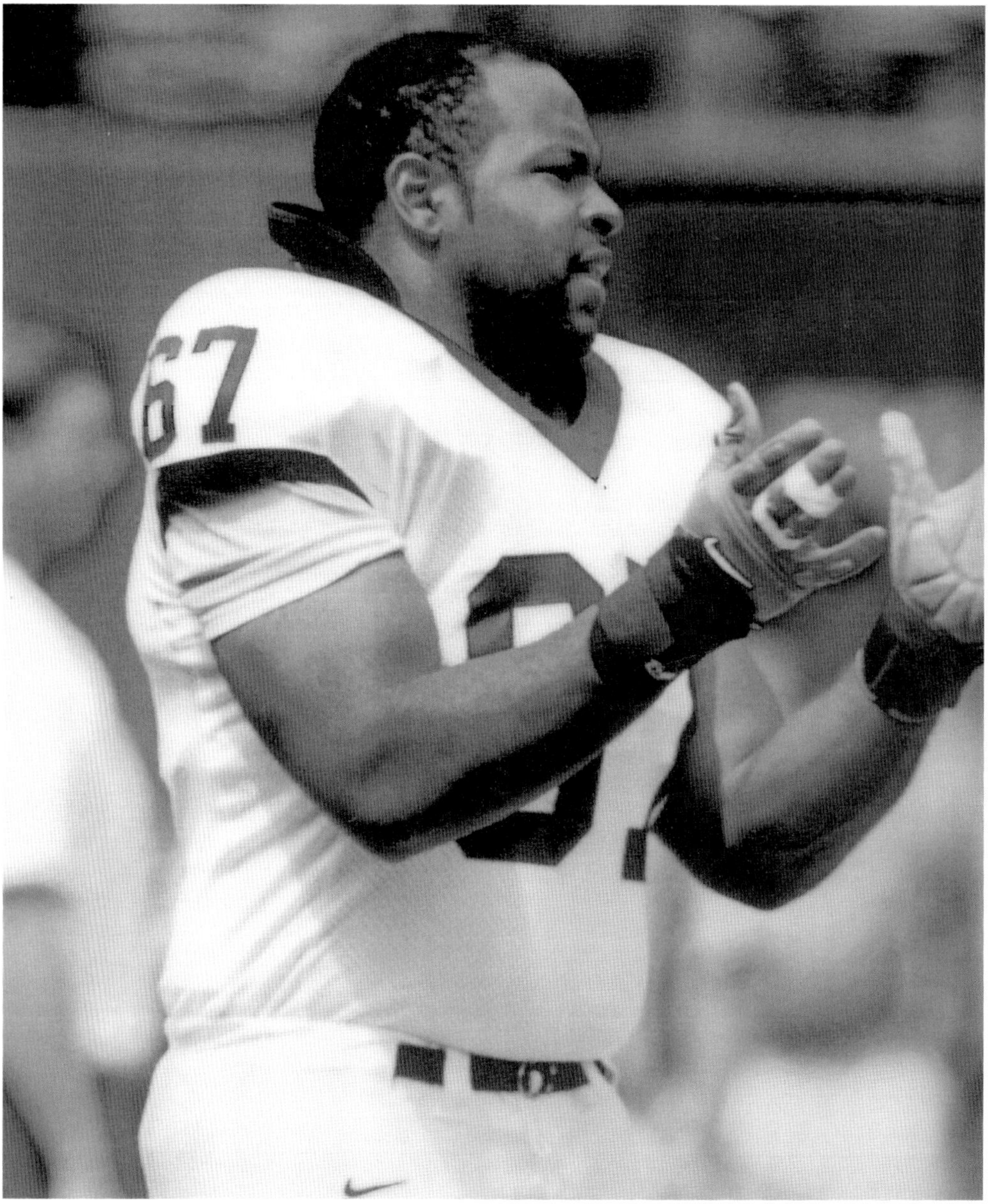

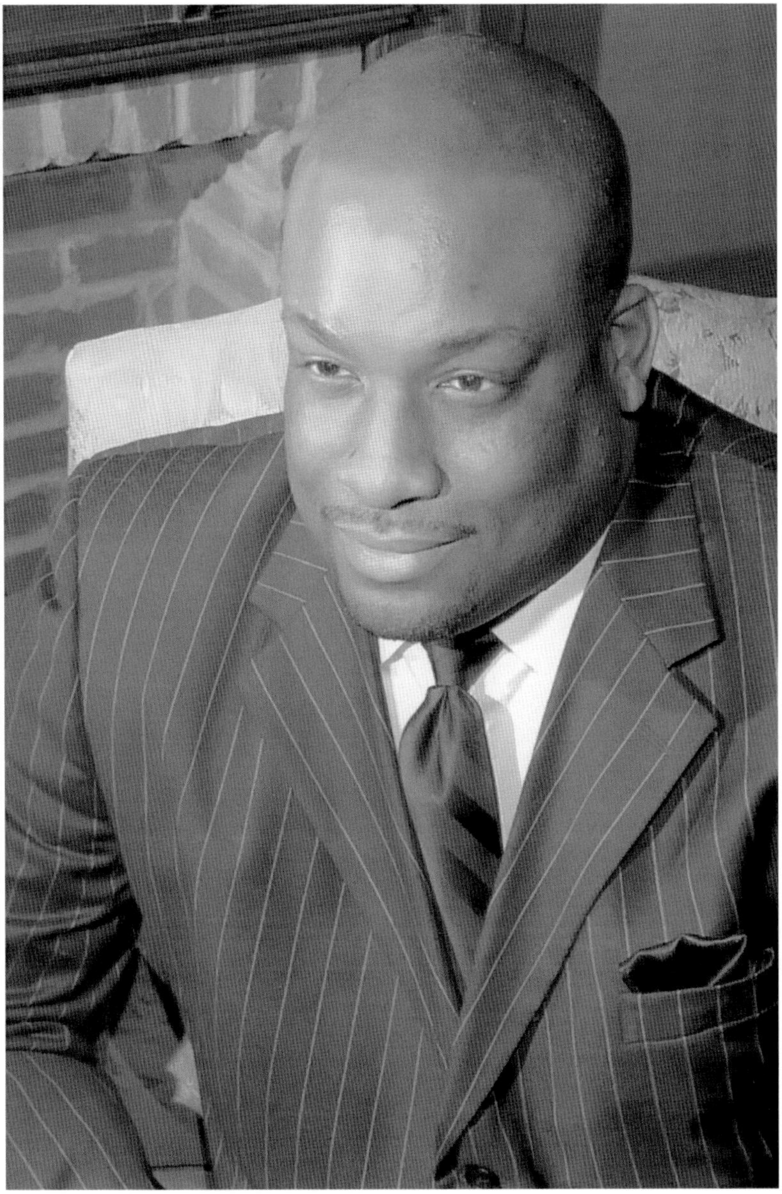

**Aaron M. Davis**
An all-star at track and basketball at Willingboro High School, Aaron M. Davis became director of the New Jersey State Athletic Control Board in 2008. The board ensures that all boxing and combative sports events are safe and meet state regulations. A graduate of Wichita State University with a degree in the administration of justice, Davis worked for four years as Kansas Boxing Commissioner, overseeing boxing, kickboxing, wrestling, and martial arts. He also served as chairman of the Code of Conduct Committee of the Association of Boxing Commissioners, which seeks uniformity of health and safety standards in combat sports. Prior to his involvement in boxing, Davis coached high school basketball and soccer, served as director of minority recruitment for Wichita State, and worked in sales and marketing for Topeka, Kansas, radio stations and as an account executive for Southwestern Bell Telephone. (Courtesy State of New Jersey.)

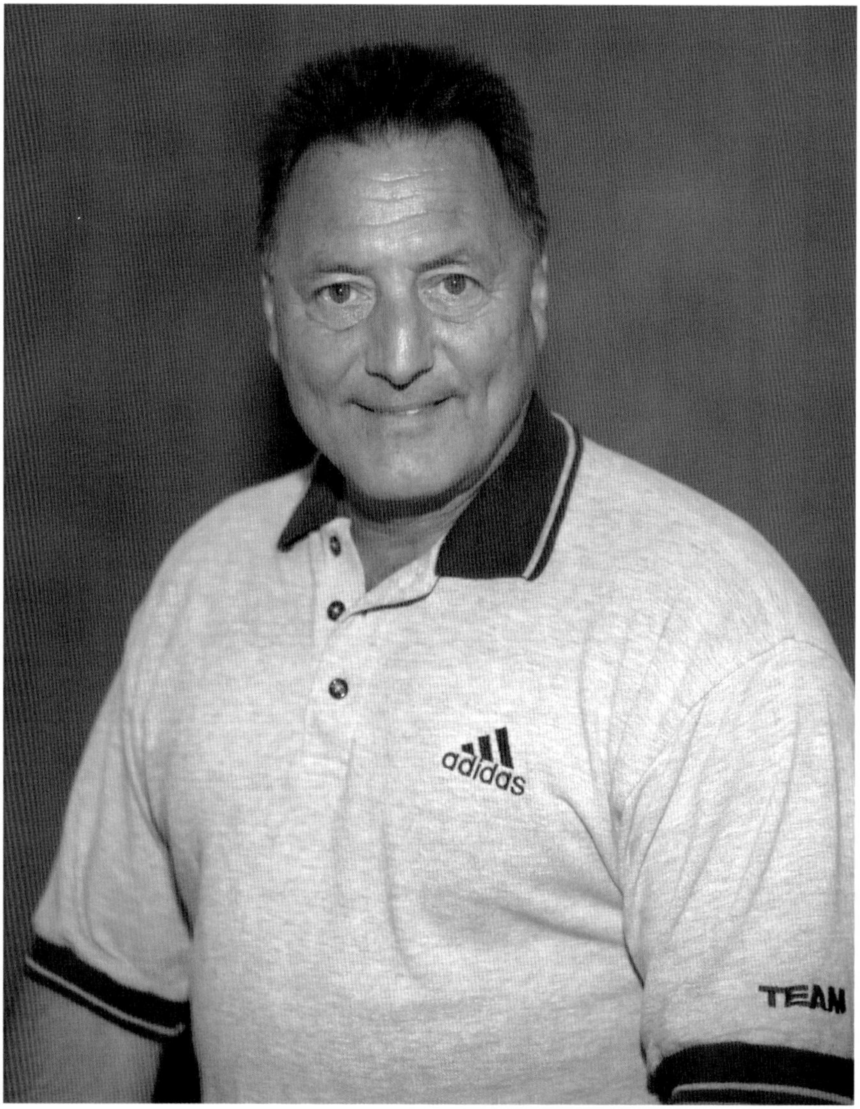


**Charles Duccilli**

Mention Willingboro sports and most people will talk about track, basketball, and football. But during the 1970s and early 1980s, legendary player Charles Duccilli made John F. Kennedy High School into a boys' soccer powerhouse. A graduate of Germantown High School, Duccilli attended Temple University, where he holds the school record for career goals with 66 (he was inducted into the Owls Hall of Fame in 1983). From 1970 to 1981, Duccilli coached at Kennedy, compiling a 135-56-19 record, winning nine championships and being named South Jersey Coach of the Year twice. As he was having success coaching at Kennedy, on the field he signed with the Philadelphia Spartans of the American Soccer League, leading the ASL in scoring with 11 goals in 1971, and five goals in 1972. In 1973, Duccilli joined the Philadelphia Atoms of the North American Soccer League, helping to win their only league title. In all, his professional career with the NASL and ASL spanned 10 years. He later coached the New York Power of the Women's United Soccer Association and both men's and women's teams at Rutgers University. Duccilli has been director of coaching for the Cape Express Soccer Club in Cape May. He also is a sales associate with Caldwell Banker. (Courtesy Charles Duccilli.)

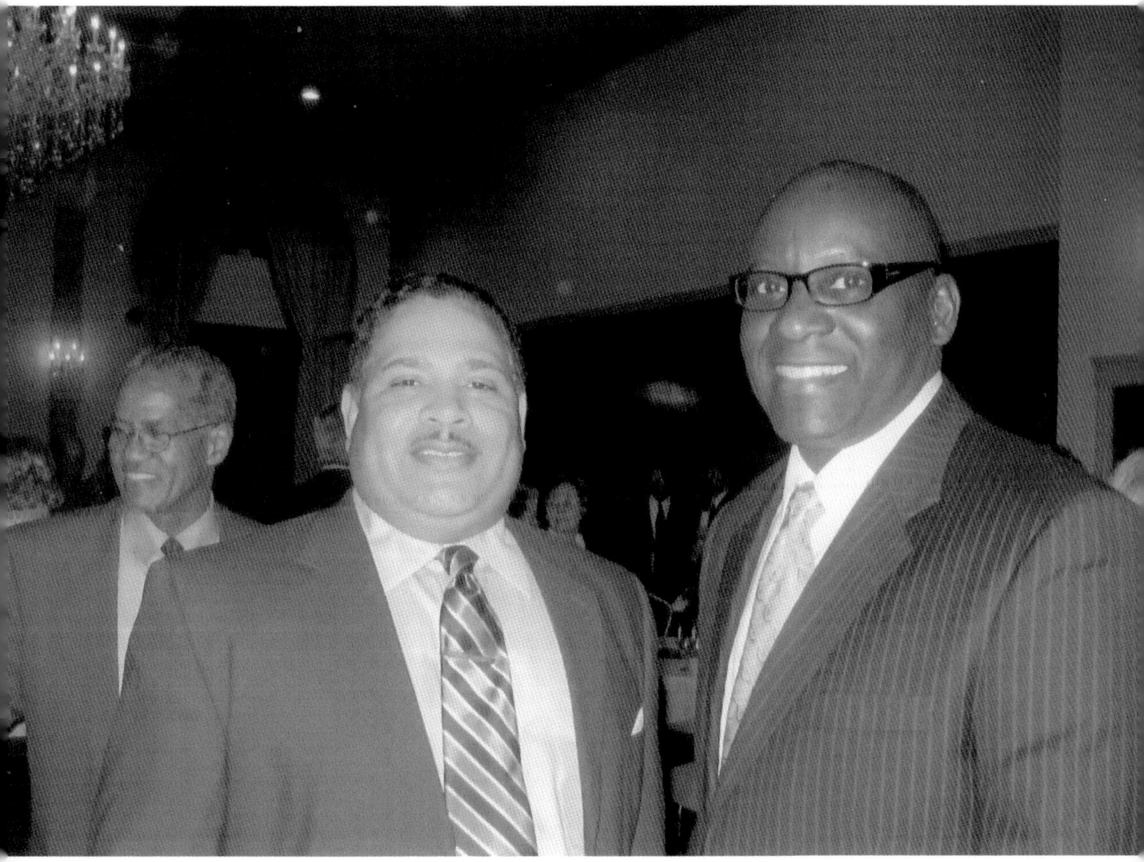

**Cleveland Lewis**

Best known as the older brother of Carl and Carol Lewis, Cleveland Lewis (right) was an outstanding athlete in his own right. Lewis played four years of soccer at Brandeis University and was an All-American and All-New England performer. He set the school's all-time scoring record with 58 goals and was named MVP of the 1976 NCAA Division III national championship game won by Brandeis. He was captain of the first national championship team in the history of the university. Following his graduation in 1978, Lewis played professional soccer with the New York Cosmos. He was inducted into the Brandeis Athletic Hall of Fame in 1993. (Courtesy Lavonne Johnson.)

### Peter Vermes

An outstanding soccer player in high school and college, Peter Vermes has played at the highest levels both here and abroad. Today, the Willingboro native is manager of Major League Soccer's Sporting Kansas City. Vermes represented the United States in the 1988 Olympics and was named US Male Soccer Athlete of the Year. He was an integral part of a young US team that qualified for its first World Cup in 40 years, and he set the stage for the progress of the US national team. During eight years with the national team, he appeared in 66 games and scored 11 goals. In 1989 and 1990, Vermes became the first American to play in the Hungarian and Dutch First Divisions. Returning to the United States, he enjoyed a stellar seven-year career with the New York/New Jersey Metro Stars, Colorado Rapids, and Kansas City. He retired from playing in 2002 and has been coaching in Kansas City ever since. (Courtesy Sporting Kansas City.)

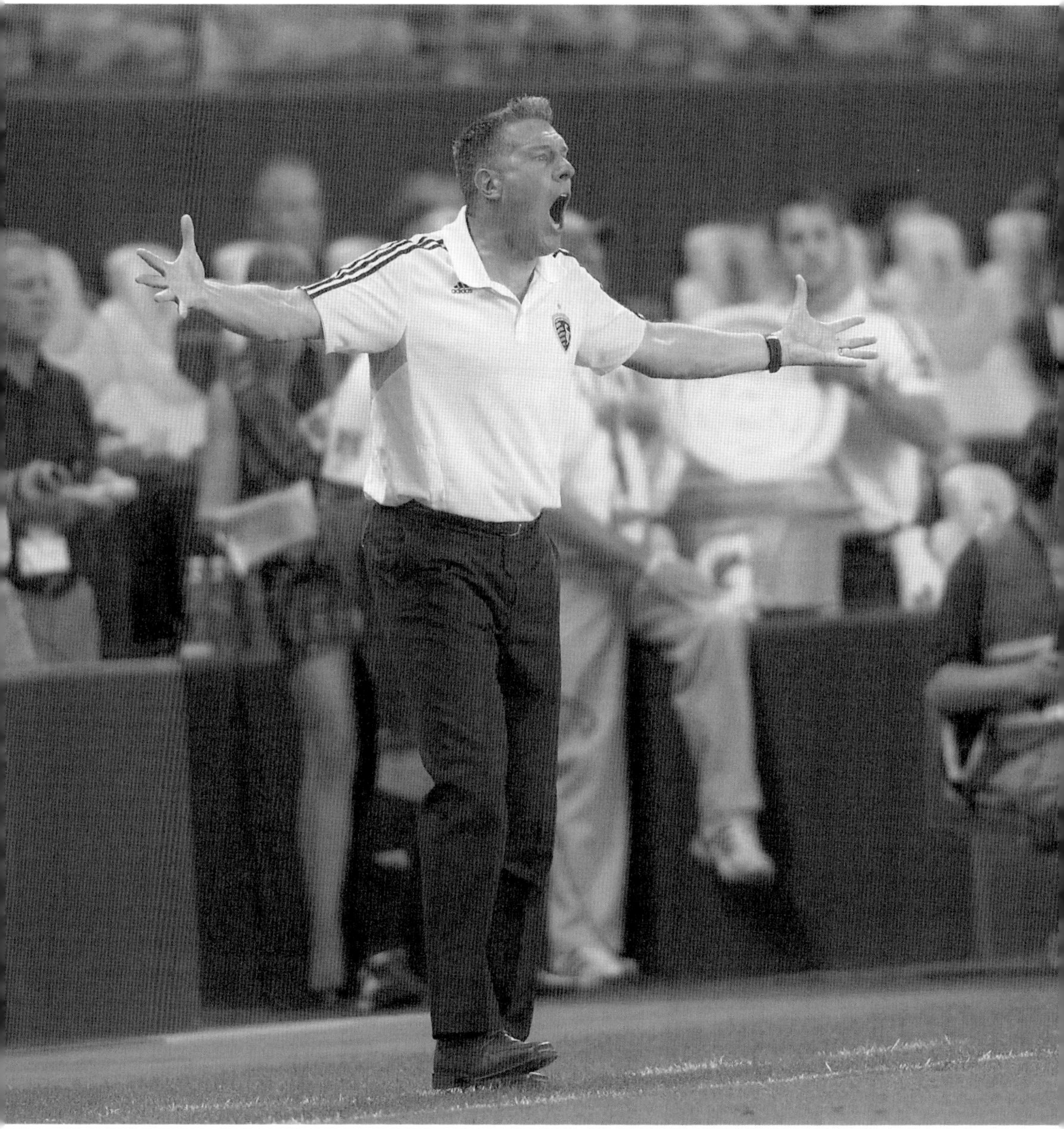

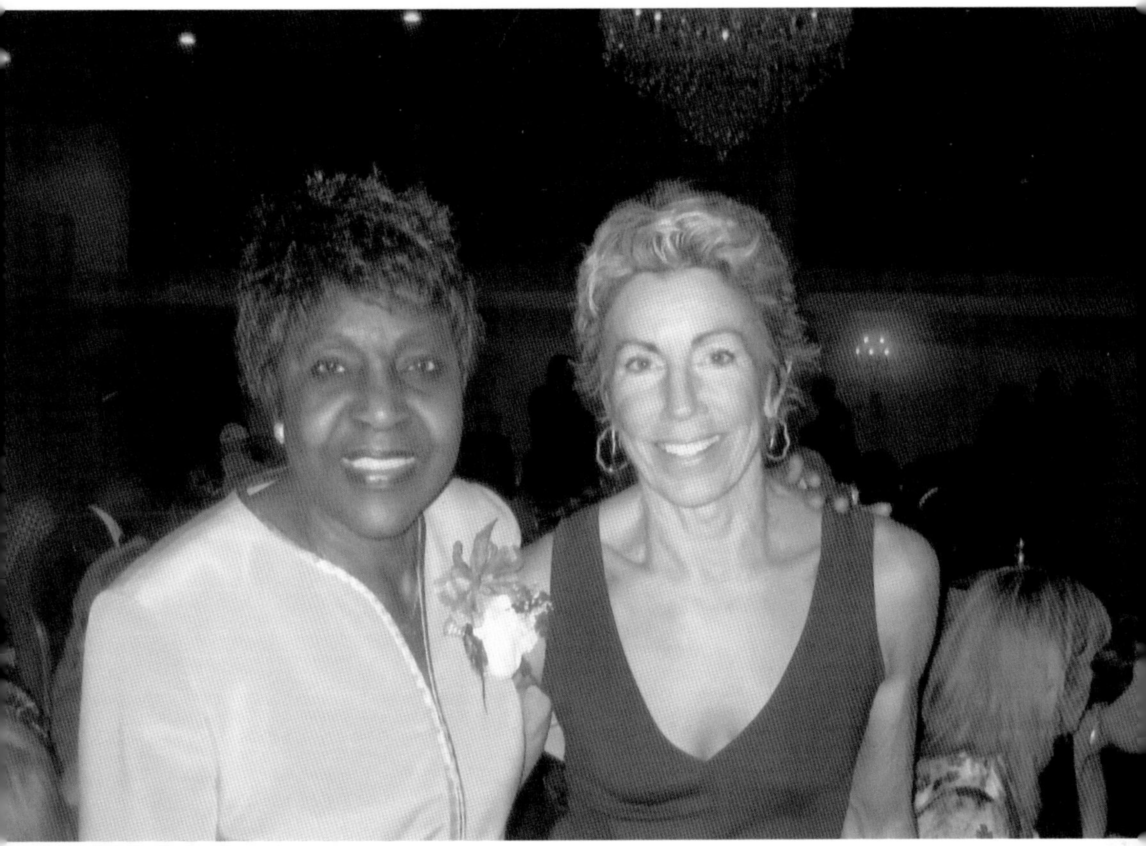

**William and Evelyn Lewis**

William and Evelyn Lewis (at left) have contributed greatly to Willingboro, especially to its youngsters. The couple met at the Tuskegee Institute in Alabama and both became world-class hurdlers, competing for the United States at the 1951 Pan American games. When they came to Willingboro to live, they shared their skills and love with the community, and their children—Mackie, Cleveland, Carl, and Carol—were encouraged to develop their athletic and academic abilities. The Lewises founded many youth athletic organizations, most notably the Willingboro Track Club, which continues to provide opportunities for young people to succeed. The two also coached rival high school track teams: Evelyn at Willingboro High, and William at John F. Kennedy High. William died of cancer in 1987. In 2008, Evelyn was inducted into the South Jersey Track and Field Hall of Fame and still inspires area youth. (Courtesy Lavonne Johnson.)

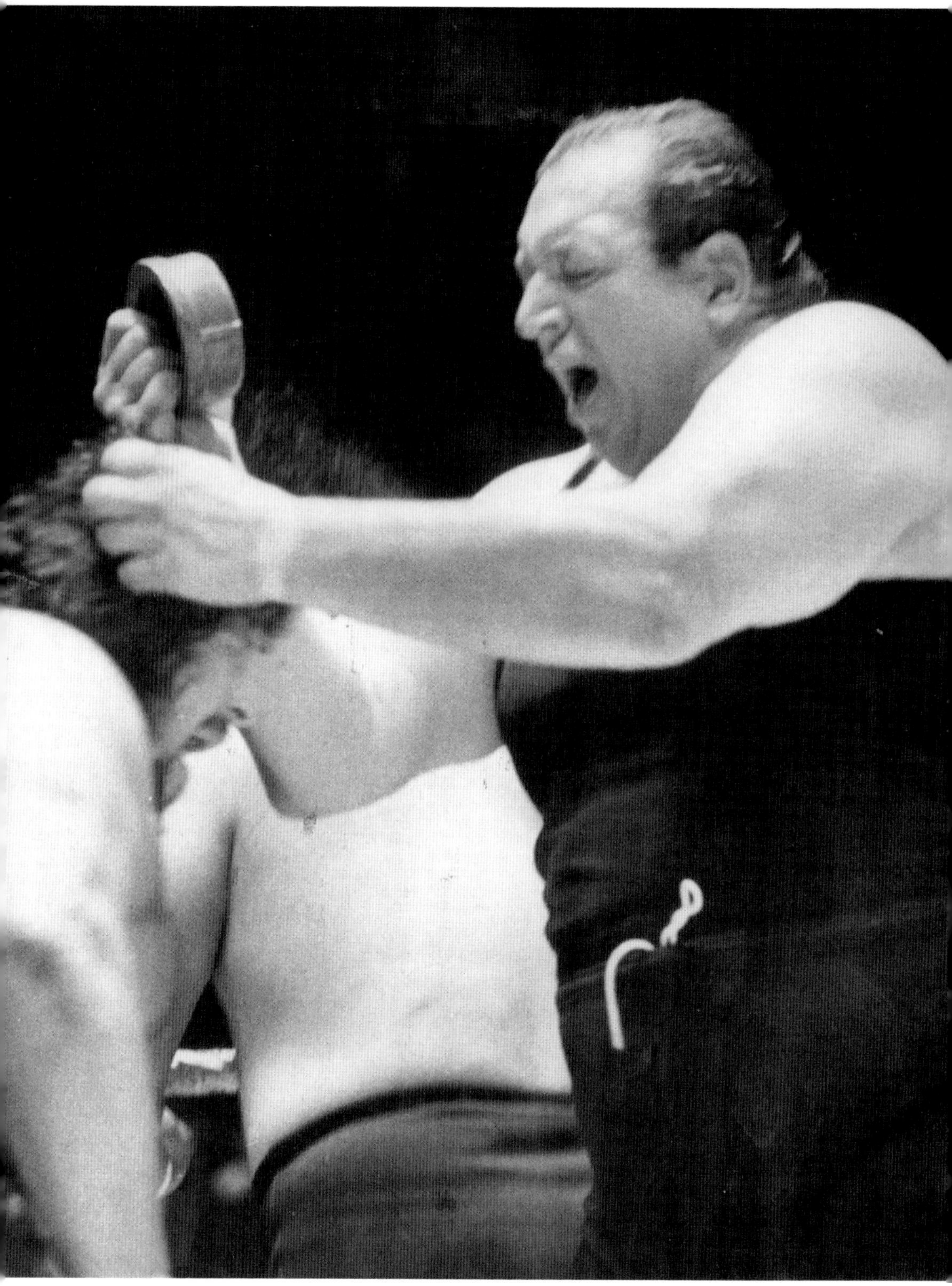

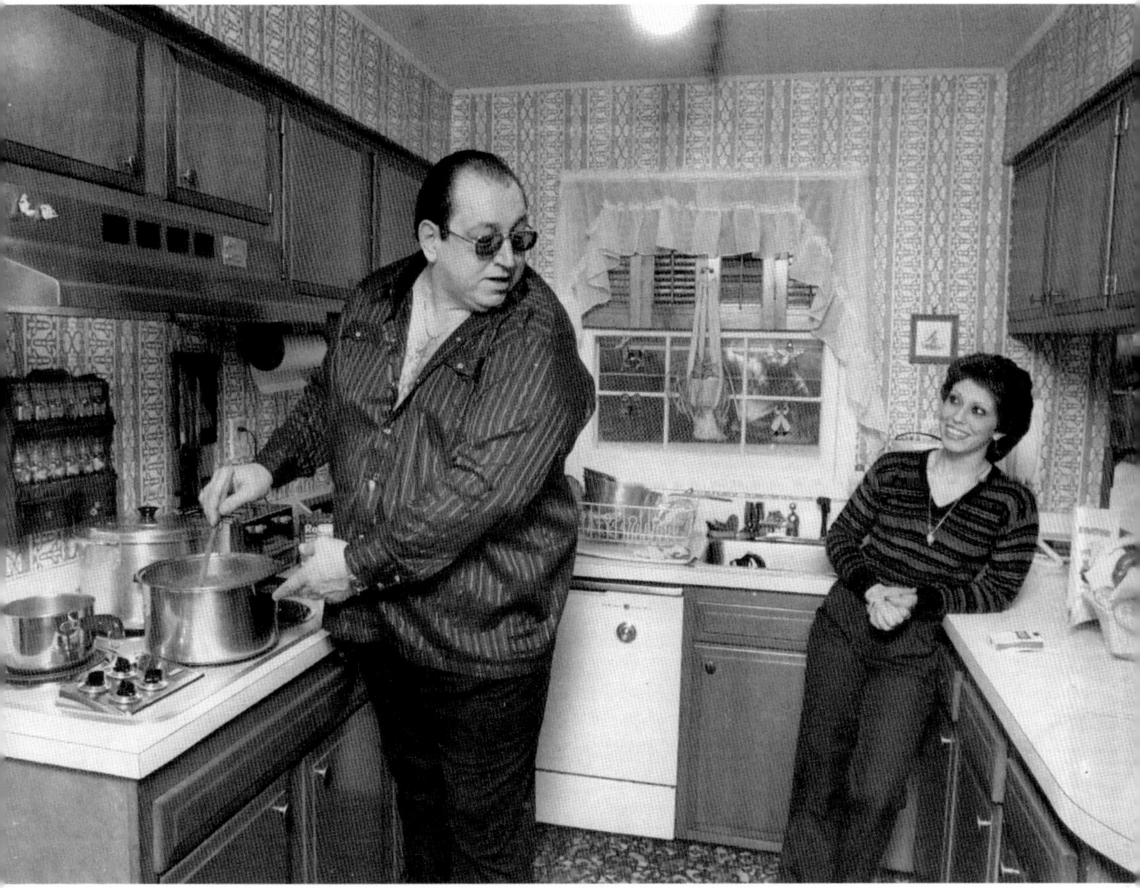

**Gorilla Monsoon** (ABOVE AND OPPOSITE PAGE)
Robert James "Gino" Marella, better known by ring name "Gorilla Monsoon," was a professional wrestler whose athletic prowess and presence transcended sport. A native of Rochester, New York, Marella began to wrestle professionally following his graduation from Ithaca College in 1959. Marella (shown on the opposite page bashing opponent Lou Albano on the head) was a giant—weighing in at upwards of 400 pounds—and for a while, he wrestled under his own name, singing in Italian before matches. He later revamped his image into a hated, bearded monster from Manchuria called Gorilla Monsoon. In 1969, his storyline changed again, becoming a fan favorite. Perhaps the most famous incident of his career occurred after a 1976 match in Philadelphia. Heavyweight champion Muhammad Ali rushed the ring and threw jabs at Marella. Marella hoisted Ali into an airplane spin and slammed him to the canvas. Marella's wrestling career began to wind down in the early 1980s, and he became a colorful commentator and backstage coordinator. Marella was inducted into the World Wrestling Entertainment Hall of Fame in 1994, and from 1995 to 1997, he served as WWE president. Marella died of heart failure on October 6, 1999, in the Willingboro home he shared with his wife, Maureen (above, at right). The couple had four children. (Both, courtesy the *Philadelphia Inquirer.*)

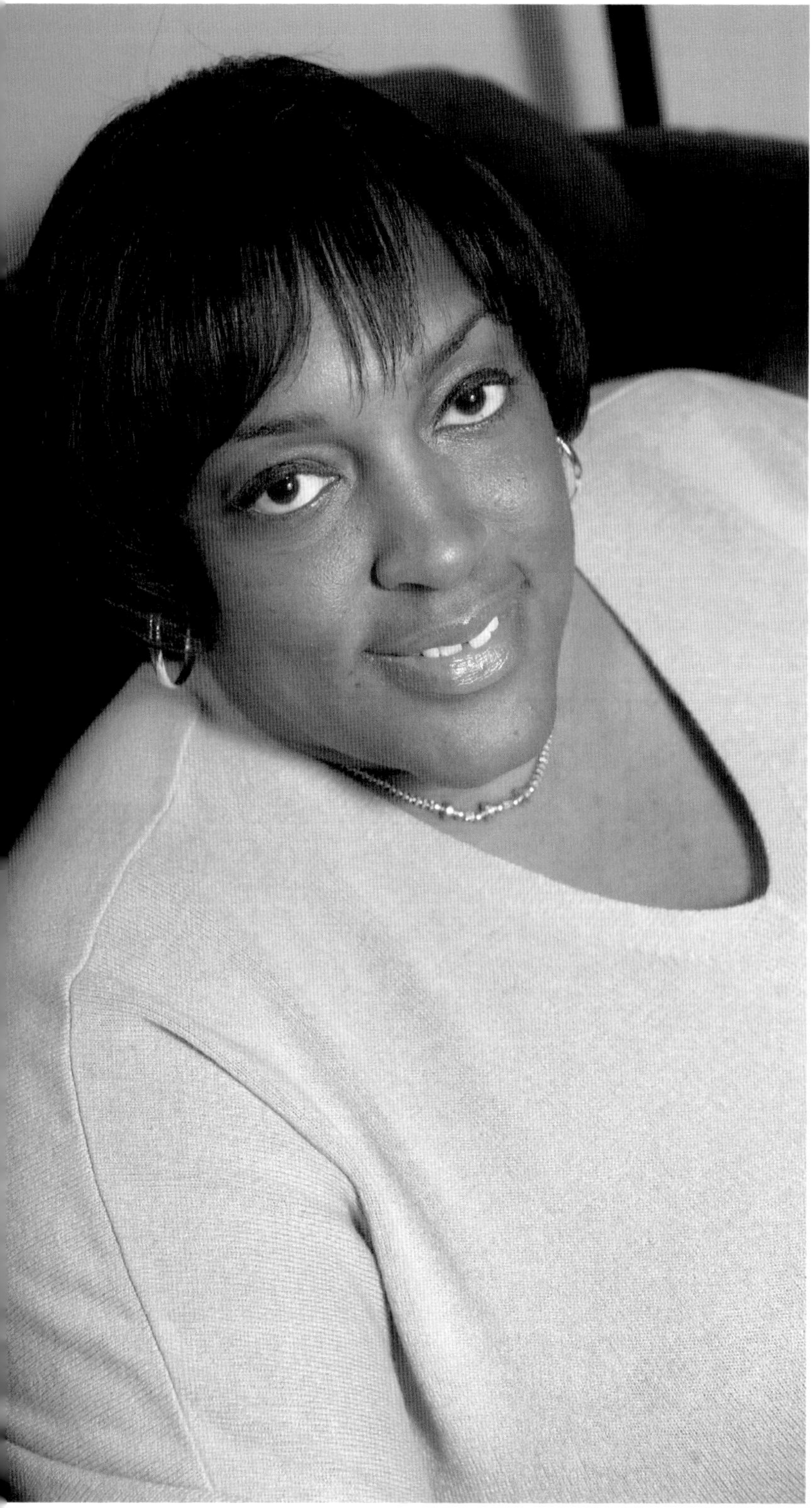

**Celeste Whittaker**
A star basketball player at Willingboro High School, Celeste Whittaker earned a bachelor's degree in journalism from the University of North Carolina at Chapel Hill. Whittaker began her career as an editorial assistant at *Business Week* magazine in New York. She then moved to the *Atlanta Journal-Constitution,* where, for eight years, she covered women's and men's basketball—including at the 1996 Summer Olympics—college football, and high school sports. Since 1998, she has been a sportswriter at the *Courier-Post* in Cherry Hill, covering the Philadelphia 76ers and college and high school sports. Whittaker has won several writing awards, and in 2009 published *The Epitome of Fatherhood: The Life of Chester M. Whittaker.* She also volunteers with the Bookmates literary program. (Courtesy Willingboro Public Library.)

# CHAPTER THREE

# Born to Shine

## Arts and Letters

In today's fast-paced, high-tech society where conversations are conducted in 140 characters or less and photographs can spread worldwide in seconds, it's easy to forget where you came from.

That's where Karen Abdul-Malik comes in. Known professionally as Queen Nur, Abdul-Malik is a nationally renowned storyteller and artist who enthralls thousands each year in the African oral tradition with presentations like *Sweet Potato Pie and Such*.

"Storytellers not only tell the community what's going on, but tell the community what their roles are," she told the *Burlington County Times*.

Willingboro is filled with musicians and poets, authors and journalists, actors, and storytellers who play a vital role in the well-being of the community. They pass on news, transport audiences to a place and time far away, and make you turn up the radio to ear-deafening levels.

Many of Willingboro's musicians began developing their skills at an early age, learning in church and from parents, and then perfecting their artistry with the renowned Willingboro Jazz Band. Under the direction of Jeffrey Lesser, the Willingboro High Jazz Band was a 13-time finalist at the Berklee College of Music High School Jazz Festival, including six wins.

Adam Blackstone, for example, took up the piano and drums at age six and bass guitar while at Willingboro High—because no one else in the band was interested in playing it. Now a top bassist, he has produced, directed, or played with a who's-who of the music industry, including Jill Scott, Justin Timberlake, and Jay-Z. Ryan Toby, Robbie Pardlo, and Claudette Ortiz were classmates when they formed City High. The group scored a Grammy-nominated single, "What Would You Do?"

On the opposite end of the musical spectrum, Mark Adamo has composed operas that have been performed around the world. His latest opera, *The Gospel of Mary Magdalene*, was scheduled to premiere with the San Francisco Opera in 2013.

A number of Willingboro natives share their gift through the written word. Poet Gregory Pardlo's first book, *Totem*, received the American Poetry Review/Honickman Prize. Bill Kent is the author of seven novels set in Philadelphia and Atlantic City, including *Street Fighter* and *Down by the Sea*. Harry Kendall began writing as part of a newspaper's project with Rutgers University to redress the imbalance of whites and blacks in the media. He is the author of two historical novels, *Truth Crushed to Earth* and *The Hot September Harvest*. And Jeff Gammage can be found in the *Philadelphia Inquirer* telling stories daily to thousands of readers.

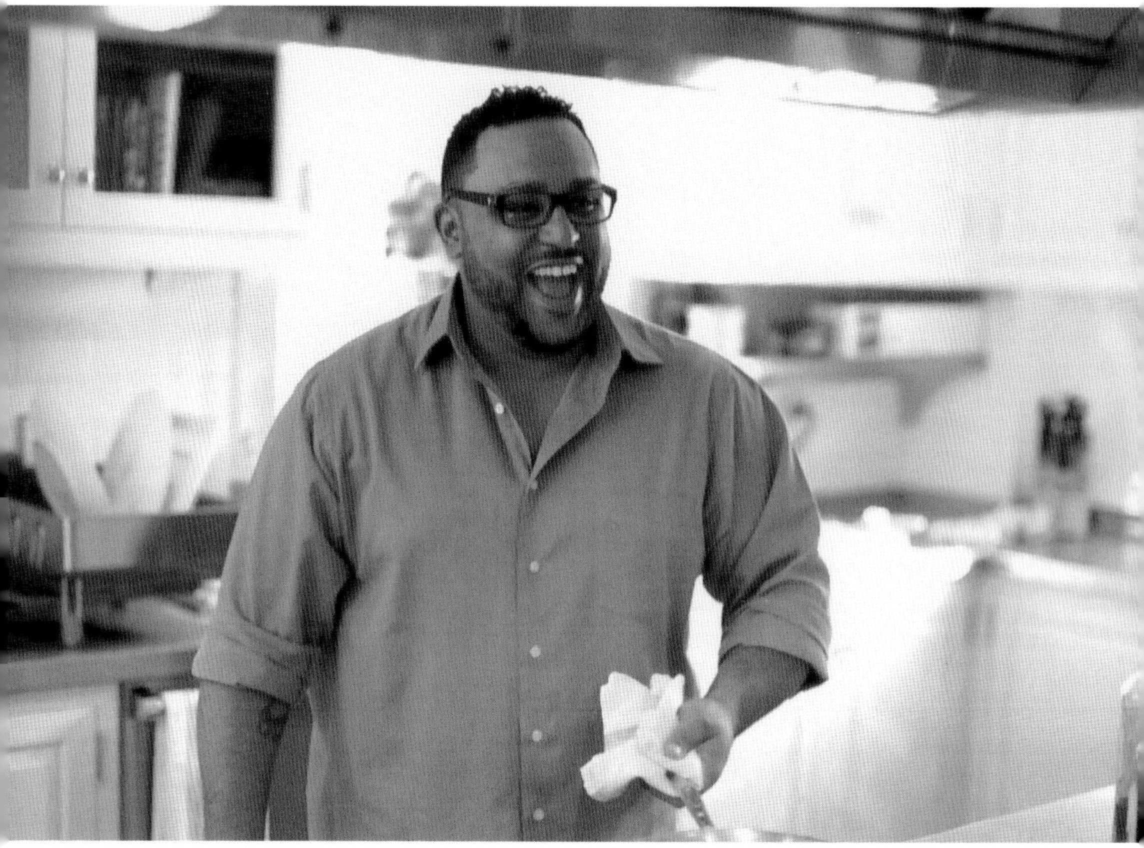

**Kevin Sbraga**

Kevin Sbraga makes things happen. The winner of season seven of Bravo TV's *Top Chef*, Sbraga is the chef and owner of the modern American Sbraga restaurant in Philadelphia. A graduate of Johnson & Wales University in Miami, Sbraga held culinary positions in Atlanta and Philadelphia before being tapped to work with award-winning chef Jose Garces. With Garces's support, he competed in the Bocuse d'Or USA culinary competition in the fall of 2008, winning the award for "Best Meat Presentation." Following the competition, Steven Starr selected him to be executive chef at Rat's Restaurant at the Grounds for Sculpture arboretum in Hamilton, New Jersey. Sbraga opened his own restaurant in October 2011. "I learned on *Top Chef* that you can't always play by the rules, and no matter what, you've got to cook from the heart and cook what's good," he said. Sbraga remains busy. In 2013, he filmed a pilot for a television show *Get Trucked*. He also planned to open a new restaurant called The Fat Ham. Sbraga resides in Willingboro with his wife, Jesmary (his restaurant's pastry chef), and their two children. (Courtesy Sbraga/Wagstaff Worldwide.)

### Mark Adamo

A native of Willingboro, Mark Adamo graduated from Holy Cross High School and the Catholic University of America, where he was awarded the Theodore Presser prize for outstanding undergraduate achievement in composition. Adamo was composer-in-residence at the New York City Opera from 2001 to 2006, where he led the VOX: Showcasing American Composers program. He also served as master artist at Atlantic Center for the Arts in May 2003, where he coached teams of composers and librettists in developing their work for the stage. His first opera, *Little Women*, premiered at the Houston Grand Opera in 1998. Since then, it has been heard in more than 70 cities worldwide, including Nagoya, Japan, where it served as the official US cultural entrant to the 2005 World Expo. In 2001, *Little Women* was nationally telecast on the PBS series *Great Performances*, and the album was acclaimed as one of the 10 best opera releases that year. His second opera, *Lysistrata*, adapted from Aristophanes's comedy with elements from Sophocles's *Antigone*, was commissioned by Houston Grand Opera for its 50th anniversary and premiered in 2005. The *New Yorker* called it "a sumptuous love story, poised between comedy and heartbreak" by "a brilliant theater composer of effortless mastery." His latest opera, *The Gospel of Mary Magdalene*, was scheduled to premiere with the San Francisco Opera in June 2013. While principally a theater artist, Adamo also has written for chorus, ballet, recital, and orchestra. Adamo is a professor at New York University and resides in Manhattan and Kent Cliffs, New York. (Courtesy Martin Gram.)

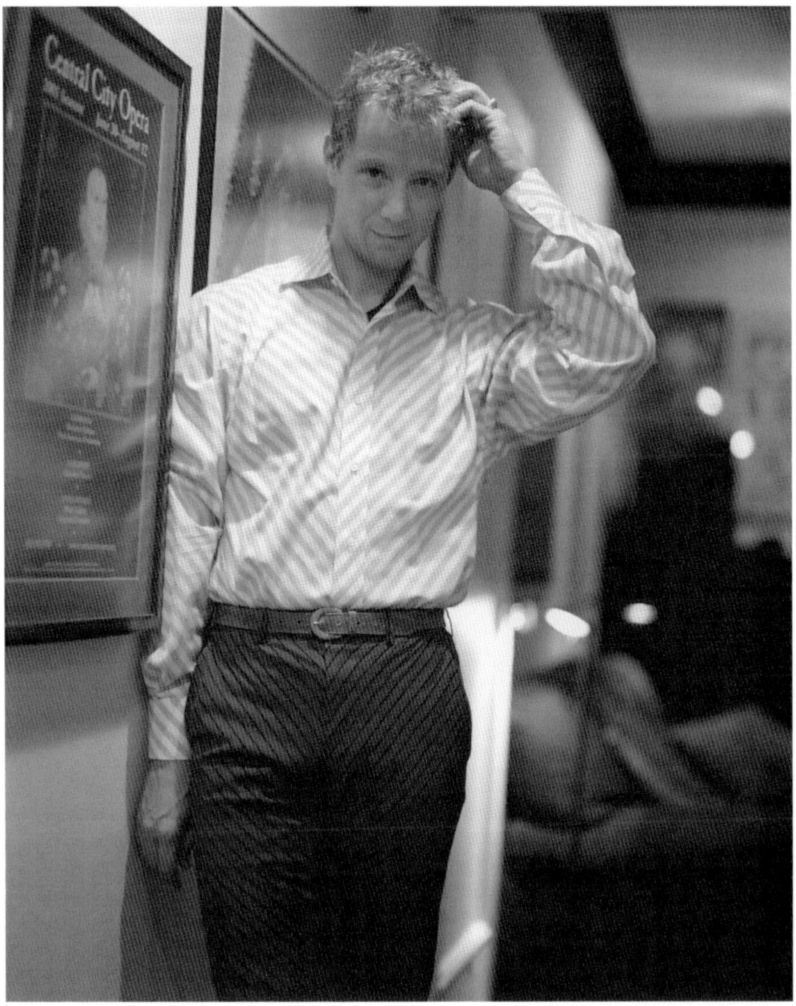

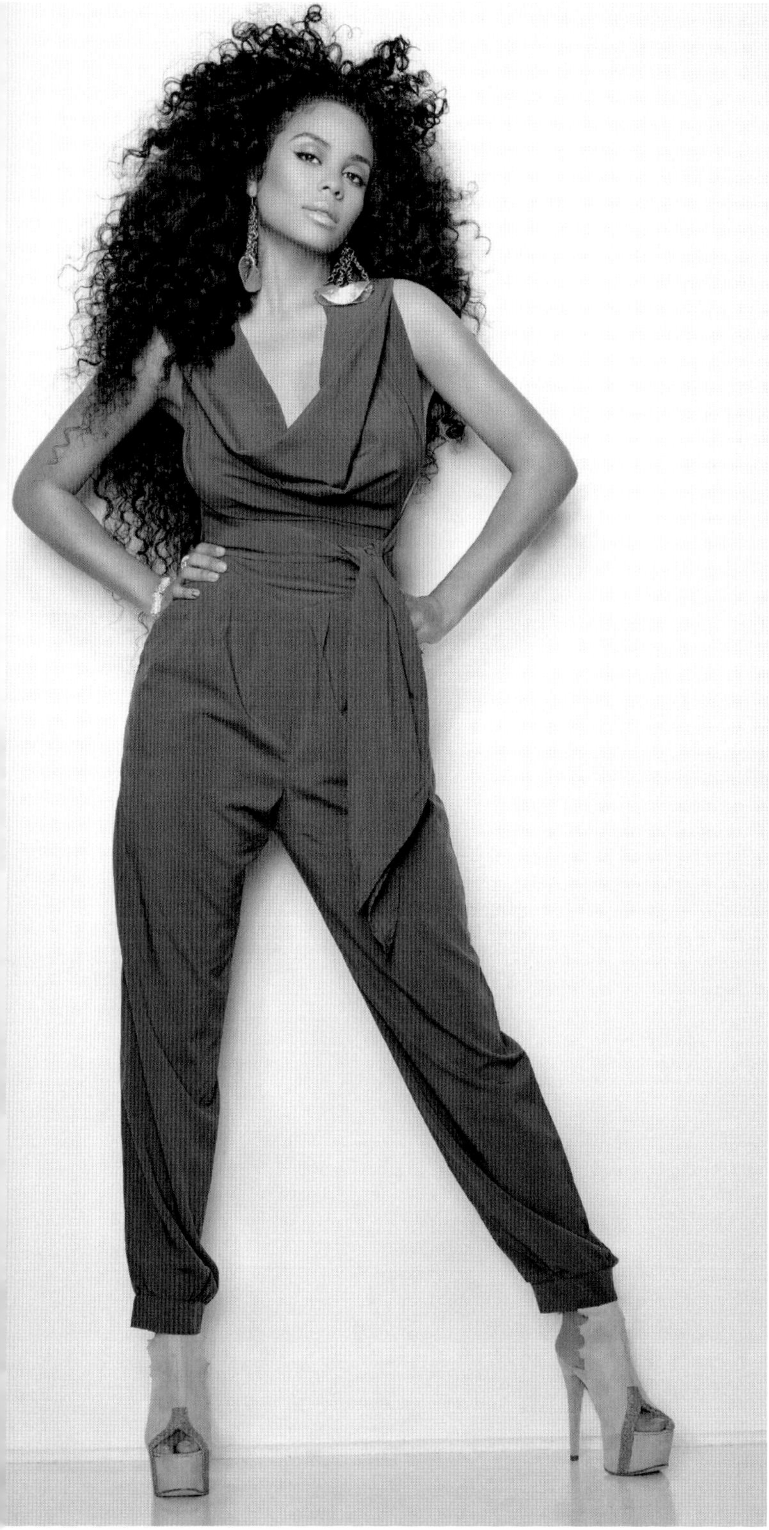

**Claudette Ortiz**
Singer and former model Claudette Ortiz made a splash on the music scene as the lead singer of the R&B/hip-hop group City High with her Willingboro High School classmates Robbie Pardlo and Ryan Toby. Ortiz began performing at age four, but her vocal abilities were rarely publicly noticed as she did not participate in school activities. Pardlo and Toby had formed a duo, and their producer, Wyclef Jean, suggested they recruit their friend Ortiz. The trio is best known for its Grammy-nominated single "What Would You Do?" from its album *City High*. The group disbanded in 2003. Ortiz first dated Pardlo, and later married Toby. Their marriage ended in 2007. Ortiz launched a solo career, and in 2006 released her first single, "Can't Get Enough," which peaked at No. 89 on the Billboard Hot 100, and No. 37 on the US R&B chart. She also worked with Wyclef Jean, Ja Rule, Nas, and Mase. Now, the single mother of three, who once considered enlisting in the US Air Force Reserve to ensure her family's financial stability, is focusing on reviving her music career. In 2013, she appeared on TV One's reality series *R&B Divas: LA*. (Courtesy D'Andre Michael.)

**Robbie Pardlo and Ryan Toby**

Robbie Pardlo (left) was one-third of the group City High, with fellow Willingboro High School classmates Ryan Toby and Claudette Ortiz. City High's first single, "What Would You Do?" was featured in the Eddie Murphy film *Life* and on MTV's *Real World*, and it earned a Grammy nomination. Sadly, drama got in the way of the group's success. Ortiz dumped high school sweetheart Pardlo for Toby and the group disbanded in 2003. Pardlo became an alcoholic, and in 2010, he appeared on the A&E show *Intervention*.

Ryan Toby (right) is the third member of the group City High. But before the trio had its album, Toby was a member of the Willingboro High School vocal program and appeared in the movie *Sister Act II: Back in the Habit*. After the group broke up, Toby and Ortiz married. They divorced in 2007. Toby has become a successful songwriter, writing for Mary J. Blige, Brian McKnight, Chris Brown, Ruben Studdard, New Edition, and Lionel Richie, among others. In 2006, he released a solo album, *Soul of a Songwriter*. (Courtesy Interscope Records.)

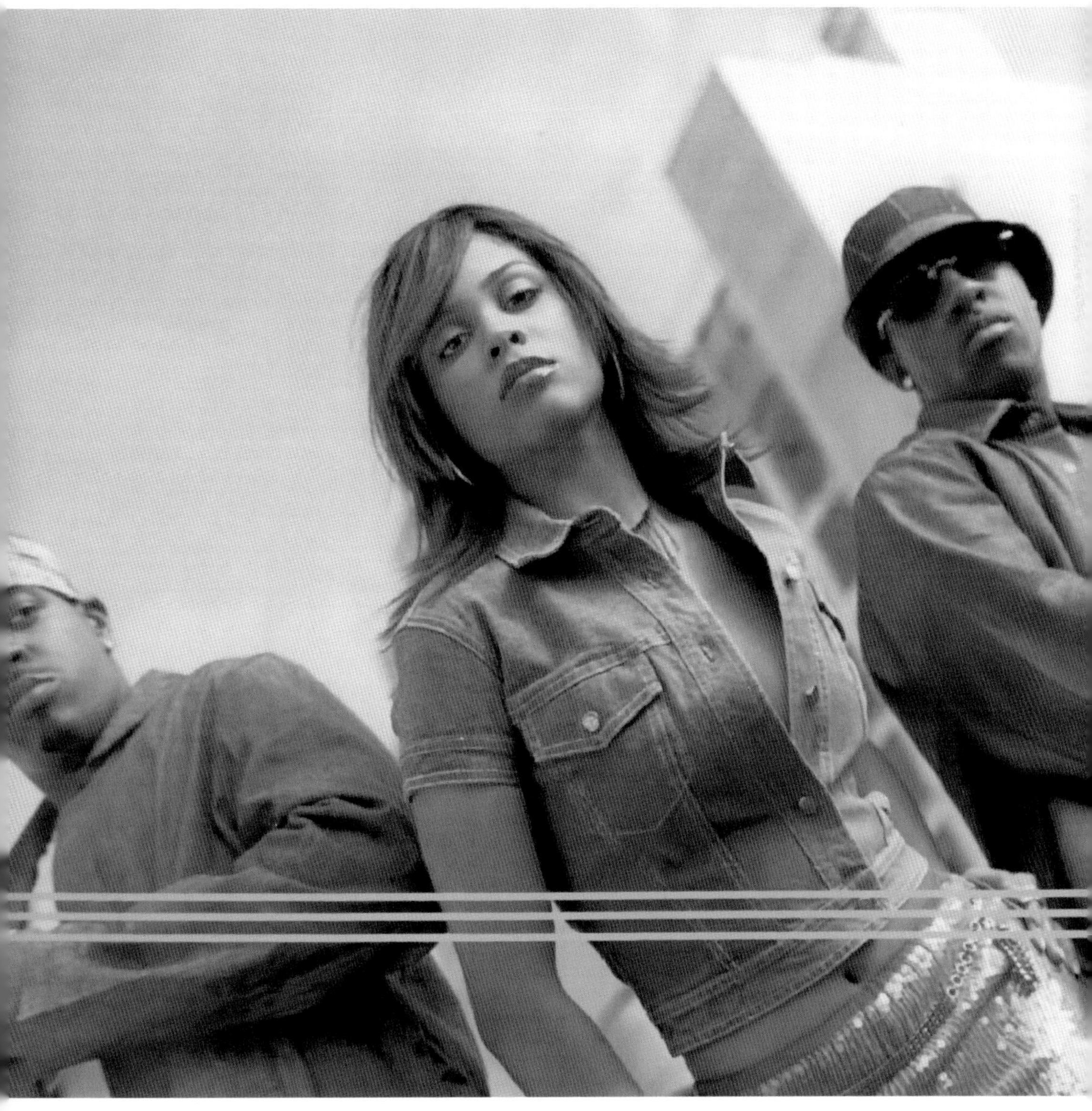

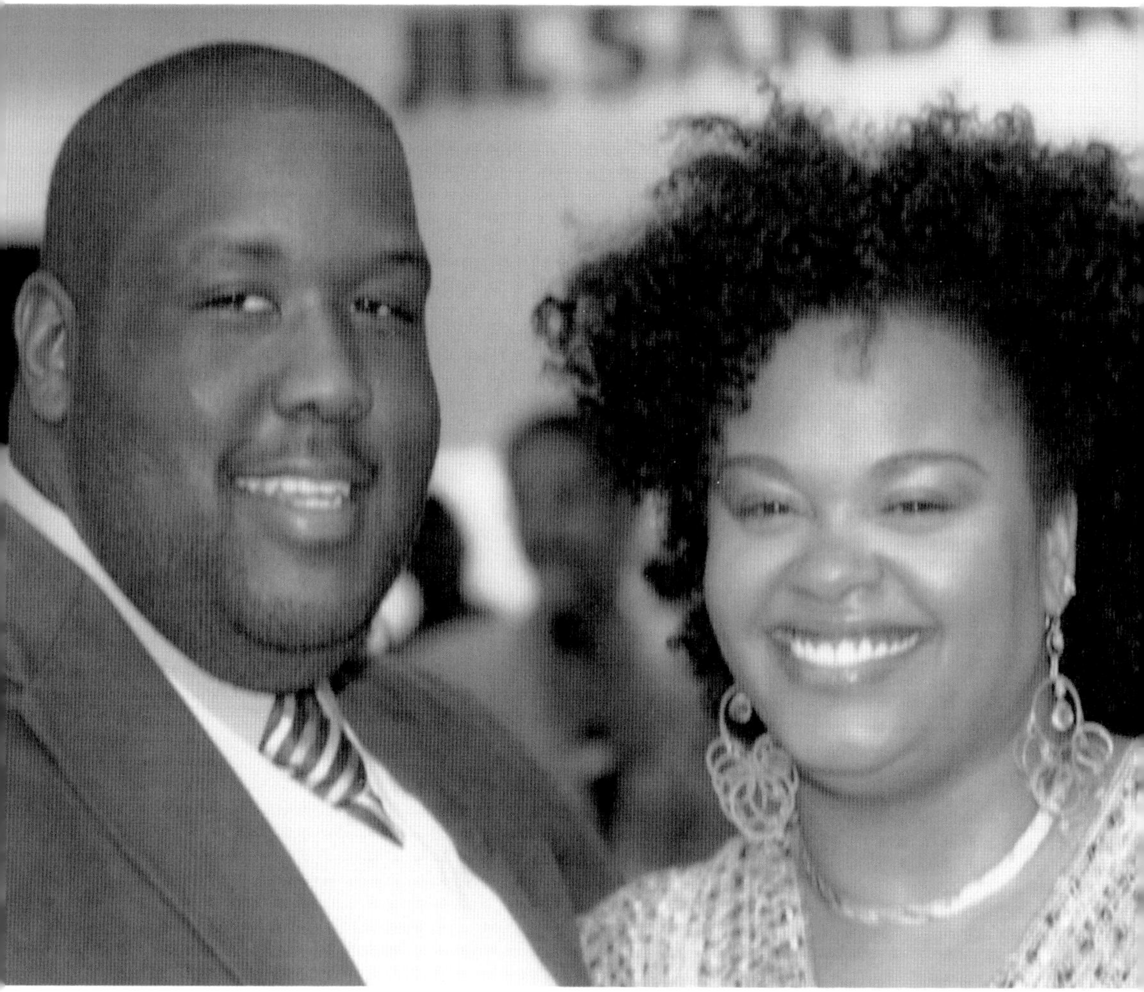

**Adam Blackstone**

If you don't immediately recognize Adam Blackstone, you sure know his music. The son of a popular Trenton jazz musician, Blackstone (at left with performer Jill Scott) fell in love with music at age six, taking up the piano and drums. He learned the bass guitar at Willingboro High School only because no one else was keen on playing it. Blackstone's musical talents earned him a college scholarship, and since then he has produced, directed, and played with performers such as Justin Timberlake, Rihanna, Jay-Z, Eminem, Kanye West, Janet Jackson, Drake, Maroon 5, the Roots, the Isley Brothers, Demi Lovato, and Jill Scott. A top bassist and one of the most sought-after talents in the industry, he also has served as an advisor on *The Voice* (NBC) and musical director on *Verses and Flow* (TV One). (Courtesy Jeffrey Lesser.)

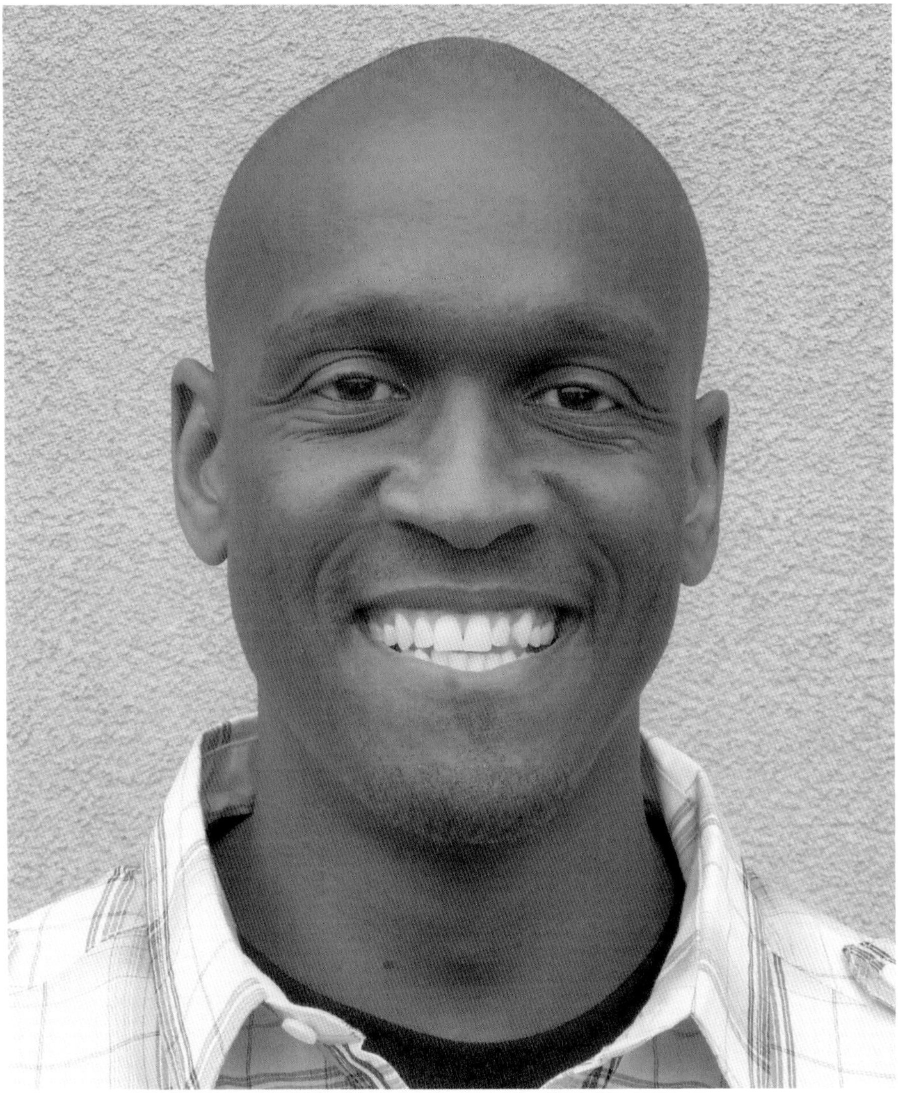

**Gervase Peterson**

Gervase Peterson became a household name in the summer of 2000 when he appeared on the first season of the reality show *Survivor*, a CBS series about 16 individuals stranded on a deserted island left to survive on their own skills. Yet the aspiring actor nearly didn't try out, as he was caring for his sick mother. Peterson became one of the most recognized cast members, and although he did not win the competition, he stayed busy in entertainment. Peterson promoted Sunkist and HeadBlade razors, served as a news correspondent for *Access Hollywood*, MTV, *The Early Show*, and the *Today Show*; appeared on programs like *Late Night with David Letterman, Nash Bridges*, and *The Hughleys*; and judged beauty pageants. Back home, Peterson worked in customer relations for an ambulance company, as well as coached at the YMCA and in Cinnaminson. He recently opened Burnz Cigar Vault and Lounge in Lawnside, writes a monthly advice column for *Jersey Man* magazine called *Say, Gerv*, acts in independent films, and makes personal appearances. In 2013, Peterson and his niece Marissa Peterson competed in *Survivor: Blood vs. Water*—his first return to the show that made him famous. "The past 12 years have been a whirlwind, but I've had fun, too."

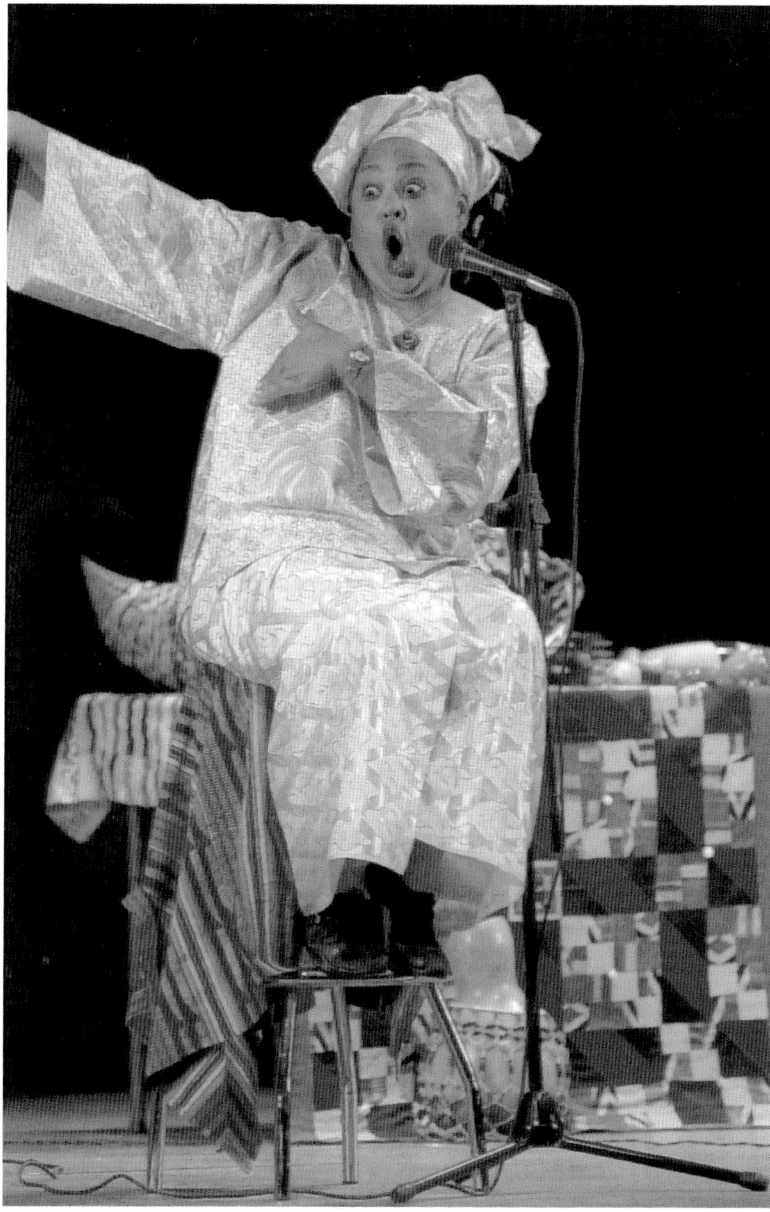

**Karen Abdul-Malik**

Karen Abdul-Malik, known professionally as "Queen Nur," is a nationally renowned storyteller and teaching artist. Abdul-Malik enthralls thousands each year in the African oral tradition at schools, churches, and festivals from Jonesboro, Arkansas, to New York City, to Washington, DC. She is a fixture at local and regional Kwanzaa and African American History Month celebrations. The mother of three and grandmother of one, Abdul-Malik received her bachelor's degree from Northeastern University. She completed graduate work at Harvard Law School, Temple University and the University of Pennsylvania. She teaches storytelling at Rutgers University's Camden campus. The recipient of numerous grants, Abdul-Malik has recorded two CDs, *Sweet Potato Pie and Such* and *Live and Storified.* (Courtesy Karen Abdul-Malik/Walter Petrule.)

### Jeffrey Lesser

A graduate of Trenton State College and Temple University, Jeffrey Lesser began his career with the East Windsor Regional School District as assistant band director. In 1985, he returned to his hometown Willingboro to teach at John F. Kennedy High School. Kennedy closed in 1990, and that year he led the new combined Willingboro High to first place at its first appearance in the prestigious Berklee College of Music High School Jazz Festival. As band director, Lesser led the Willingboro High School Jazz Band to 13 Berklee finals, including 6 first-place finishes. He has helped hundreds of students to appreciate musical performance through entertaining marching, concert, and jazz bands. In 1997, Lesser was named New Jersey Outstanding Jazz Educator of the Year. Currently, Lesser is supervisor of arts education for East Brunswick Public Schools. A composer and arranger, he writes for Forte Publications. A trumpet player, Lesser has performed with the Greater Trenton Symphony Orchestra and with his top-40 group Trilogy, appearing on the ABC soap opera *All My Children*. (Courtesy Jeffrey Lesser.)

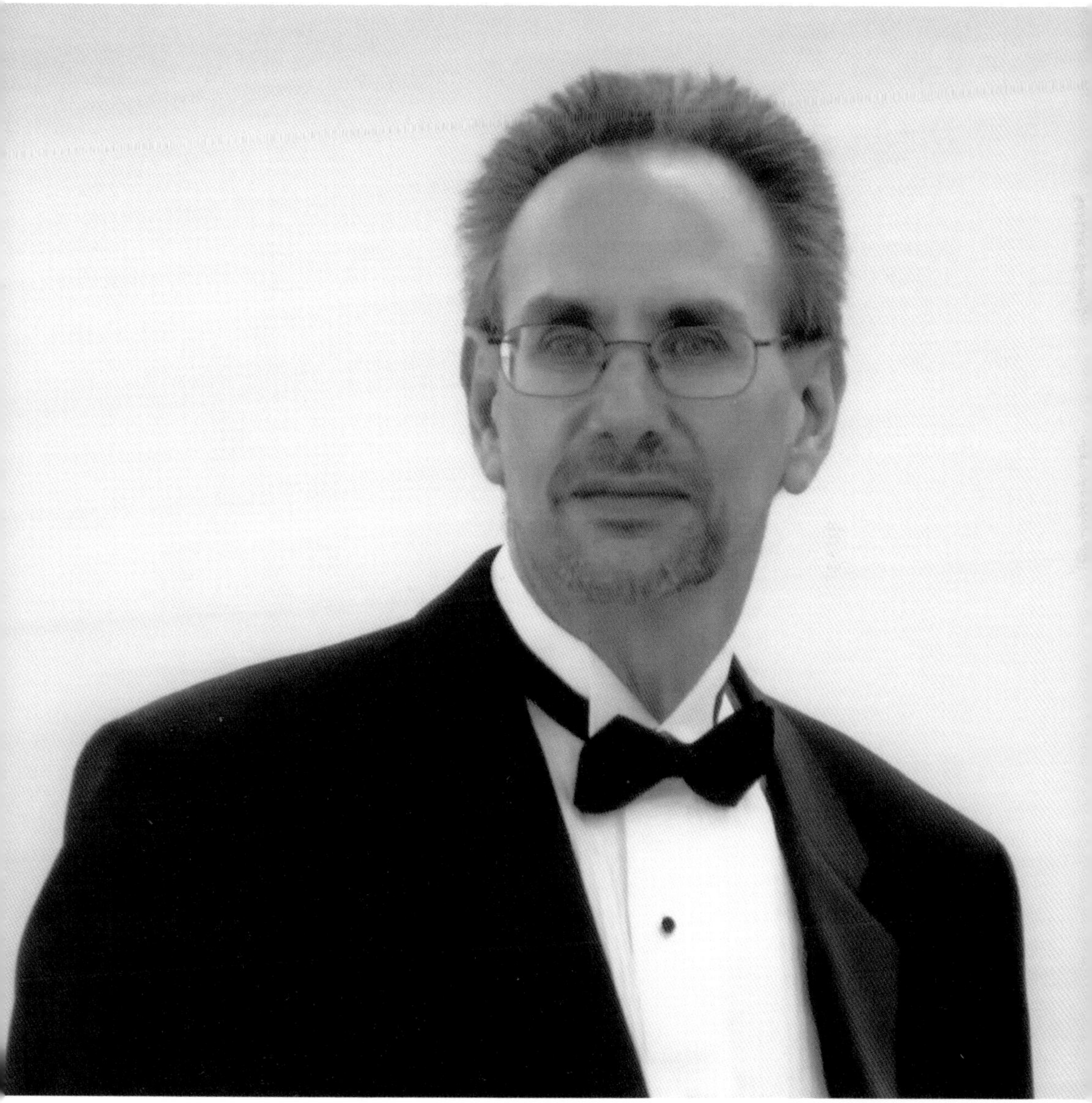

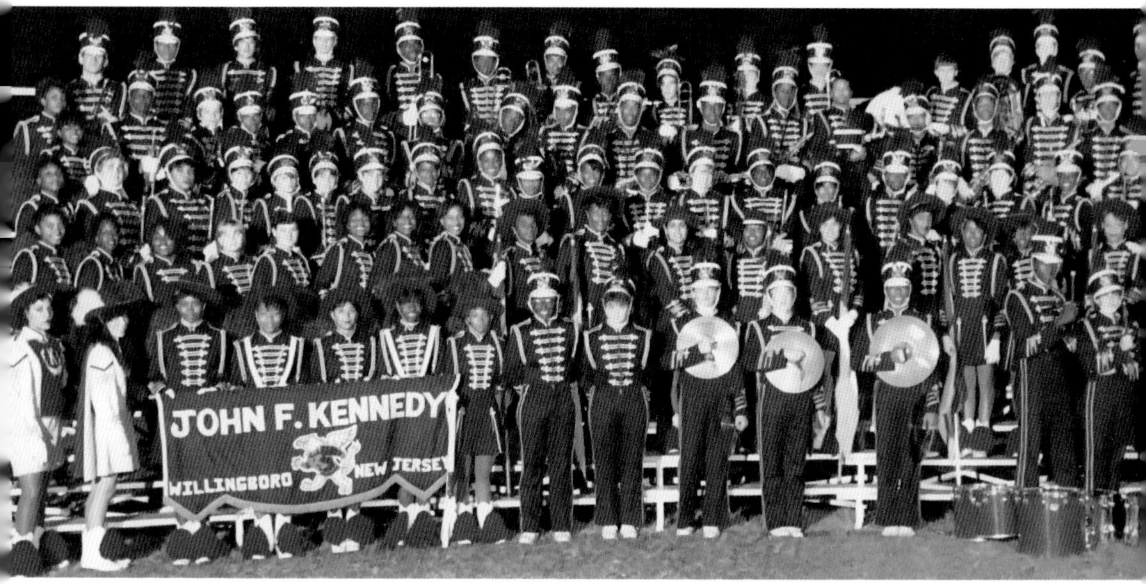


**High School Bands**

Willingboro has a rich musical heritage in its schools, beginning with John F. Kennedy High School (seen here above at a 1988 championship) and continuing at Willingboro High School. The Willingboro High School Jazz Band (below) has been a finalist 13 times at the Berklee College of Music High School Jazz Festival and a finalist 19 times at the International Association for Jazz Education New Jersey State Jazz Festival. It has served as the opening act for the Willingboro Township Jazz Festival and hosted concerts by the Count Basie Orchestra and the Mingus Big Band. Many students have won individual awards at festivals and continue their musical careers in performance and education. (Both, courtesy Jeffrey Lesser.)

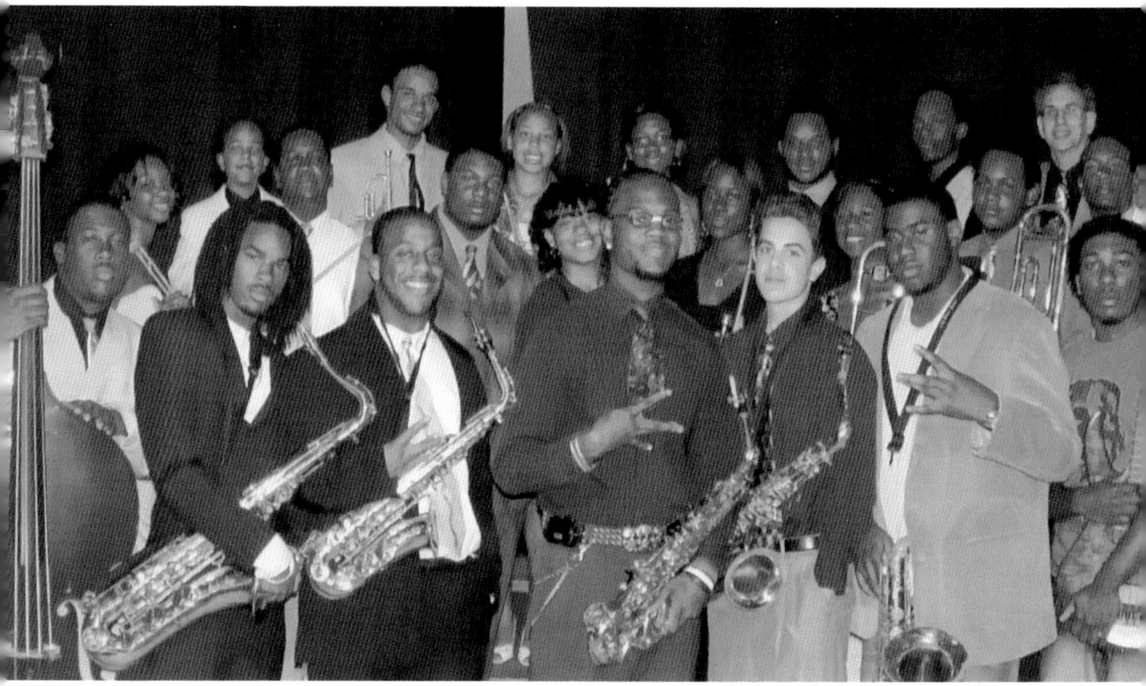

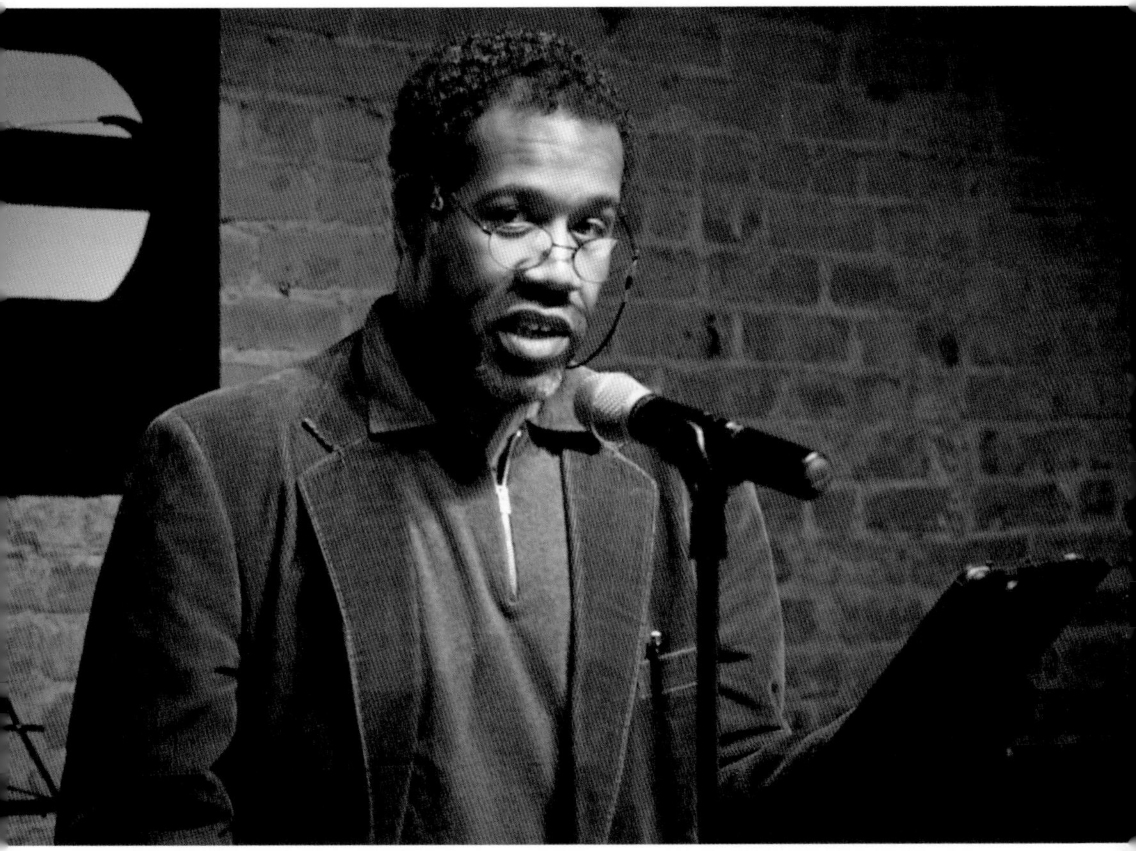

**Gregory Pardlo**

Gregory Pardlo's first book, *Totem*, received the American Poetry Review/Honickman Prize in 2007. His poems have appeared in *American Poetry Review*, *Boston Review*, *Callaloo*, *Gulf Coast*, *Harvard Review*, the *Nation*, *Ploughshares*, and *Best American Poetry 2010*, as well as several anthologies, including *Angles of Ascent*, the Norton Anthology of Contemporary African American Poetry. Pardlo is the recipient of a New York Foundation for the Arts Fellowship and a fellowship in translation from the National Endowment for the Arts. He has received other fellowships from the *New York Times*, the MacDowell Colony, the Lotos Club Foundation and Cave Canem. He is an associate editor of *Callaloo*, and his second collection, *Digest*, is forthcoming from Four Way Books. (Courtesy Haimy Assefa.)

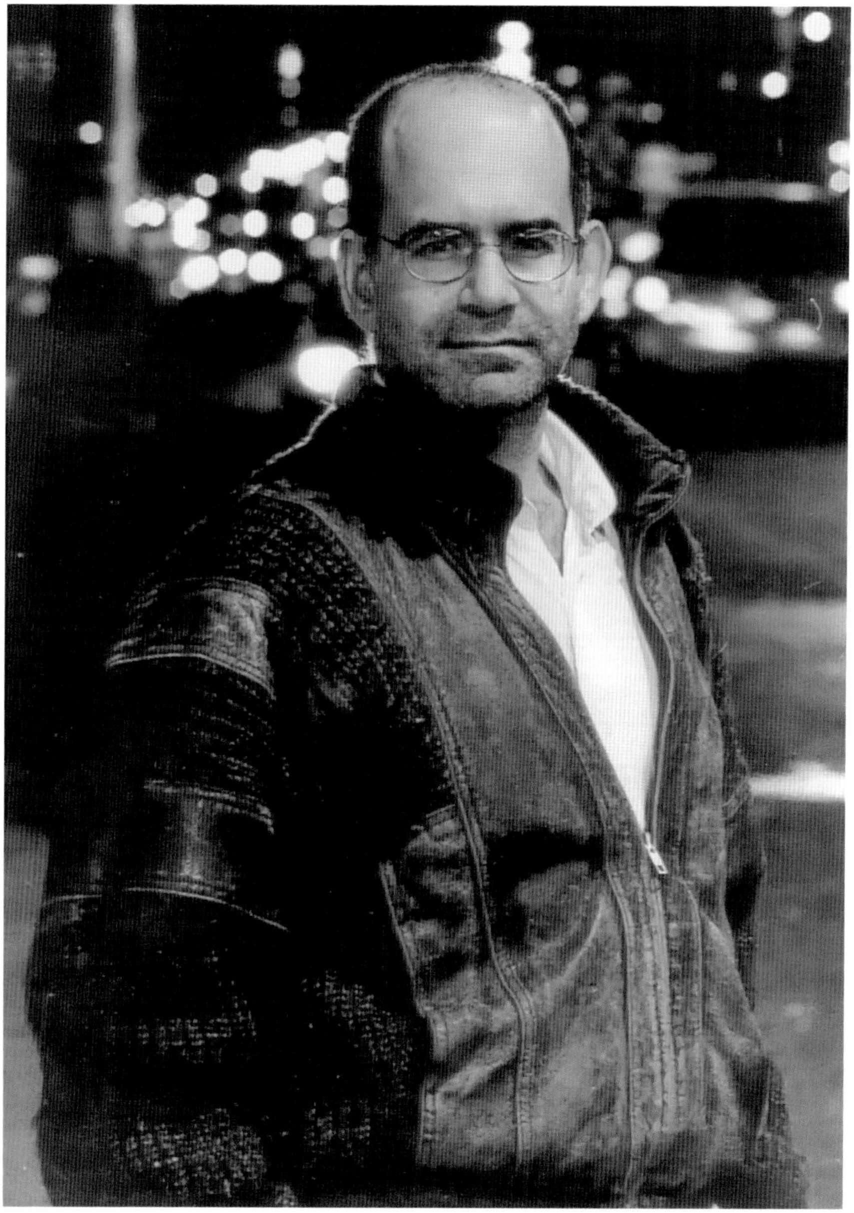

**Bill Kent**

Born in Hackensack and raised in Willingboro, Bill Kent is a writer, journalist, and teacher. A graduate of Oberlin College, Kent has been a reporter and freelance writer for the *New York Times*, *Philadelphia Inquirer*, *Washington Post*, and more than 40 other regional and national publications. He is the author of seven novels set in Philadelphia and Atlantic City, including *Street Money*, *Street Fighter* and *Down by the Sea*, as well as a history of Atlantic City. Along the way, Kent has flown a kite off the Great Wall of China, served as an apprentice to a novelist, studied archaeology in Israel, earned a black belt in karate, and swam with the Atlantic City Polar Bear Club on New Year's Day. Kent teaches novel writing at the University of Pennsylvania and lectures on history and biography. He resides in Wynnewood, Pennsylvania, with his wife and son. (Courtesy Willingboro Library.)

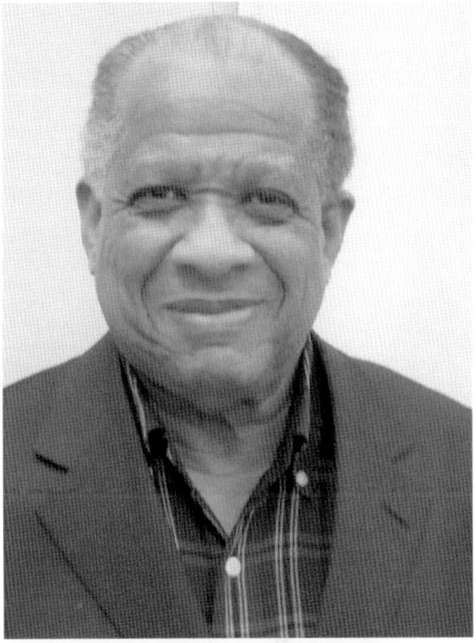

**Harry Kendall**
Born in western Pennsylvania, Harry Kendall began writing as part of a newspaper's project with Rutgers University to redress racial imbalance in the media. After earning a bachelor's degree in journalism from Rutgers, he worked for newspapers in New Jersey and Philadelphia and later received a master's of fine arts degree from Vermont College. Kendall has written two historical novels, *Truth Crushed to Earth* and *The Hot September Harvest*. Kendall is chairman of the Willingboro Library Board of Trustees.

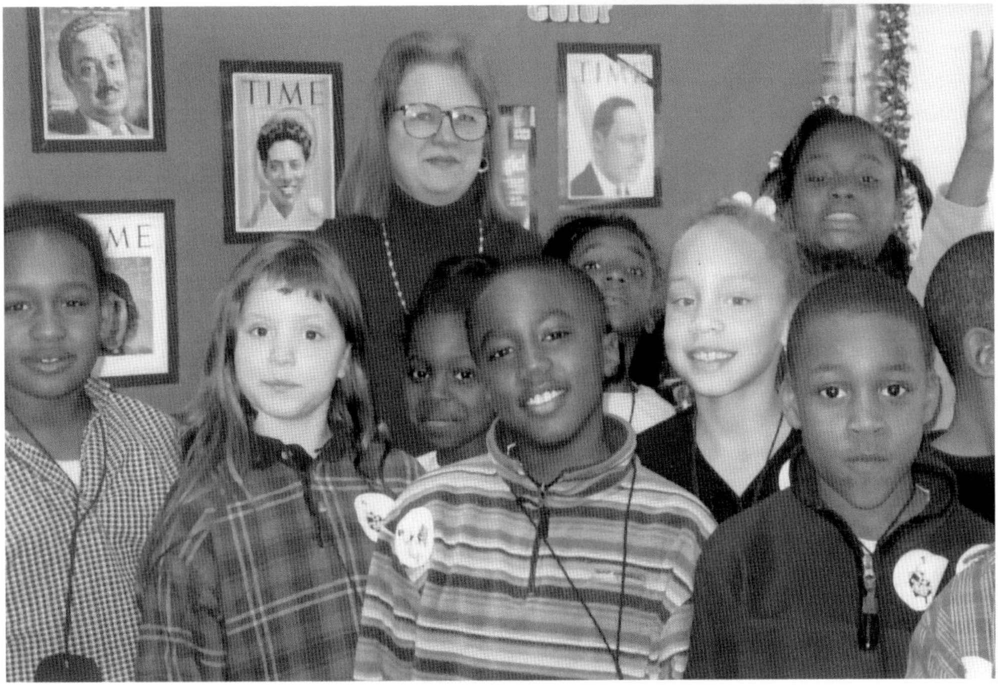


**Christine M. Hill**
Christine M. Hill (back row, center) is the assistant director of the Willingboro Library, where she was previously children's librarian. Hill formerly worked at the Free Library of Philadelphia and Mercer County Library, and received her master's degree in library service from Columbia University. Hill also is the author of seven young adult biographies from Enslow Publishers. *John Lewis: From Freedom Rider to Congressman* and *Gwendolyn Brooks: Poetry Is Life Distilled* were named Best Children's Trade Books in the Social Studies by the National Council of Social Studies Teachers. (Courtesy Willingboro Library.)

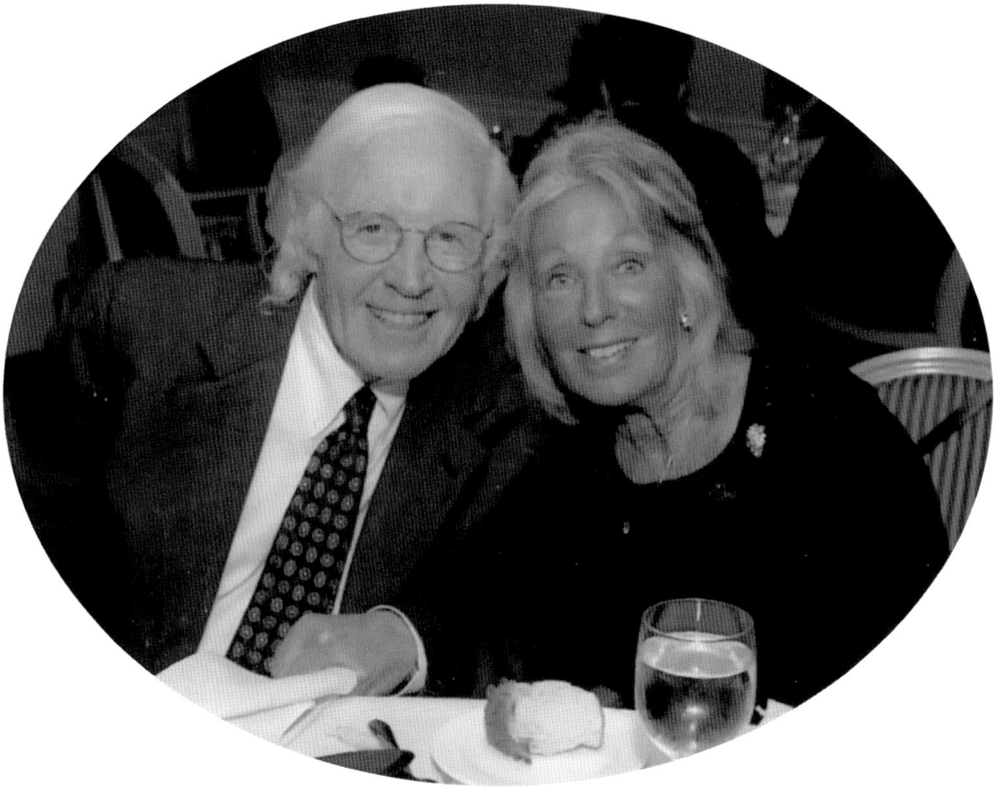

**Sally Friedman**

For more than 40 years, Sally Friedman has shared poignant, personal stories in the pages of local, regional, and national publications. Often drawing on her own family for inspiration, Friedman makes people feel as if they are reading dispatches from a friend or loved one. A graduate of the University of Pennsylvania, Friedman and her husband, retired New Jersey Superior Court Judge Victor Friedman, were among Willingboro's pioneers, moving into a Cape Cod in Pennypacker Park in 1960. She taught eighth-grade English at Levitt Junior/Senior High School for one year before staying home to raise her children full time. Friedman became active in the League of Women Voters and the literary American Association of University Women. She found her writing talent in 1964 and began freelancing in 1971. Today, the mother of three and grandmother of seven can be found in publications such as the *Burlington County Times*, the *Philadelphia Inquirer*, the *New York Times*, *Ladies Home Journal*, *Family Circle*, the *Huffington Post*, and *SJ Magazine*, among many others. (Courtesy Sally and Victor Friedman.)

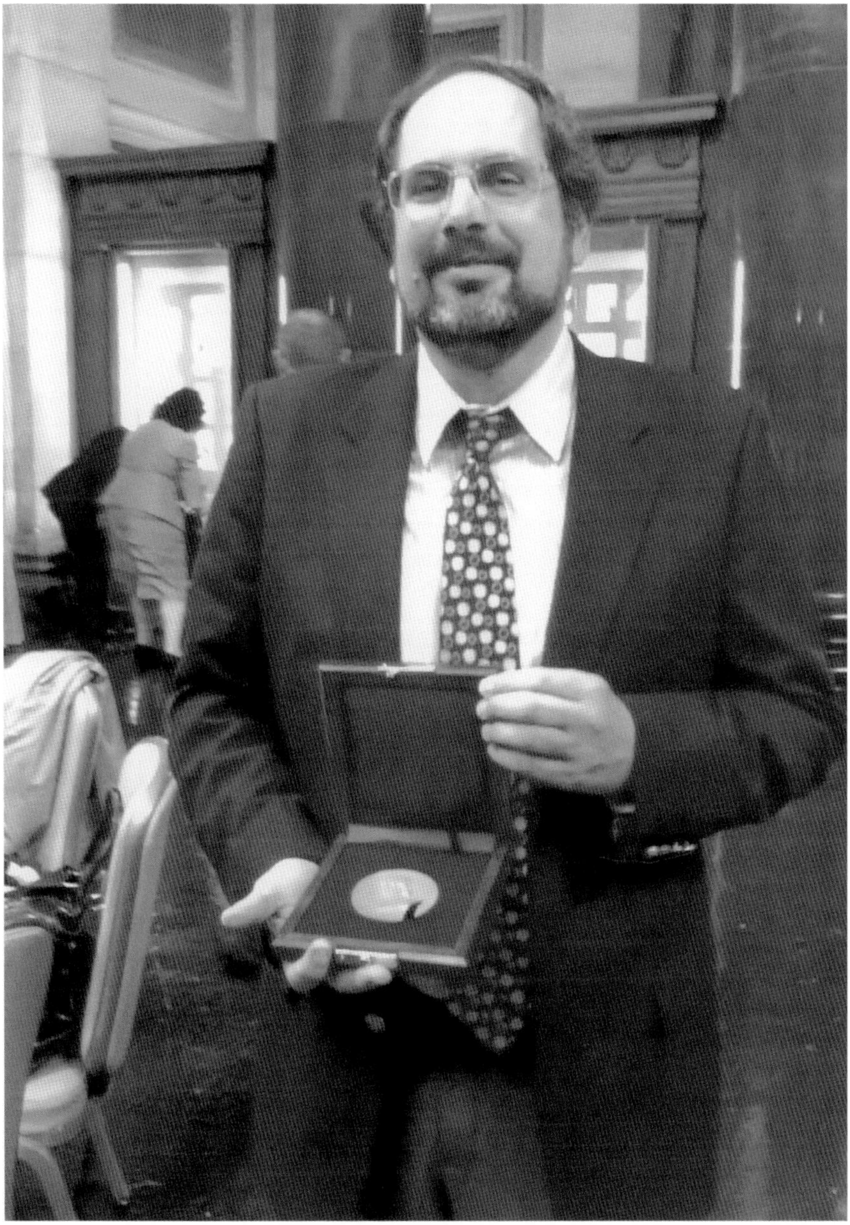

**Jeff Gammage**

Jeff Gammage is a staff writer at the *Philadelphia Inquirer*, where he was part of a five-reporter team that won the 2012 Pulitzer Prize for Public Service, awarded for an investigation into violence in the city public schools. The same year, James Madison University presented him with the Ronald E. Carrier Distinguished Alumni Award, which recognizes alumni who have demonstrated significant achievements of enduring value to society. Gammage is the author of *China Ghosts*, a memoir of adopting his two daughters from China, published by William Morrow, and he has written about Chinese adoption for publications including the *New York Times* and *Adoptive Families* magazine. He is a 1978 graduate of John F. Kennedy High School and grew up in Buckingham Park. He and his family live in Elkins Park, Pennsylvania. (Courtesy Jeff Gammage.)

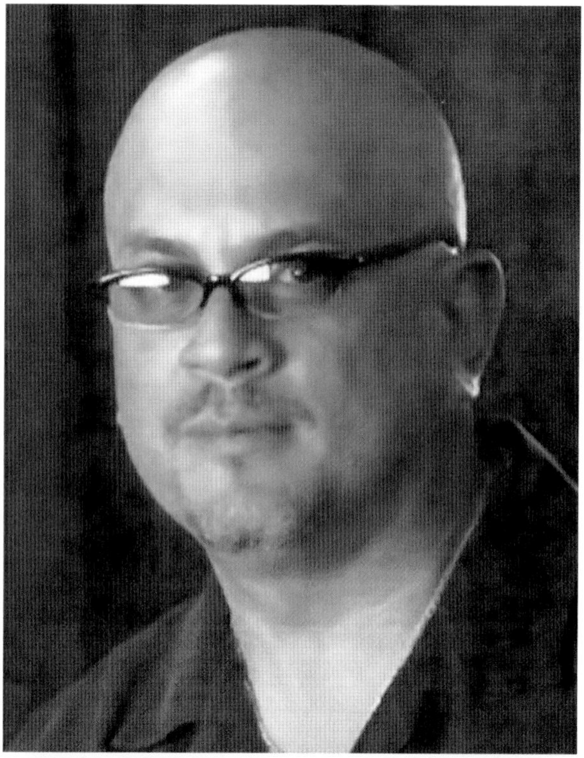

### Edgardo Cintron

Percussionist Edgardo Cintron is a second-generation musician known as much for his affable personality and generous spirit as for his musicianship. The leader of the Latin pop orchestra Cintron, he is a mainstay at the Willingboro, Newark, and Cape May Jazz festivals. The son of a guitarist in a US military band, Cintron was studying French horn and guitar by age five. By 12, he was traveling up and down the East Coast with his father's band. In 1988, he formed his own 12-piece band, the Tiempo Noventa Orchestra. Cintron and his band have recorded a number of albums, including *From Fathers to Sons, Nuestro Amigo, Summer Heat,* and *Straight No Chaser.* (Courtesy Jeffrey Lesser.)

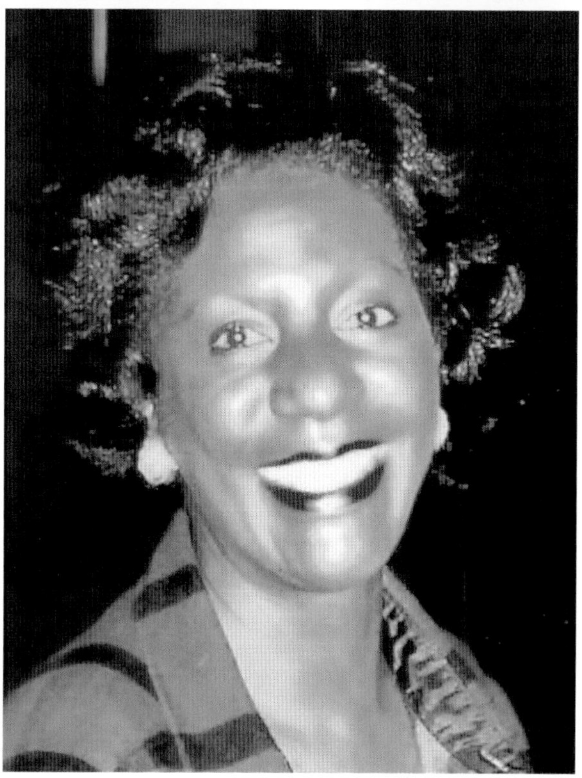

### Alma Day

Actress and writer Alma Day has performed at the Freedom Theatre in Philadelphia, as well as the Crossroads and George Street Theatres in New Brunswick. She frequently appears at the Willingboro Library, having performed shows called *A Holiday Celebration of the Arts* and *Faces of Women's History.* Day also has written and starred in one-woman tributes to abolitionist Sojourner Truth and author Zora Neale Hurston. (Courtesy Willingboro Library.)

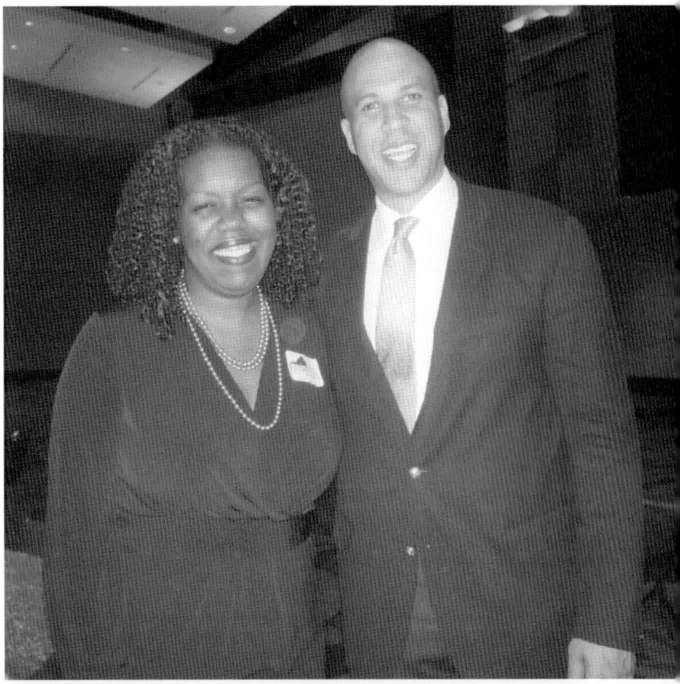

**Lisa Helem**

Lisa Helem (seen here with Newark mayor Cory Booker) is a journalist and lawyer. The oldest of three children, Helem participated in the Jack and Jill of America and the Willingboro track and soccer clubs. An honors student at Holy Cross High School, Helem attended Duke University, where she double-majored in English and African American studies. After graduation, she wrote for publications including *Newsweek*, the *Philadelphia Inquirer*, the *Atlanta Journal-Constitution*, *Essence Magazine*, and the *Burlington County Times*. Helem graduated from the University of Michigan Law School and in 2013 was press secretary for Justin Fairfax, a candidate for attorney general of Virginia. (Courtesy Lisa Helem.)

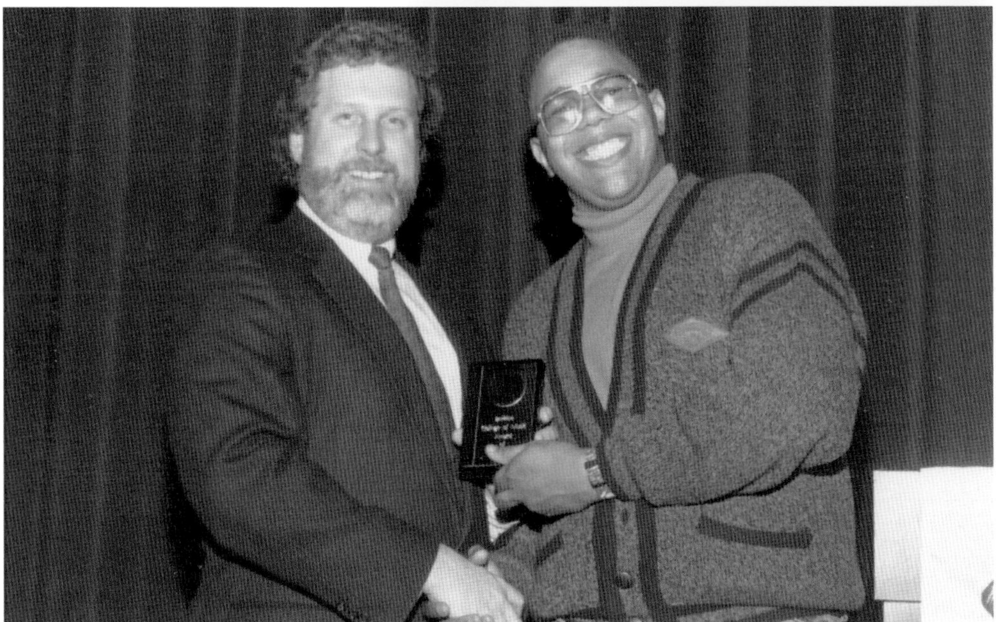

**Kendall Brunson**

A star trumpet player in the Willingboro High School Jazz Band, Kendall Brunson (right) won the outstanding musicianship award at the prestigious 22nd annual Berklee College of Music High School Jazz Festival. Brunson, whose twin brother, Randall, also played trumpet in the band, was noted for his ability to play screaming octaves, such as in the band's high-voltage version of Maynard Ferguson's "Give It One." Brunson is currently a recreation supervisor at the busy Willingboro Department of Recreation. (Courtesy Jeffrey Lesser.)

### Christine King

Walk into the Willingboro Library and one will find residents of all ages combing the stacks and using the computers. Numerous meetings are being held. An art exhibit attracts attention. Behind it all is Christine King, who, as library director, oversaw the planning and construction of the state-of-the-art, environmentally friendly library at the Willingboro Town Center in 2003. A native of Philadelphia, King taught in the city public school system before turning to library sciences in the early 1980s. She worked at numerous libraries throughout South Jersey before becoming Willingboro's director in 1997—only the second person to hold that job in the institution's 54-year history. King serves on the executive board of the New Jersey Library Association and has served on the Black Caucus of the American Library Association. She is the recipient of numerous awards, and is seen here (front row, left) with members of the Willingboro Library Board of Trustees. Other members are, from left to right (first row) Harry Kendall, Ardeth Holder, Martha Hall, and Parthenia Cogdell, (second row) Jennifer Crawford-Reid, Patricia Lindsay-Harvey, James Byrd, Grover McKenzie, and Joseph Jacobs.

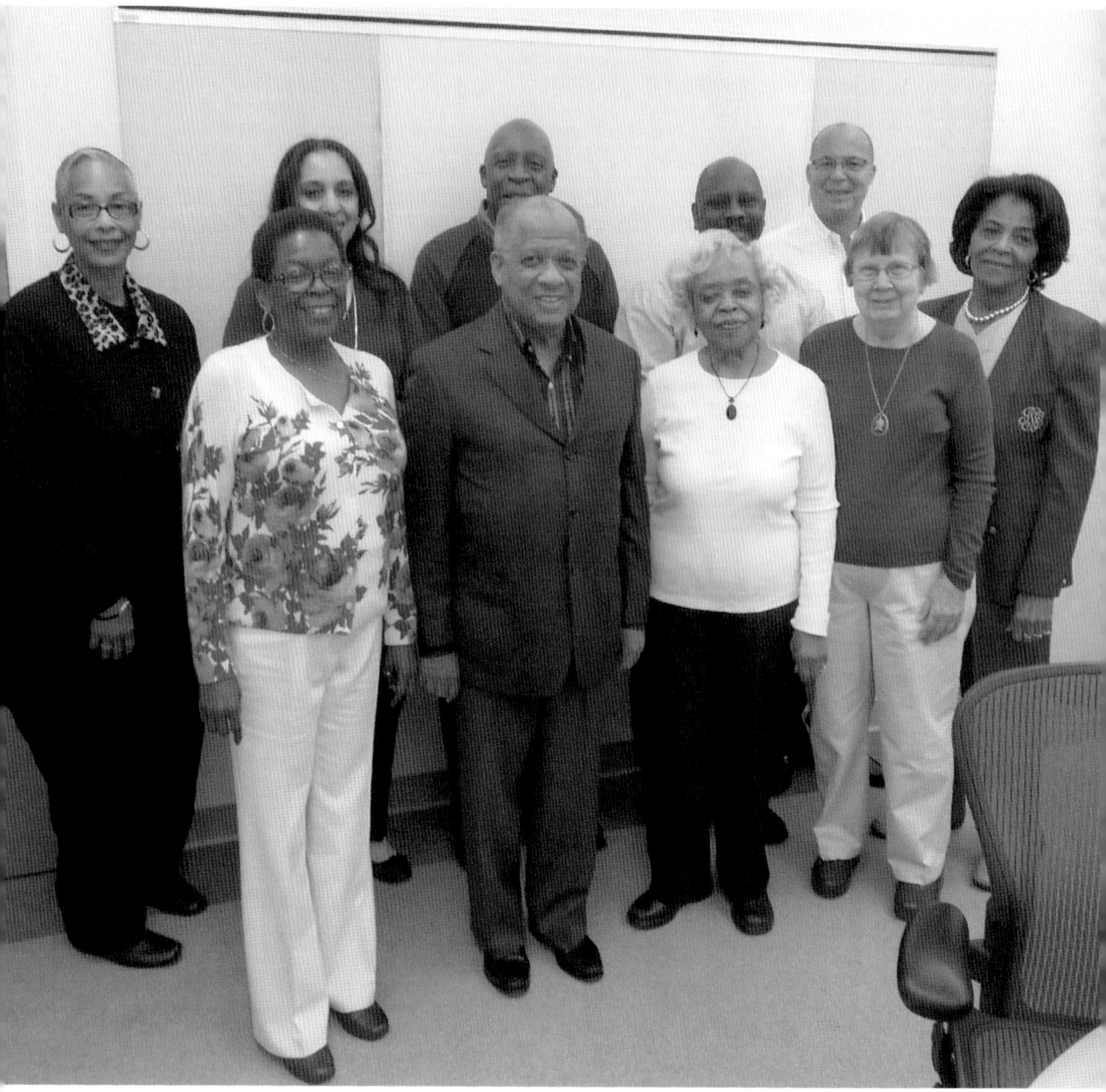

# CHAPTER FOUR

# Healing the Community

## Mind, Body, and Spirit

Dr. Meyer Abrams had a problem. To develop an active practice, Dr. Abrams, a general and thoracic surgeon, had to maintain two offices and privileges at four hospitals scattered throughout Philadelphia. He dreamed of having one office and treating patients at one nearby hospital. But where?

Levitt and Sons' new Levittown would be attracting thousands of new residents, and existing hospitals in Riverside and Mount Holly were not equipped to handle the influx. In 1961, Dr. Meyer and a select group of physicians who shared his vision opened Rancocas Valley Hospital. Over the years, the hospital tripled in size and changed hands many times. But one thing remained constant: the desire to care for a community in mind, body, and spirit.

Many of these doctors became mainstays in the community, like Dr. Bernard Blank, whose patients waited for him well into the night in the family living room, and Dr. Edward Messey, who likened his interaction with patients as an exchange of gifts: he provided diagnosis and treatment and, in return, received satisfaction knowing he made their lives better.

Over the years, new physicians would open practices. Dr. Louis Ruvolo, referred to by colleagues as "a doctor's doctor," is one of the first physicians in South Jersey to specialize in the treatment of peripheral vascular disease. Dr. Arnold Baskies, a surgical oncologist, is the recipient of major awards in cancer research, and is widely recognized in his role in providing leadership in cancer prevention and treatment in New Jersey. Dr. Eduardo Fernandez, who emigrated from Cuba following the Communist revolution, gave up a career in veterinary medicine to treat people who really needed his help. A hematologist and oncologist for the past two decades, Dr. Fernandez believes that to truly heal someone, one must recognize the interdependence between his or her physical, spiritual, and emotional needs.

Then there is Dr. Ann Marie Stephenson. Daughter of long-time township councilman Paul Stephenson, Dr. Stephenson volunteered as a candy striper at Rancocas Hospital (now Lourdes Medical Center of Burlington County), bringing patients their meals, providing companionship, and assisting nurses. Eighteen years later, the gastroenterologist with a master's degree in business administration returned home to Willingboro to practice medicine.

Dr. Stephenson is just one of a new generation of doctors choosing the Willingboro area to apply their knowledge and expertise and to continue a commitment to compassionate caring started by physicians like Dr. Meyer Abrams.

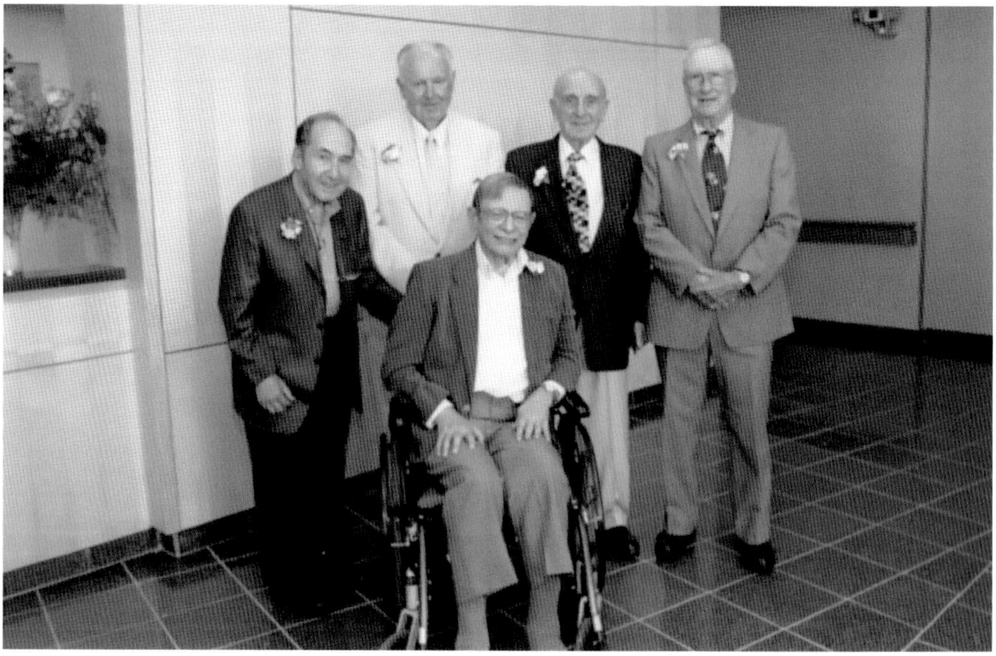

## Dr. Meyer Abrams

A 34-year-old general and thoracic surgeon in Philadelphia, Dr. Meyer Abrams was constantly on the road. In order to develop an active practice, he had to operate at four hospitals and maintain two offices. He longed for a new model: one hospital to bring all his patients and a single office. In the fall of 1958, Dr. Abrams and a group of like-minded fellow physicians took their first look at Willingboro. Three years later, Dr. Abrams's group of 11 opened Rancocas Hospital. These medical pioneers had the courage and vision to give of themselves and invest in the community and its future, and, today, the hospital continues to provide much-needed medical care to the area.

Pictured here are, from left to right, (first row in wheelchair) Dr. Abrams; (second row) Dr. Jack Rosenberg, Dr. John Gallagher, Dr. Gabriel Tatarian, and Dr. Stanton Oliver. Other founders were Dr. Jonas Brachfeld, Dr. Conrad Brahin, Dr. Irwin Smith, Dr. Lionel Gold, and Dr. Joseph Ziegler. (Courtesy Lourdes Health System.)

## Dr. Andrew Blank

Andrew Blank graduated from the Philadelphia College of Osteopathic Medicine in 1987 and completed an internship at the University of the Health Sciences in Kansas City and residency at Delaware Valley Medical Center. Board-certified in family medicine, he joined his father at Sunset Road Medical Associates in 1989. When not practicing medicine, one often can find Dr. Blank in the kitchen or his garden and with his family.

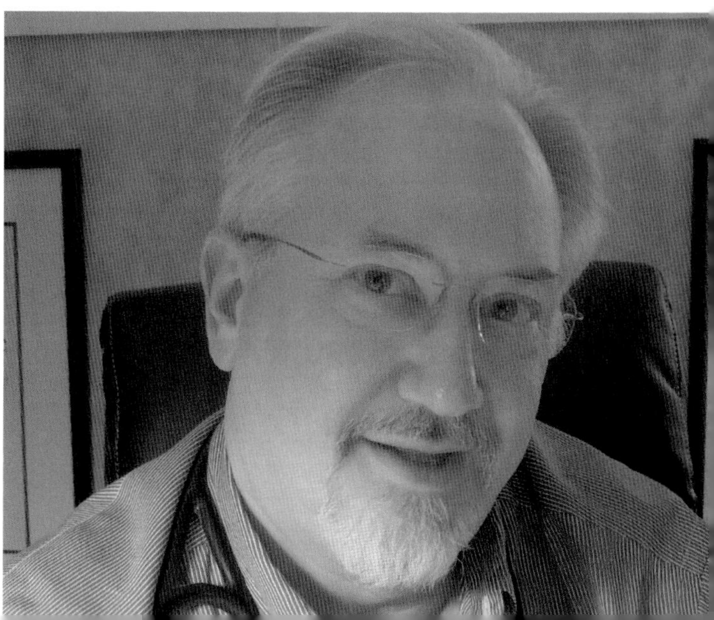

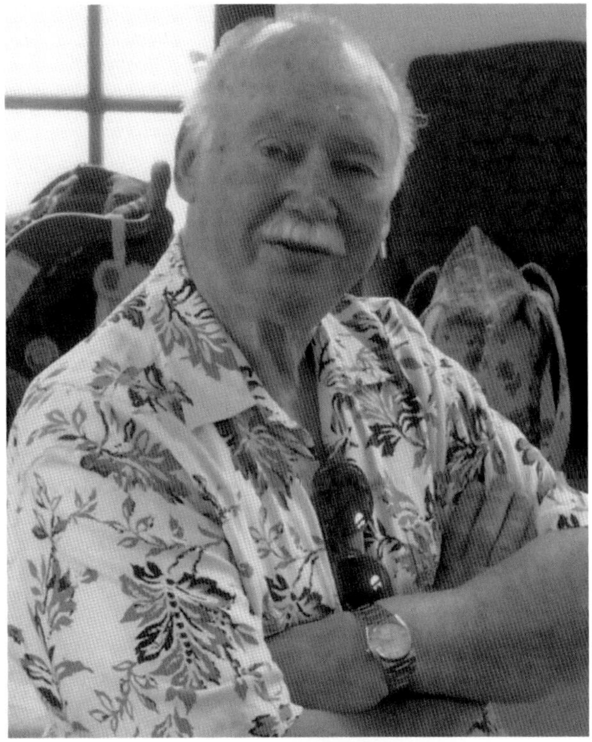

**Dr. Bernard Blank**
Doctors like Bernard Blank aren't often found any more. A 1957 graduate of the Philadelphia College of Osteopathic Medicine, Dr. Blank set up his home and office at Sunset Road and Levitt Parkway. He did it all: treated patients in the office—who sometimes waited in the family living room until one or two in the morning—delivered babies, and rounded at nearby hospitals. Visits cost $4. Two of his sons, Benjamin and Andrew, became physicians themselves, with Andrew later joining him in practice. He retired after more than 50 years in medical practice, and died in December 2011. "He had time for everybody," said son Andrew. "He treated his patients like family, and we try to do that today." (Courtesy Dr. Andrew Blank.)

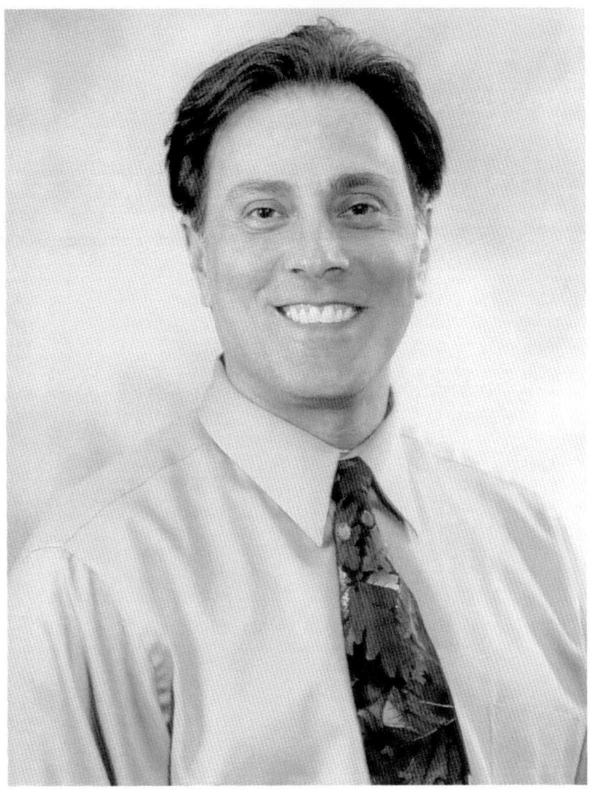

**Dr. John Hamaty**
Selected one of the top physicians in South Jersey by *South Jersey* magazine in 2004 and 2005, Dr. John Hamaty is chief of cardiology at Lourdes Medical Center of Burlington County. A member of Lourdes Cardiology Services (South Jersey Heart Group), Dr. Hamaty has received numerous teacher of the year awards from the UMDNJ School of Osteopathic Medicine, where he directs the cardiovascular fellowship program. (Courtesy Lourdes Health System.)

### Dr. Ann Marie Stephenson

On any given day, Dr. Ann Marie Stephenson might see an old classmate, a family friend, or fellow church member. But for the Willingboro-born gastroenterologist, it's all a part of being home. Eighteen years after volunteering as a candy striper at Rancocas Hospital, she returned to the hospital to start practicing medicine.

A graduate of Willingboro High School and Spelman College, Stephenson completed a joint medical-master of business administration degree at the Philadelphia College of Osteopathic Medicine and St. Joseph's University. Following a residency in internal medicine and fellowship in geriatrics, Dr. Stephenson traveled to Chicago to specialize in gastroenterology. After spending one Thanksgiving home with her family, she decided Willingboro was the place to start her career. "I am pleased to say I am a product of Willingboro," she said. (Courtesy Lourdes Health System.)

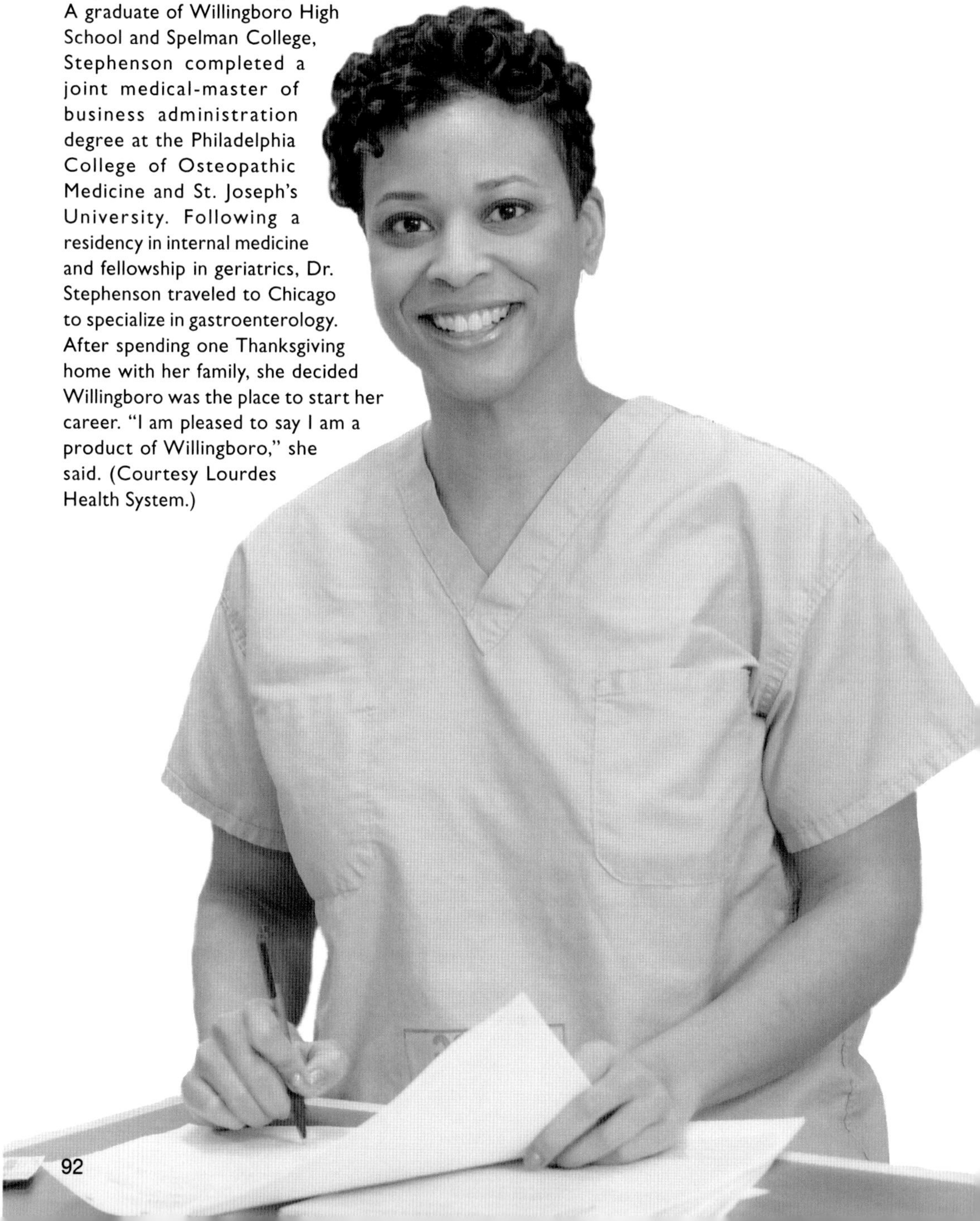

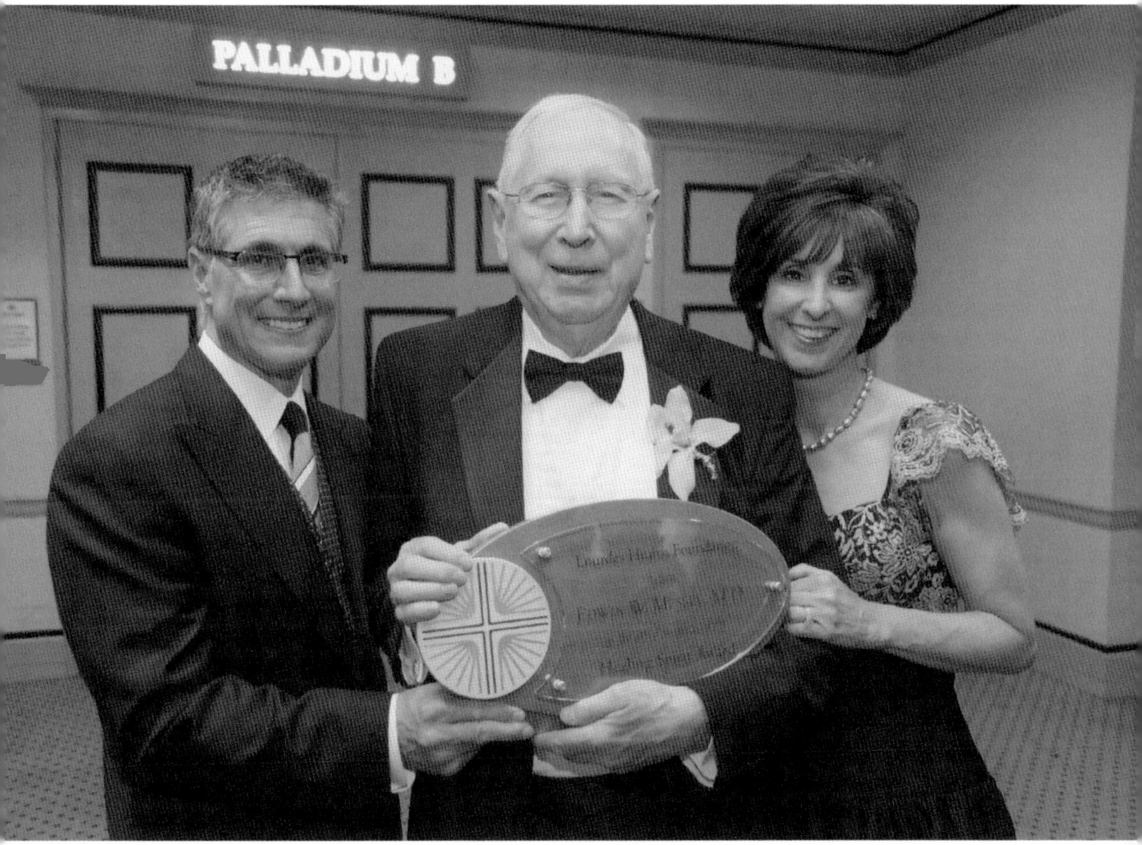


**Dr. Edwin Messey**

For four generations of Willingboro residents, Edwin Messey (center) was the only physician they ever knew. Whether he was treating a cold or a more serious condition, Messey's clear passion for medicine made him a beloved fixture in the community. "I often likened the interaction between me and my patients to exchanging gifts," he explained. "I provided them with a diagnosis, treatment and care, and in return I received the satisfaction of knowing I've made a positive impact in their lives." Dr. Messey's giving spirit also benefitted the broader medical community. A 1959 graduate of Hahnemann Medical College, he welcomed medical students into his practice to hone their clinical skills. Dr. Messey was active on several hospital committees and served as president of the Burlington County Medical Society. For two years, he hosted a society-sponsored radio talk show called *Ask Your Doctor.* Dr. Messey also served on the Burlington County Special Services School District Board of Education and the Willingboro Rotary, and he was president of the Willingboro Art Alliance. Dr. Messey retired in 2011, and his dedication and compassion earned him Lourdes Health System's 2012 Healing Spirit Award. (Courtesy Lourdes Health System.)

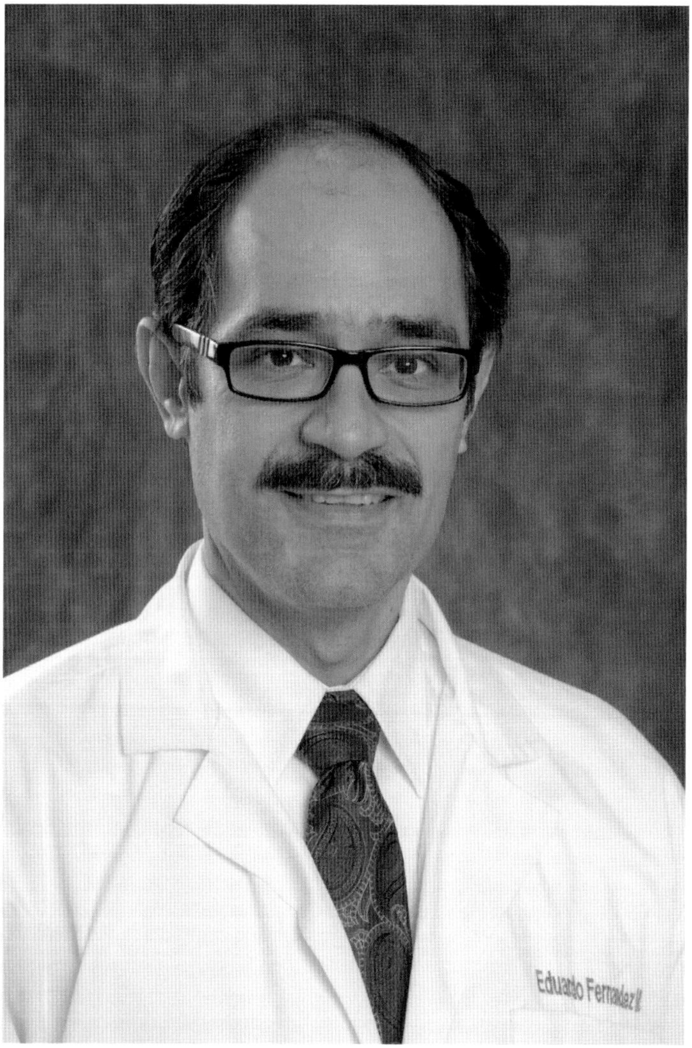

**Dr. Eduardo Fernandez**

Dr. Eduardo Fernandez believes that one has to go beyond medical science to truly heal a patient, recognizing the interdependence between the individual's physical health and spiritual, social, and emotional needs. A hematologist and oncologist in practice for nearly two decades, Dr. Fernandez was only a year old when his parents emigrated from Cuba after the Communist revolution. They left their home, personal belongings, and family members behind to start a new life in the United States. Eventually settling in Elizabeth, New Jersey, he began to develop an interest in science, particularly veterinary medicine. A veterinarian he was working with convinced him to follow in the footsteps of his father and grandfather and pursue a career in medicine. Dr. Fernandez earned a bachelor's degree in biology and Spanish from Lehigh University and a medical degree from Robert Wood Johnson Medical School. A clinical assistant professor at Robert Wood Johnson, Dr. Fernandez serves as medical director for Compassionate Care Hospice and volunteers his time for many community programs, including screenings for cancer. In April 2013, he received the Healing Spirit Award from Lourdes Health System. "I am passionate about volunteering and community service," he said. "I try to live by the motto that my life has meaning because of the good things I can do for others. My greatest reward is often a thank you card sent from a patient or family member; then I know I have done my best." (Courtesy Lourdes Health System.)

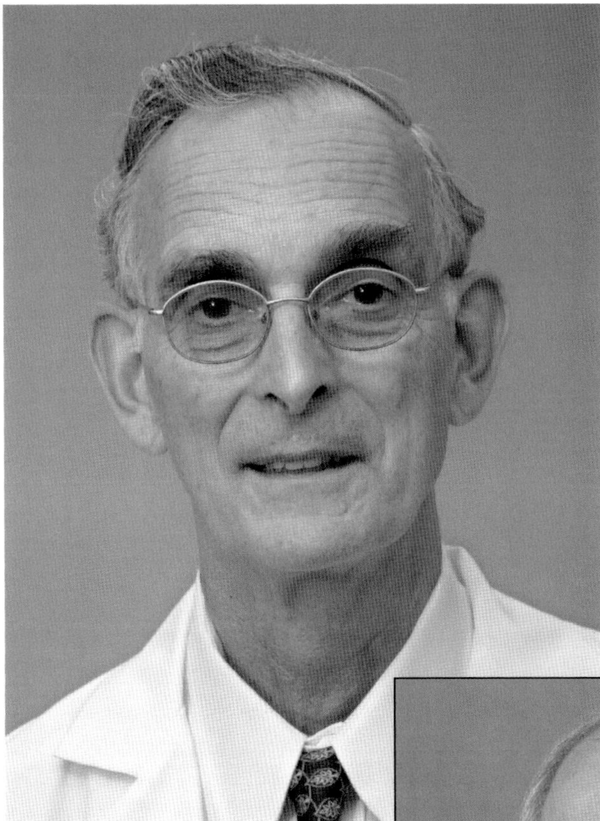

**Dr. Louis Ruvolo**
"A doctor's doctor" and "the glue that holds the staff together" are just two of the many compliments that colleagues offer about surgeon Dr. Louis Ruvolo. A native of Brooklyn who earned his medical degree from Indiana University, Dr. Ruvolo was one of the first surgeons in South Jersey to specialize in the treatment of peripheral vascular disease and founded the area's first noninvasive diagnostic vascular disease laboratory. He and his wife, Clara, have three children. (Courtesy Lourdes Health System.)

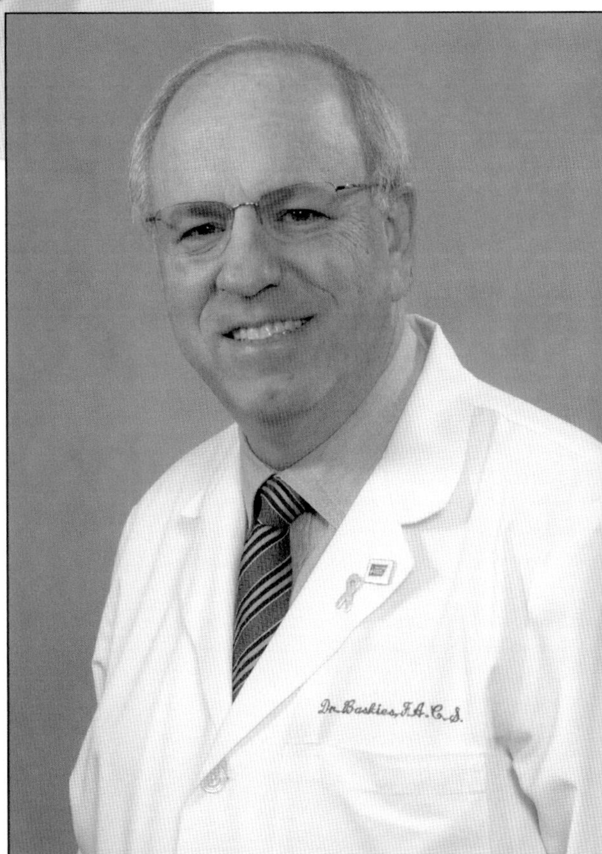


**Dr. Arnold Baskies**
Dr. Arnold Baskies has spent more than 30 years giving people with cancer a new lease on life. A graduate of the Boston University School of Medicine, Dr. Baskies specializes in surgical oncology, including the treatment of breast, thyroid, and skin cancers. He is widely recognized as a leader in cancer prevention and treatment in New Jersey. He served as chief medical officer and president of the Eastern Division of the American Cancer Society. (Courtesy Lourdes Health System.)

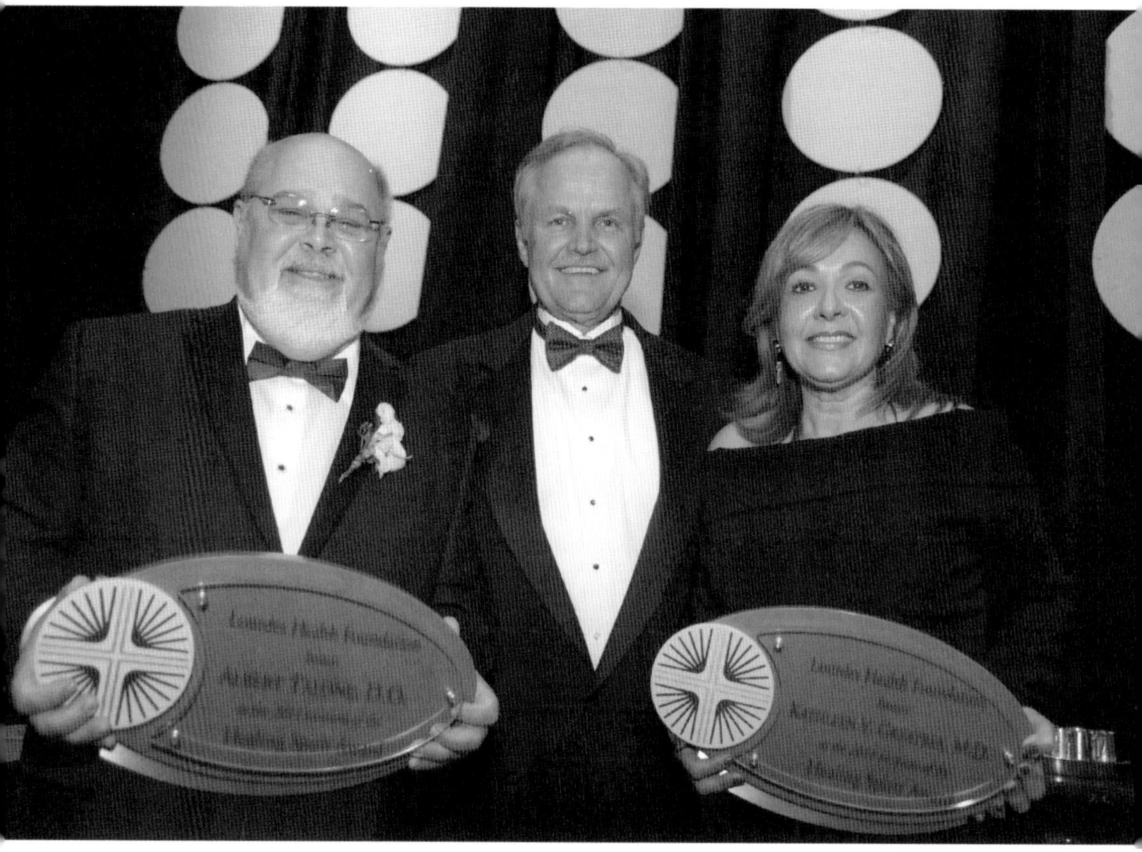

### Dr. Albert Talone

For more than 35 years, Dr. Albert Talone has been the epitome of a family practitioner—caring and compassionate to his patients and a role model to fellow physicians. He believes the focus of care is to spend adequate time and assure quality care for all patients. "Medicine is a constantly evolving art and science," he said. "It is always exciting. There's always something new to learn." A native of Trenton, Dr. Talone graduated from Holy Cross High School and the Philadelphia College of Pharmacy. He was drafted during the Vietnam War, where he served as a medical specialist airman in the US Air Force Reserve. After completing military service, Dr. Talone attended Kansas City University of Osteopathic Medicine, where he obtained a deep appreciation of preventive and community medicine as a primary care physician. Dr. Talone joined Dr. Bernard Blank at Sunset Road Medical Associates and served as an attending physician at Rancocas Hospital. In 1980, he served as president and chief of the medical staff. In this position, Dr. Talone helped to combine the professional staffs of Rancocas and Zurbrugg Memorial Hospital after the two facilities merged. In 2011, Dr. Talone received the Healing Spirit Award from Lourdes Health System for his devotion to his patients and the community. Dr. Talone (left) is pictured with Lourdes Health System president and chief executive officer Alexander J. Hatala (center) and fellow honoree Dr. Kathleen V. Greatrex. (Courtesy Lourdes Health System.)

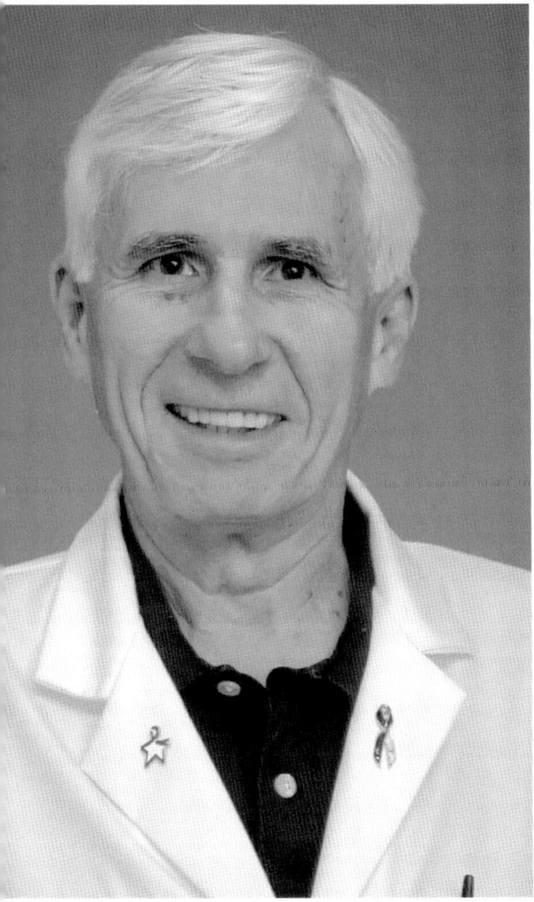

**Dr. Donald Petroski**
A graduate of the Hahnemann University School of Medicine, Dr. Donald Petroski has been serving the Willingboro community since 1975. A gastroenterologist, Dr. Petroski served as chairman of the Department of Internal Medicine at Lourdes Medical Center of Burlington County. He currently is chief of gastroenterology. Dr. Petroski has been at the forefront of many innovations in GI, including capsule endoscopy. He is a member of the Lourdes Health System Foundation Board. (Courtesy Lourdes Health System.)

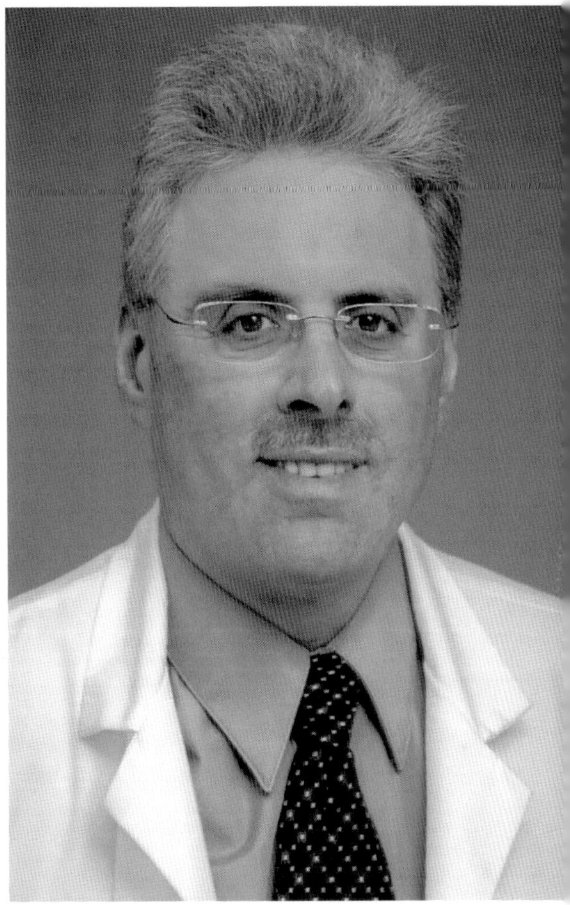

**Dr. Stuart Mest**
A graduate of the University of Pennsylvania and Penn State University, Dr. Stuart Mest began practicing at Lourdes Medical Center of Burlington County in 1989. A past president of the hospital's medical staff, Dr. Mest is chairman of the Department of Medicine and medical director of Respiratory Care. Recently, Dr. Mest has advocated testing for a hereditary disorder that can lead to emphysema, even in people who have never smoked. (Courtesy Lourdes Health System.)

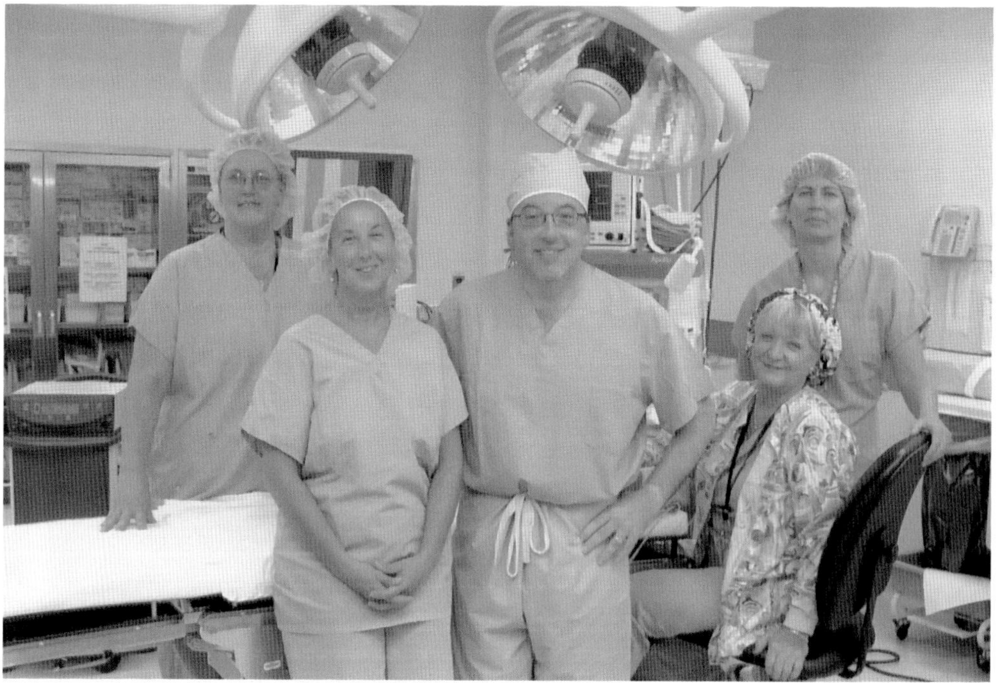

**Dr. Adam Perzin**

Named a "top doc" by *South Jersey* magazine in 2006 and 2008, Adam Perzin (center) is chief of urology at Lourdes Medical Center of Burlington County. A graduate of Temple University and the University of Medicine and Dentistry, Dr. Perzin is president of Delaware Valley Urology, one of the largest urology practice groups in the Delaware Valley. (Courtesy Lourdes Health System.)

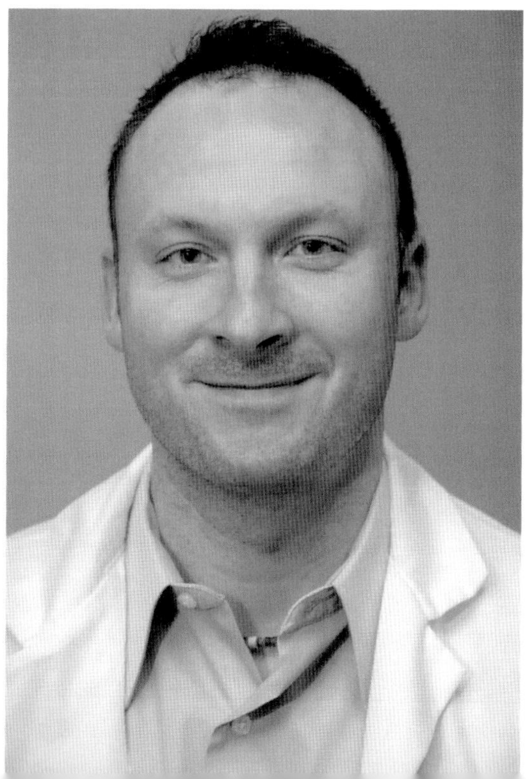

**Dr. Sean McMillan**

Orthopedic surgeon Sean McMillan is among the new doctors who chose to practice in Willingboro. A former team physician for the Boston Red Sox (at AAA Pawtucket), high schools, and even professional wrestling, Dr. McMillan is chief of orthopedics at Lourdes Medical Center of Burlington County. Dr. McMillan specializes in sports medicine and osteoarthritis prevention. Dr. McMillan is one of a handful of surgeons in South Jersey to perform a new procedure called "reverse total shoulder replacement." (Courtesy Lourdes Health System.)

# CHAPTER FIVE

# To Serve and Protect

## Willingboro's First Responders

It all started with a man and his horse.

In the late 1800s, flamboyant sheriff Edwin Van Sciver patroled the town on his white stallion, rounding up any rowdies who might be disturbing the peace. At that point, it was about all the protection the roughly 750 residents needed.

But times changed. As farmland gave way to row upon row of houses and the population soared from 850 in 1950 to 11,000 in 1960 to 40,000 in 1970, there was a clear need for first responders.

In 1959, Charles Van Kirk saw the need for ambulance service in the growing town—if someone had a medical emergency, a squad from Beverly, Burlington, or Rancocas responded. Van Kirk placed an advertisement in the *Burlington County Times* looking for interested people. The Levittown Emergency Squad was formed in April 1960 in the home of William and Ethel Smith. Charter members obtained second mortgages to pay for the first ambulance, a 1955 Cadillac. Calls to 877-HELP came to the Smith house. Ethel Smith answered the line, called members, and dispatched the ambulance. As call volume increased, additional ambulances were purchased and stationed at volunteers' homes and Rancocas Hospital. In 1969, the squad and fire department gained their own home at Charleston Road and John F. Kennedy Way. Today the squad, a mixture of paid staff and volunteers, answers 3,600 calls annually, responding to car accidents, fires, and medical emergencies large and small.

The Levittown Fire Department was formed in January 1960 by a group that included Harry Jackson, Woody Addis, and George Derr (who continues to run calls today). The first fire truck, a used 1941 pumper, was purchased for $3,000. The department continued to grow with more equipment and volunteers. In August 1964, nearly three dozen firefighters bravely tried to save Strawberry Mansion, built in 1839 on the site of Gov. William Franklin's 14-room Colonial summer home. But the most famous fire in Willingboro history occurred four months later, when the municipal building burned, destroying township offices, the police department, and library. A new municipal building opened three years later. More recently, firefighters spent nearly eight hours in the aftermath of an explosion at a metals plant that killed one employee and injured several others. Today, the fire department relies primarily on paid staff and responds to 1,100 calls a year.

Marshall Roser became Willingboro's first police chief in October 1958. A one-man force, Roser patroled the new neighborhoods and the quickly disappearing rural homesteads, answering all calls. As the town grew to become one of the largest in South Jersey, so did the police force, numbering 70 officers. They would deal with the traffic accidents, sometimes high-profile violence, drugs—and later, gangs—that came with the influx of people. The department would develop a special operations SWAT team and walking, bicycle, and motorcycle patrols to put officers more in touch with the community.

Sheriff Van Sciver would be proud.

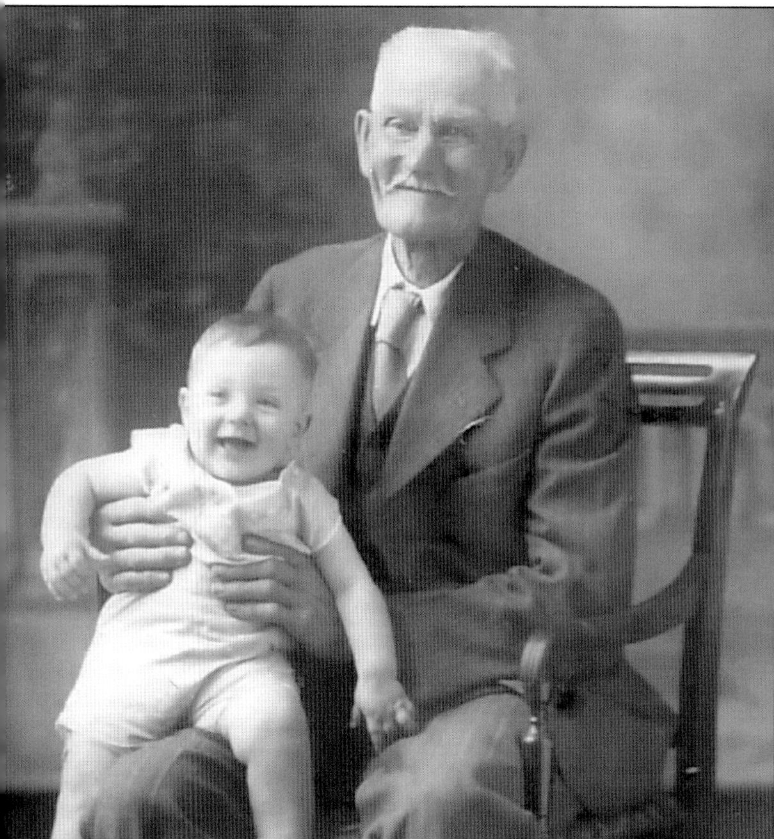

### Edwin Van Sciver

In the late 1880s, Edwin Van Sciver served as the town sheriff, riding down country lanes aboard a white stallion, pistols at his side. His handlebar mustache and fancy side arms gave him a flamboyant flair. Occasionally, boats traversing the Delaware would drop off what Van Sciver and locals referred to as "river rats," drunken and rowdy individuals who would disturb the peace and make a general nuisance. The galloping lawman would chase them away, preserving law and order. (Courtesy Willingboro Historical Society.)

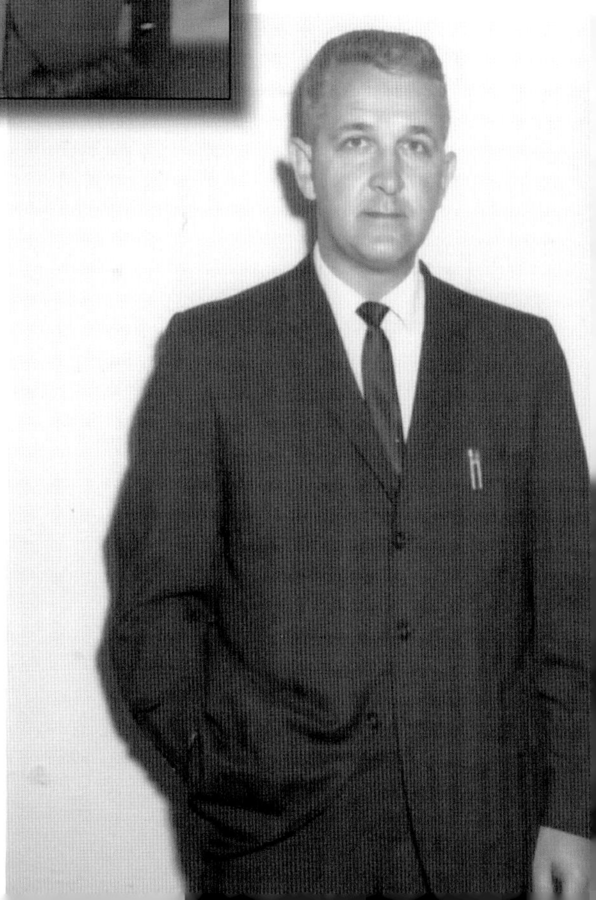

### Chief Marshall Roser

Marshall Roser became Willingboro's first police chief in October 1958. A one-man force, Roser patroled the new neighborhoods and the quickly disappearing rural homesteads, answering all calls. Police records show it took Roser only a week to issue the town's first ticket, to a man involved in a traffic accident. To serve the hundreds of children moving in every year, he helped organize the Levittown Youth Sports and Athletic Association. By the time Roser retired in 1969, the department had grown to nearly 50 full- and part-time officers. (Courtesy Willingboro Police Department.)

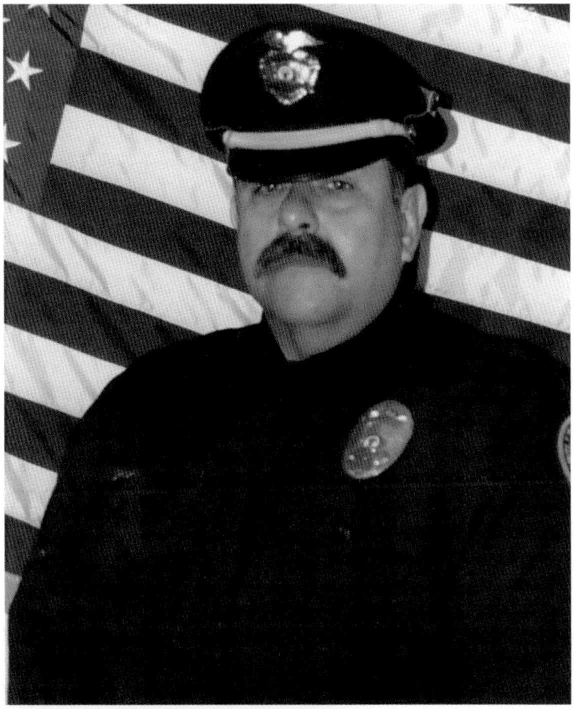

**Capt. Gerald Valenta**
A member of the police force since June 1978, Gerald Valenta is commander of the patrol division. Valenta has been a detective, a member of the department special response team, and an instructor at the Burlington County Police Academy. Each uniformed officer under Valenta's command is assigned to a specific area of town and is equipped with the latest technology, including live-scan fingerprint and mobile video systems and laptop computers. (Courtesy Willingboro Police Department.)

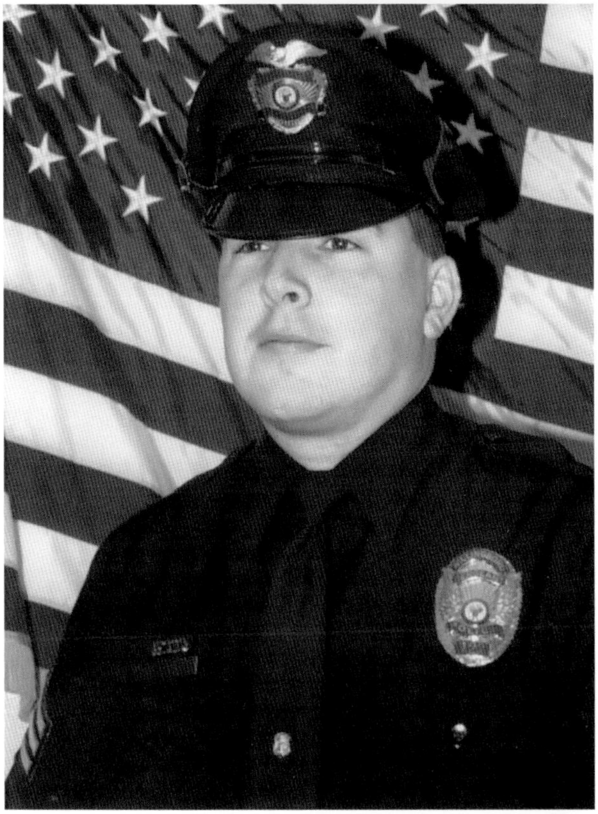

**Lt. Joseph Dey**
A township native and former lifeguard, Joseph Dey joined the Willingboro Police Department part time in 1988. He became a full-time officer in 1991. Dey has been a member of the department and county SWAT teams, as well as the fire department's underwater recovery/dive team. Dey is the administrative lieutenant in charge of the department's records division. (Courtesy Willingboro Police Department.)

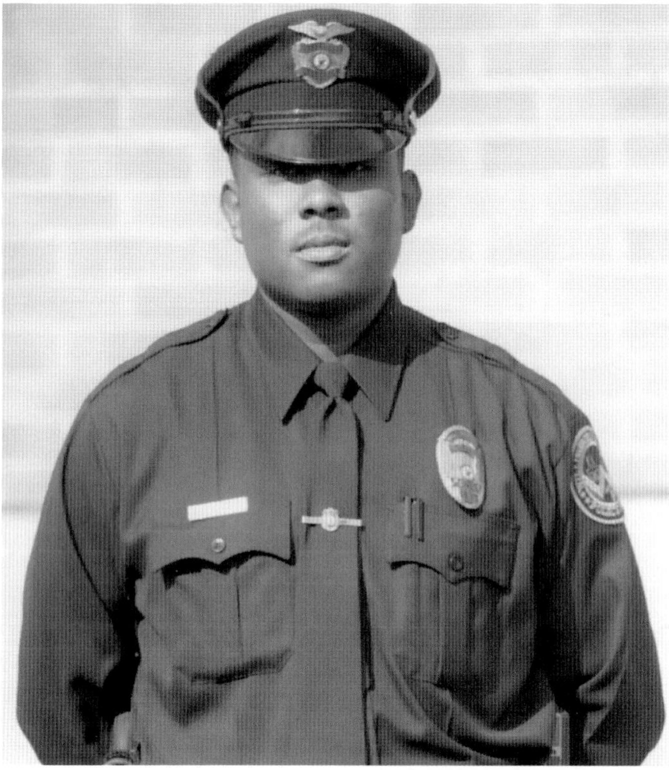

**Capt. Kenneth Strother Jr.**
Kenneth Strother Jr. is commander of the criminal investigations division in the Willingboro Police Department. Strother started as a special officer in 1992. He studied political science at Rowan University before becoming a full-time patrol officer in 1994. Strother coached basketball at Life Center Academy and served as president of the Willingboro Lodge of the Fraternal Order of Police. (Courtesy Willingboro Police Department.)

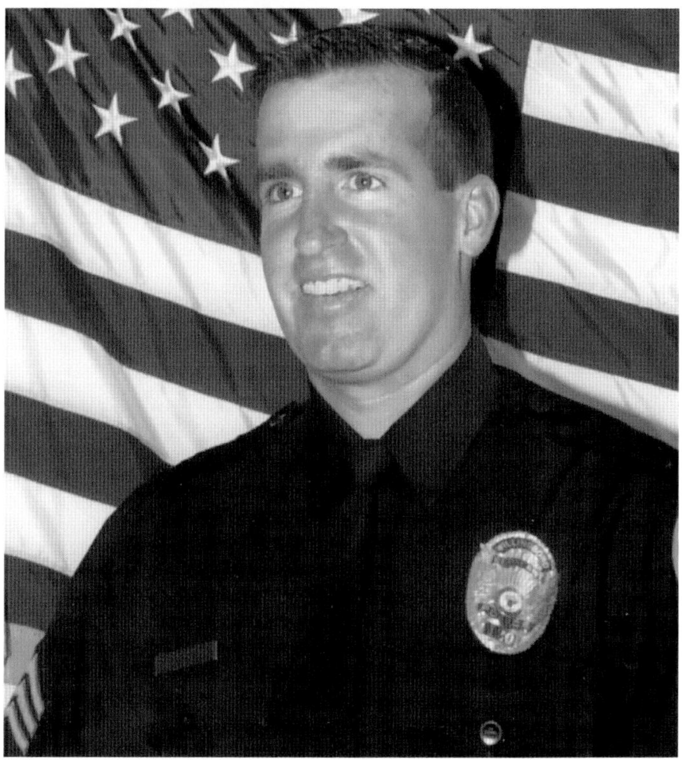

**Capt. Michael Randall**
Michael Randall helps lead the police department's patrol division. Randall has served on the department's special response tactical team and the bicycle patrol unit. He has trained more than 200 police officers across Burlington County and the state on the proper use of mountain bicycles. His three-day course covers riding, agility, and balance, and how to interact with the public while on this very visible patrol. (Courtesy Willingboro Police Department.)


102

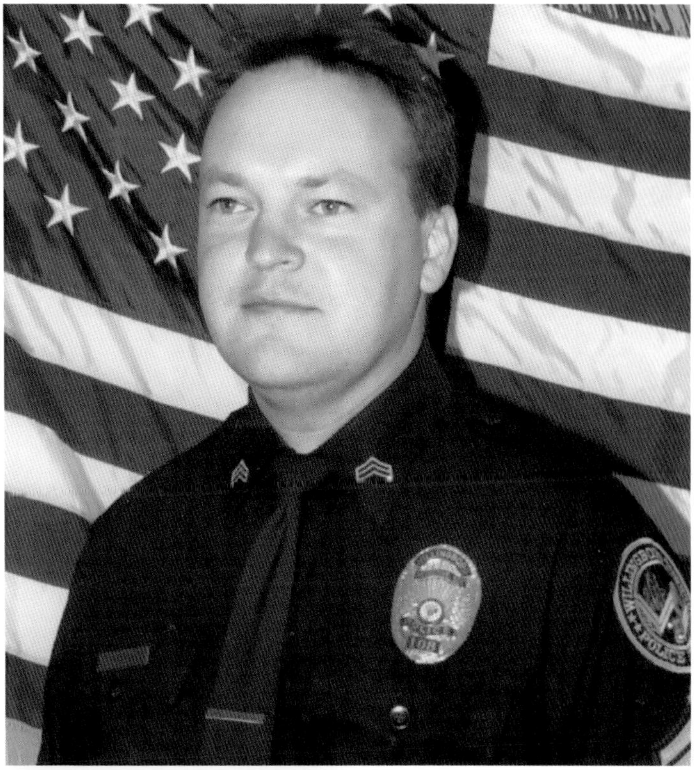

**Lt. Timothy Ryan**
A full-time Willingboro police officer since June 1987, Timothy Ryan is a lieutenant in the criminal investigations division. Ryan is a certified Drug Abuse Resistance Education (DARE) officer and served on the department's special response team. He enjoys reading, listening to music, and spending time with his family. (Courtesy Willingboro Police Department.)

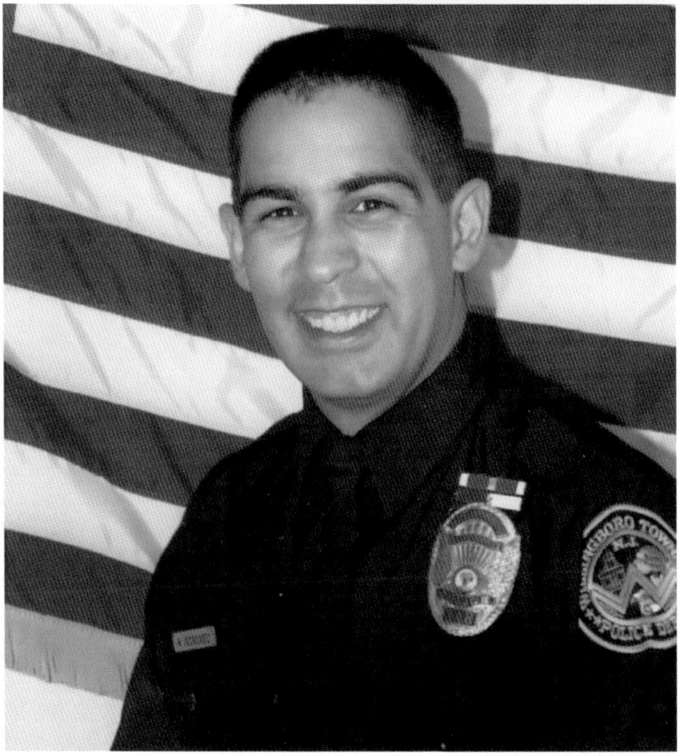

**Patrolman Mario Rodriguez Jr.**
Mario Rodriguez Jr. has been a member of the police department since 1996. Prior to joining Willingboro, he served as a dispatcher with another department. Besides his regular patrol duties, Rodriguez participated in the DARE program with township youth. Rodriguez also is a volunteer EMT with the Willingboro Emergency Squad. (Courtesy Willingboro Police Department.)

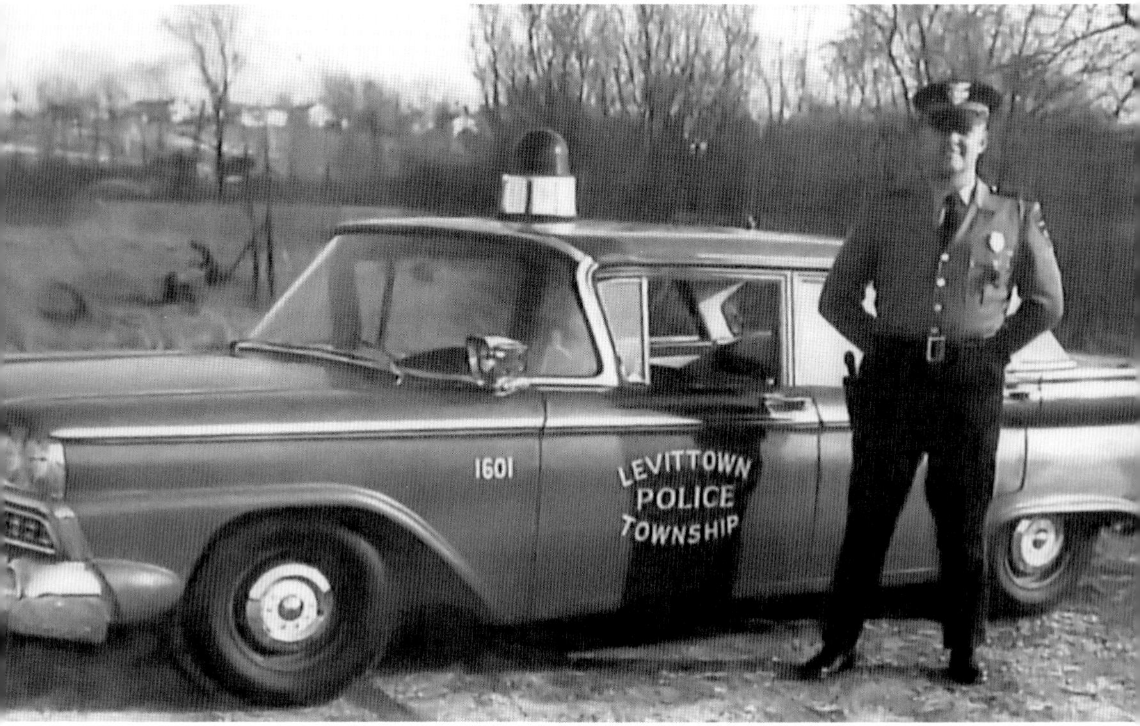


**Chief Richard Van Sciver**
Richard Van Sciver, the grandson of flamboyant 1880s constable Edwin Van Sciver, was the fourth sworn member of the fledgling Levittown Police Department, joining in June 1959. He became chief of the Willingboro department in 1987. Van Sciver retired in 1990. (Courtesy Willingboro Library.)

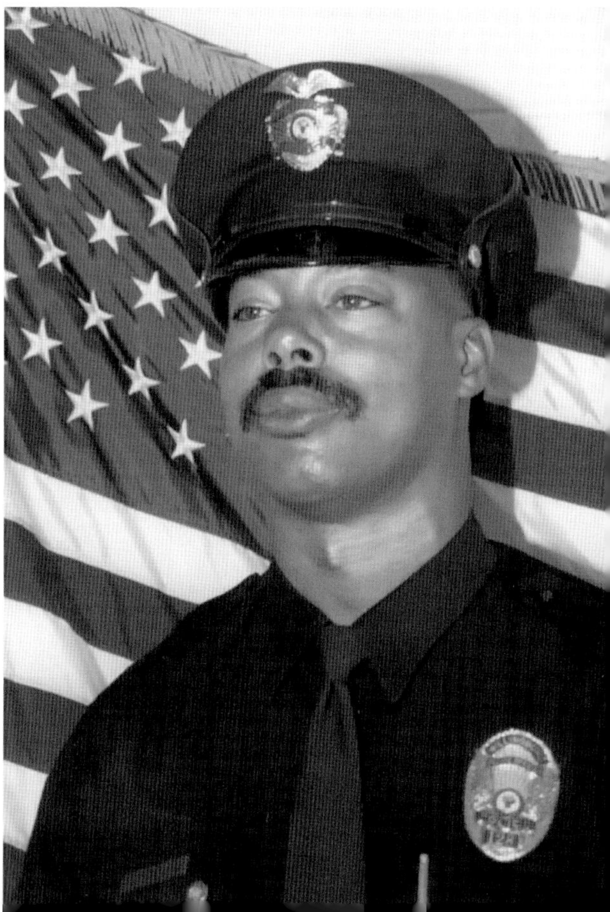

**Sgt. Eric Bowman**
At six-feet, eight-inches tall, Eric Bowman is a towering figure in the police department. This has served him well, from patroling the streets to keeping children on the straight and narrow as a school resource officer. Bowman began in law enforcement in 1990 and joined Willingboro in 1993. Bowman previously served as a township DARE officer. (Courtesy Willingboro Police Department.)

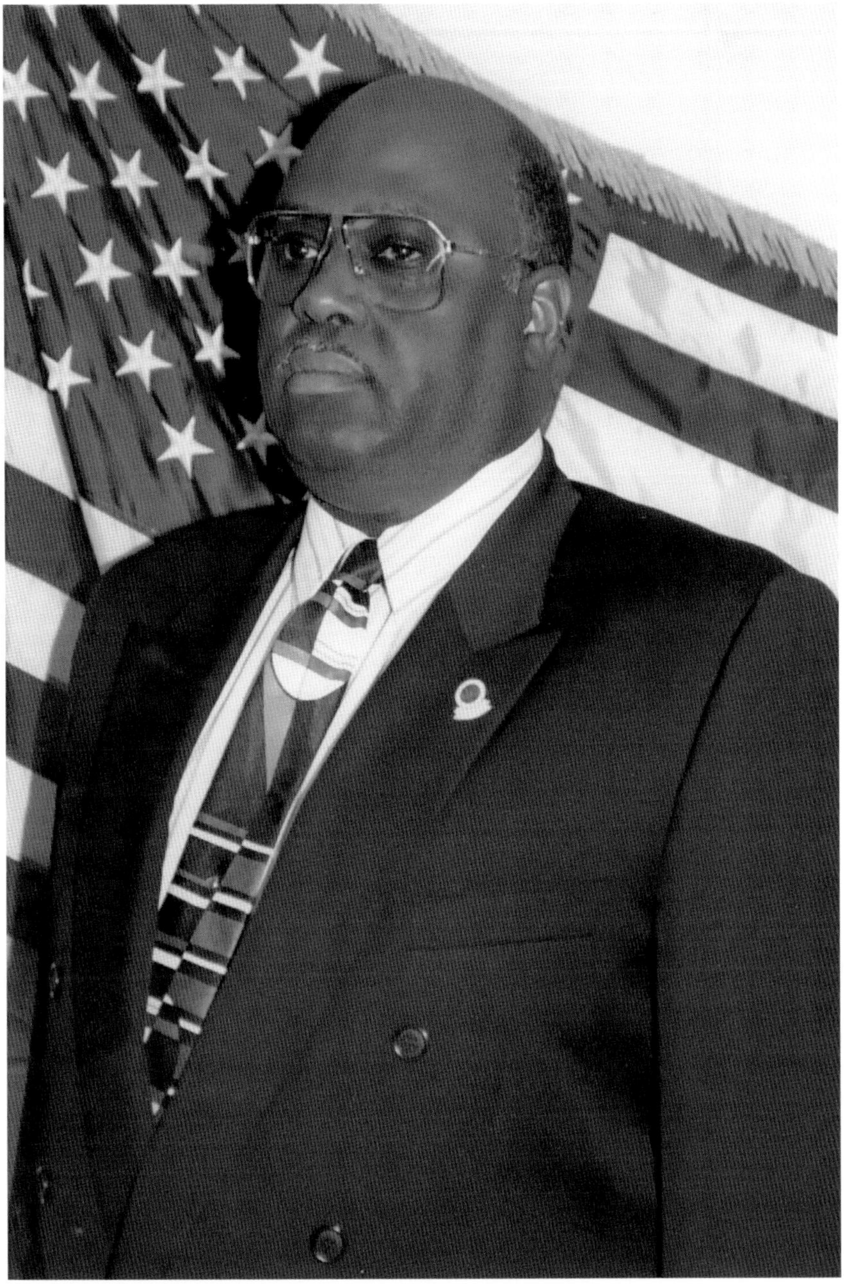

**Director Benjamin Braxton**

A graduate of Edison State College, Benjamin Braxton spent 27 years in the Philadelphia Police Department, rising to become the commanding officer of the highway patrol. Braxton also served as administrative assistant to the first deputy police commander, supervisor of the expressway command and tactical unit, and sergeant of civil affairs. He served as police chief in Ohio for a year before become director of public safety in Willingboro in 1994. Braxton focused on community policing, with foot, bicycle, and motorcycle patrols, and a strong relationship with the schools and neighborhood watch. Braxton retired in 2007. He ran unsuccessfully for Burlington County Sheriff. (Courtesy Willingboro Police Department.)

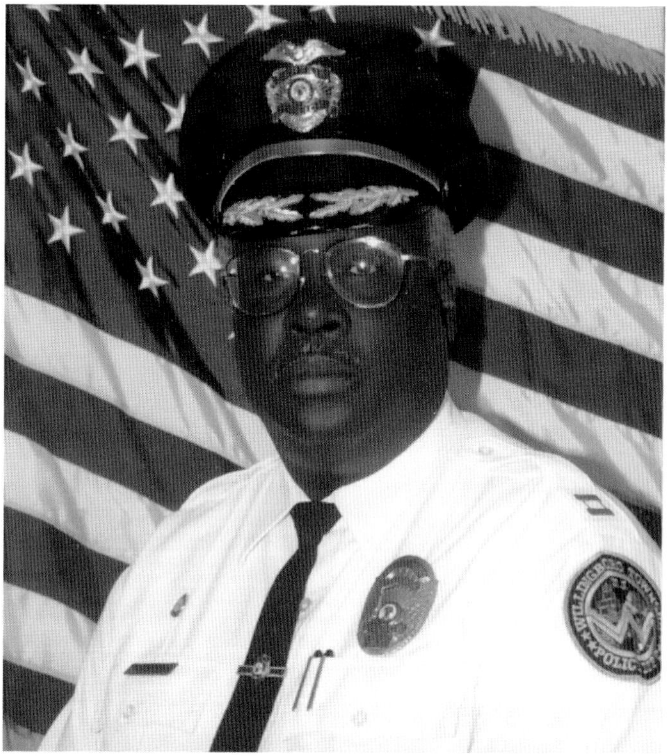

**Director Gregory Rucker**
Township native Gregory Rucker joined the Willingboro Police Department in 1978 and rose through the ranks to command the investigations division. Rucker sought to establish greater relationships with the community, and formed the Captain's Table at Memorial Junior High School to create bonds between youth and officers, among other initiatives. He retired in 2003 but in 2007 returned as director of public safety. (Courtesy Willingboro Police Department.)

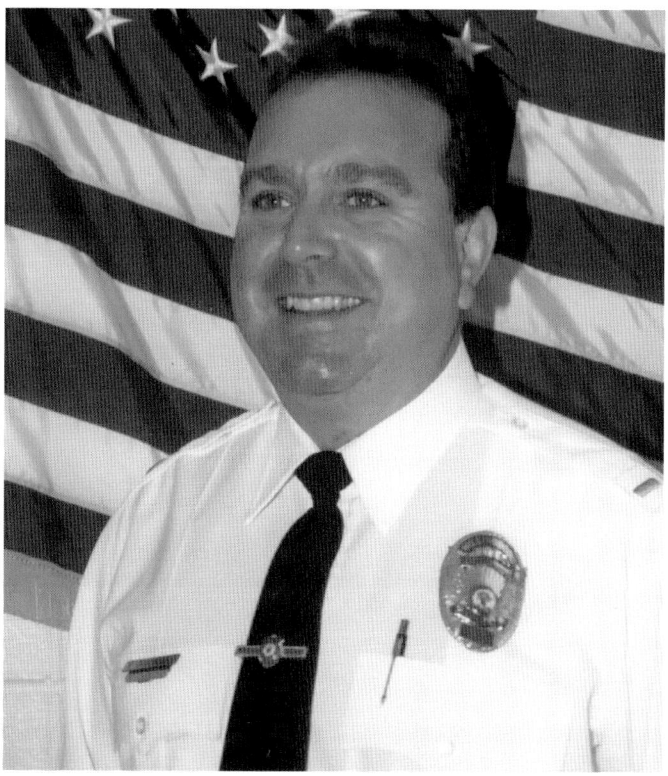

**Capt. Brian Cantwell**
Brian Cantwell joined the police department in April 1981. Currently a captain in the patrol division, Cantwell was one of the first officers assigned to walk a beat. He also was assigned to the detective division, supervised the narcotics unit, and trained new recruits. (Courtesy Willingboro Police Department.)

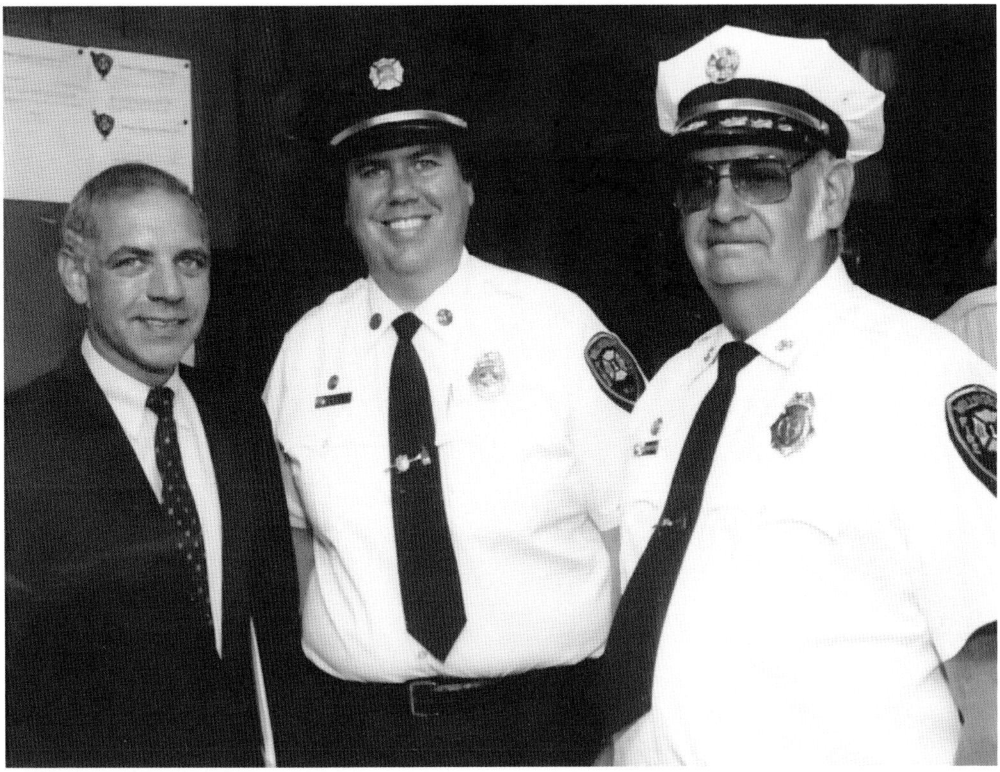

**Norman Cheeseman**

When Norman Cheeseman (at right) joined the Willingboro Fire Department in 1961, the all-volunteer company did not even have a firehouse. During his 47 years of service, he is credited with helping secure a firehouse and make the transition from all volunteers to a department with full-time, paid staff. Known for his kind ways and ability to tell jokes and puns, Cheeseman was chief for 12 years and was on the Willingboro Board of Fire Commissioners for 12 years, with 9 spent as chairman. Even though he retired in 2003 to Magnolia, Camden County, Cheeseman and his wife, Barbara, regularly attended monthly meetings and dinner events. Cheeseman died in April 2008 at age 79. (Courtesy Willingboro Fire Department.)

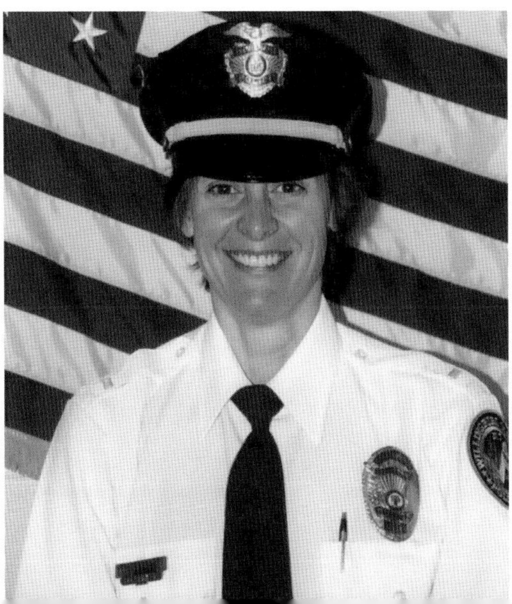

**Capt. Donna Dimitri**

Hired in 1979, Donna Dimitri was the Willingboro Police Department's first female officer. Dimitri served in both the patrol and detective divisions and was involved in many high-profile cases, including a 12-year-old girl who disappeared from her home only weeks before she was due to give birth. In 1995, the Burlington County Prosecutor's Office honored Dimitri for assisting victims of domestic violence. She retired in 2011 as a captain. (Courtesy Willingboro Police Department.)

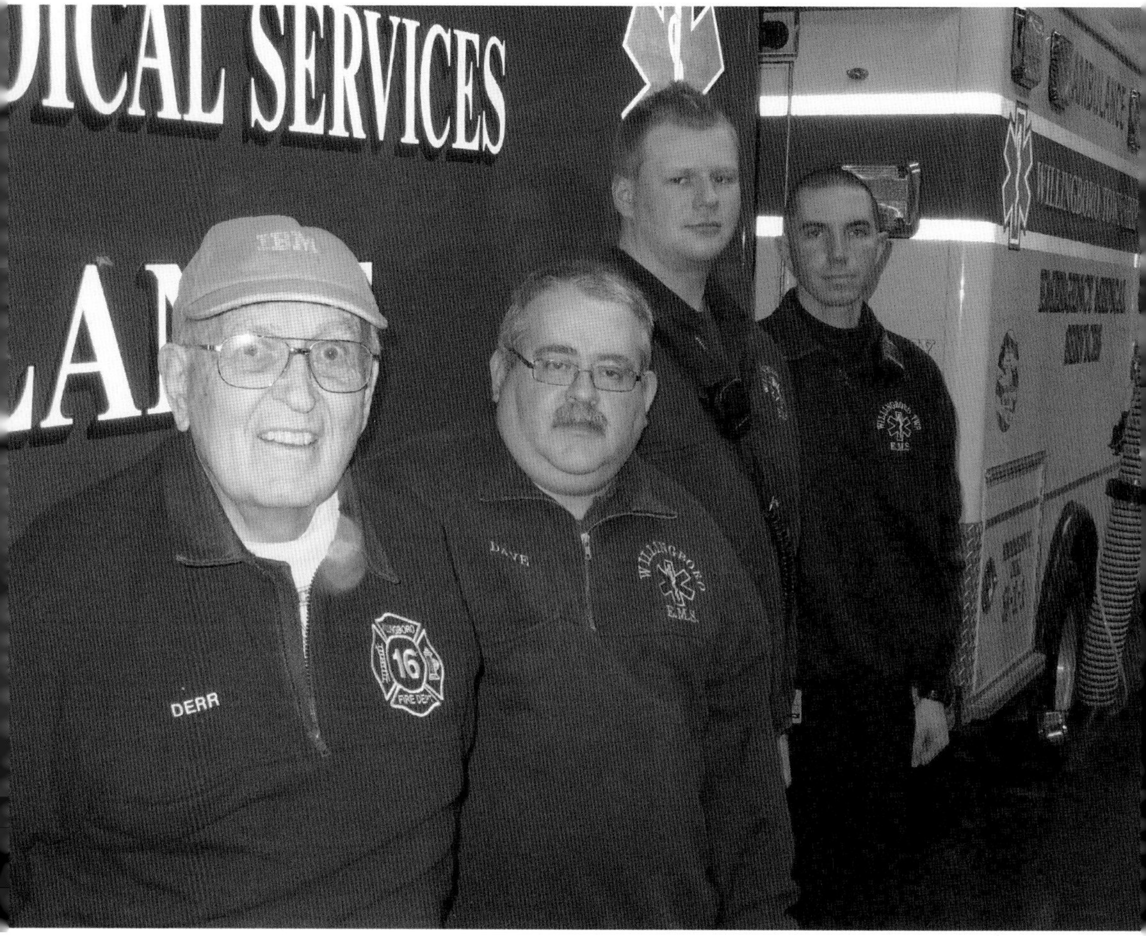


**George Derr**

One of the founders of the Levittown Volunteer Fire Company in January 1960, George Derr (far left) continues to extinguish fires. He twice served as president of the department. In 1973, he helped organize the Willingboro Board of Fire Commissioners and served on the panel for seven years, including as chairman. Derr fondly recalls each and every piece of equipment the department acquired and many memorable incidents, including how two successive nights of storms triggered 165 calls for help, flooded streets, and even knocked out two fire trucks. Derr also was responsible for integrating the department in 1969, accepting Ray Holden as its first black firefighter. Holden was promoted to lieutenant in 1971, and more African Americans began to join the department.

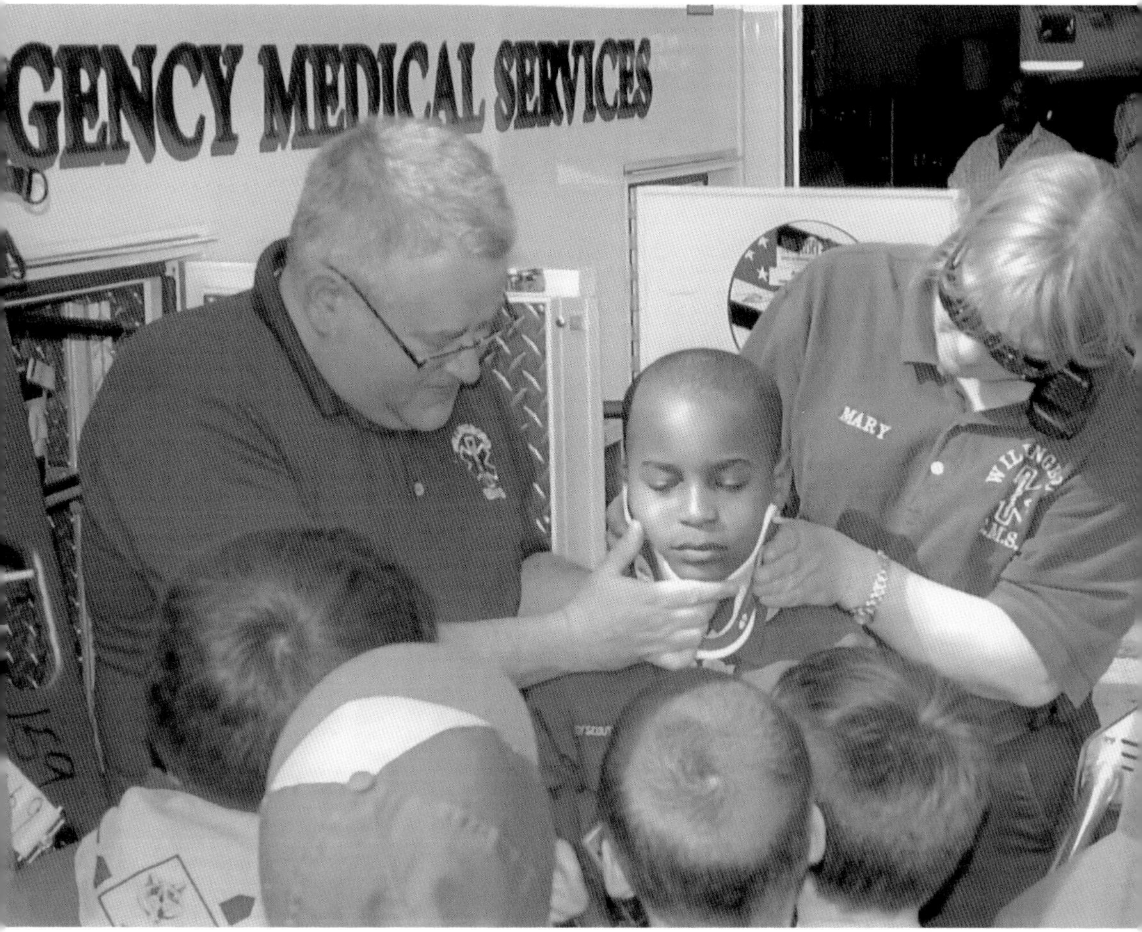


**David Nelinson**

David Nelinson (left), an emergency medical technician, has served Willingboro since 1980 as a member of the fire department and emergency squad. A graduate of John F. Kennedy High School, Nelinson has served as chief, logistics coordinator, and historian of the emergency squad, as well as a fire police captain and treasurer of the fire department. Nelinson works for Burlington County Central Communications. Nelinson's wife, Denise, a trauma data abstractionist, has served as president of the emergency squad and as a fire commissioner. (Courtesy Willingboro Emergency Squad.)

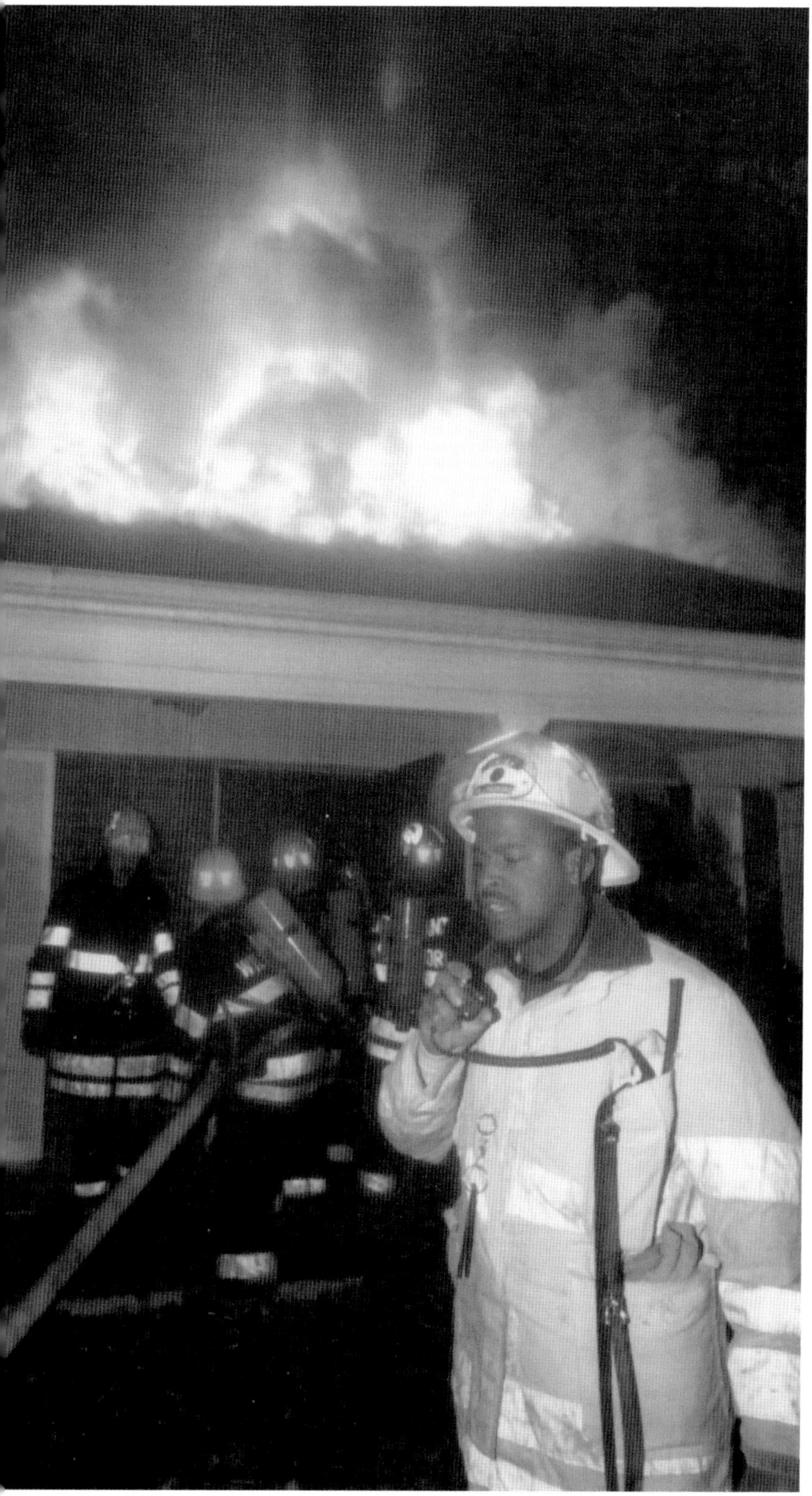

**Anthony Burnett**
Anthony Burnett began volunteering with the Willingboro Fire Department as a junior firefighter in 1981, at age 16. He rose to chief of the volunteer department in 1992–1993, and then was hired as the first paid chief in August 2002. Burnett oversees three full-time captains and 16 firefighters who work 24-hour shifts, as well as 20 volunteers who assist on nights and weekends, and a fire police unit. The department responds to about 1,100 calls per year, from house fires to traffic accidents, and performs community outreach. Recently, Burnett arranged for the birthday party of the four-year-old son of a US Army sergeant who was deployed to Kuwait before she could take him to the firehouse for a visit. The boy and his family received a special tour, even getting to work the fire hose. (Courtesy Willingboro Fire Department.)

### Gus Maier

Gus Maier was a life member of the Willingboro Emergency Squad, serving as president for 10 years—longer than any other member. A paramedic, Maier (at right, with past squad captain Robert Ruotolo) saved countless lives on the Willingboro squad and as a supervisor at Memorial Hospital of Burlington County for 14 years. Maier held a bachelor's degree in business management and ran his own sales management firm. He also served the community as president of the Willingboro Rotary in 1997 and 1998. Maier passed away in 1999. (Courtesy Willingboro Emergency Squad.)

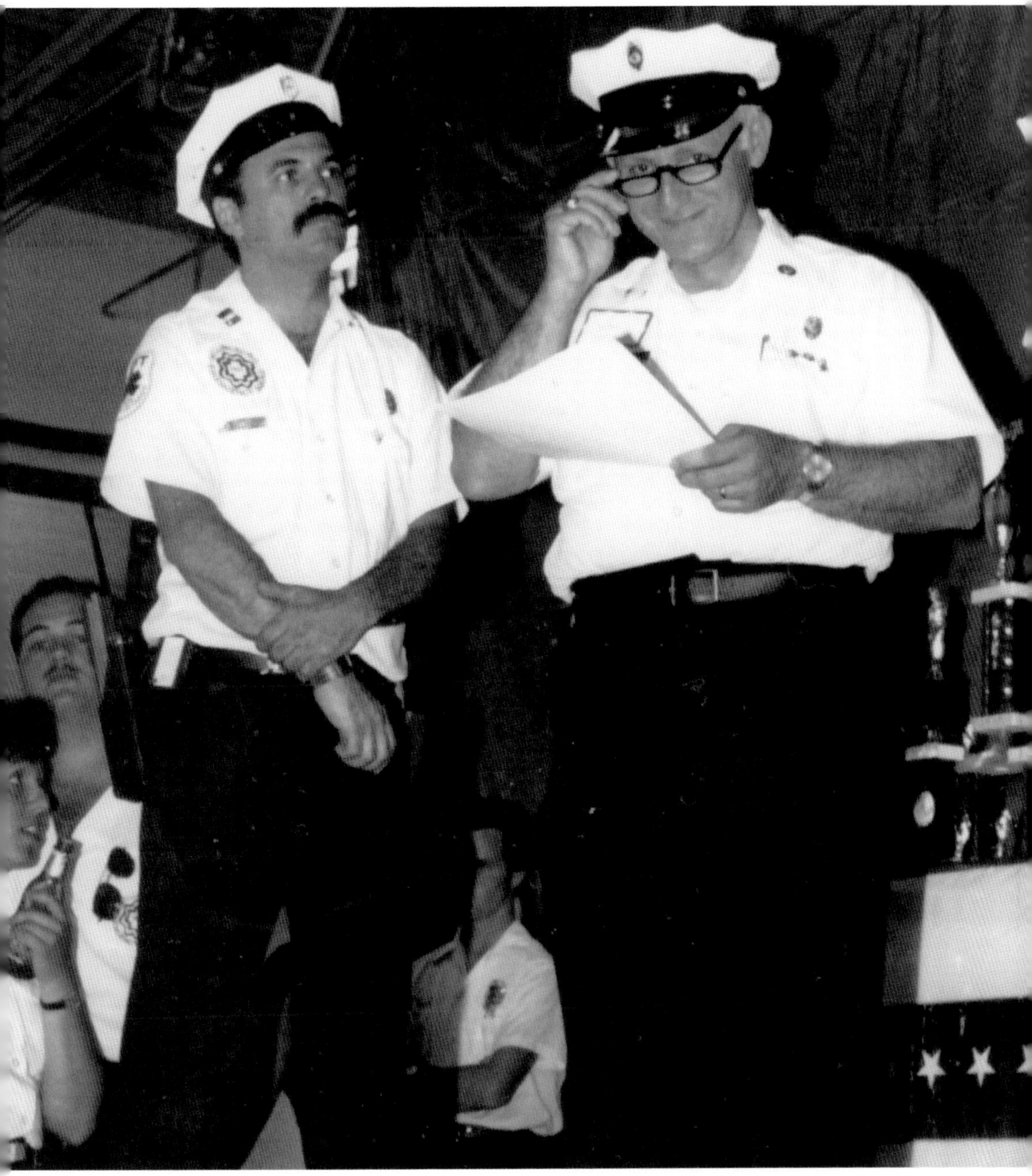

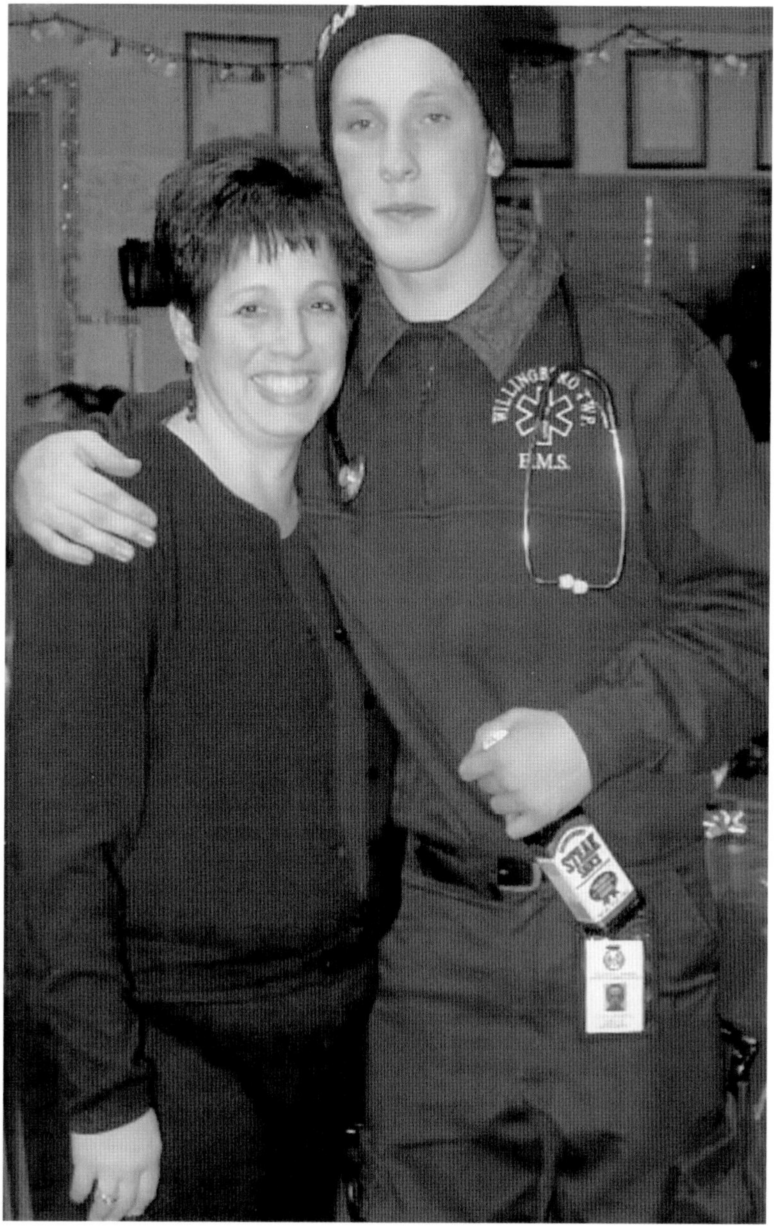


**Janine Maier Stringfellow and Brendan Stringfellow**

For members of the Willingboro Emergency Squad, saving lives is a family affair. A paramedic and life member of the squad, Janine Maier Stringfellow (left) is the daughter of longtime president Gus Maier. A pharmaceutical and medical sales representative for 18 years, Maier Stringfellow also followed in her father's footsteps serving as president of the Willingboro Rotary in 2008 and 2009. Brendan Stringfellow (right) is a third-generation member of the squad, following parents Janine Maier Stringfellow and Joe Stringfellow and grandfathers Gus Maier and Mason Stringfellow. A student at Arcadia University, he was honored for helping to safely deliver a baby born at home and saving a life using cardiopulmonary resuscitation. Brendan also is an EMT with the Bellmawr Emergency Squad. (Courtesy Willingboro Emergency Squad.)

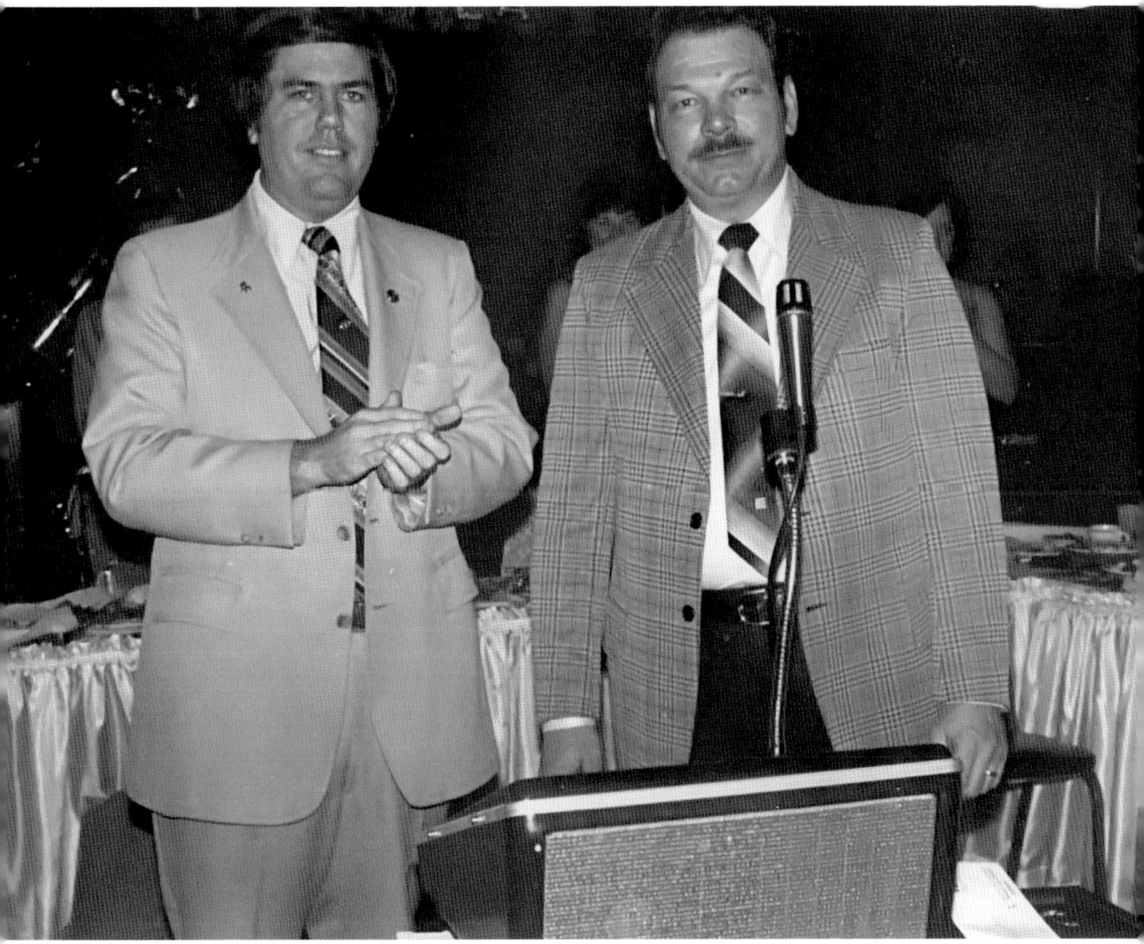

**George Richardson**

George Richardson served as president of the Willingboro Fire Department from 1973 to 1976, 1980 to 1981, and 1986 to 1988. Seen here at the left (with fellow department president George Baxter Jr.), Richardson helped organize the Willingboro Board of Fire Commissioners in 1973, serving as chairman from 1988 to 1989. Richardson also served on the Willingboro School Board. (Courtesy Willingboro Fire Department.)

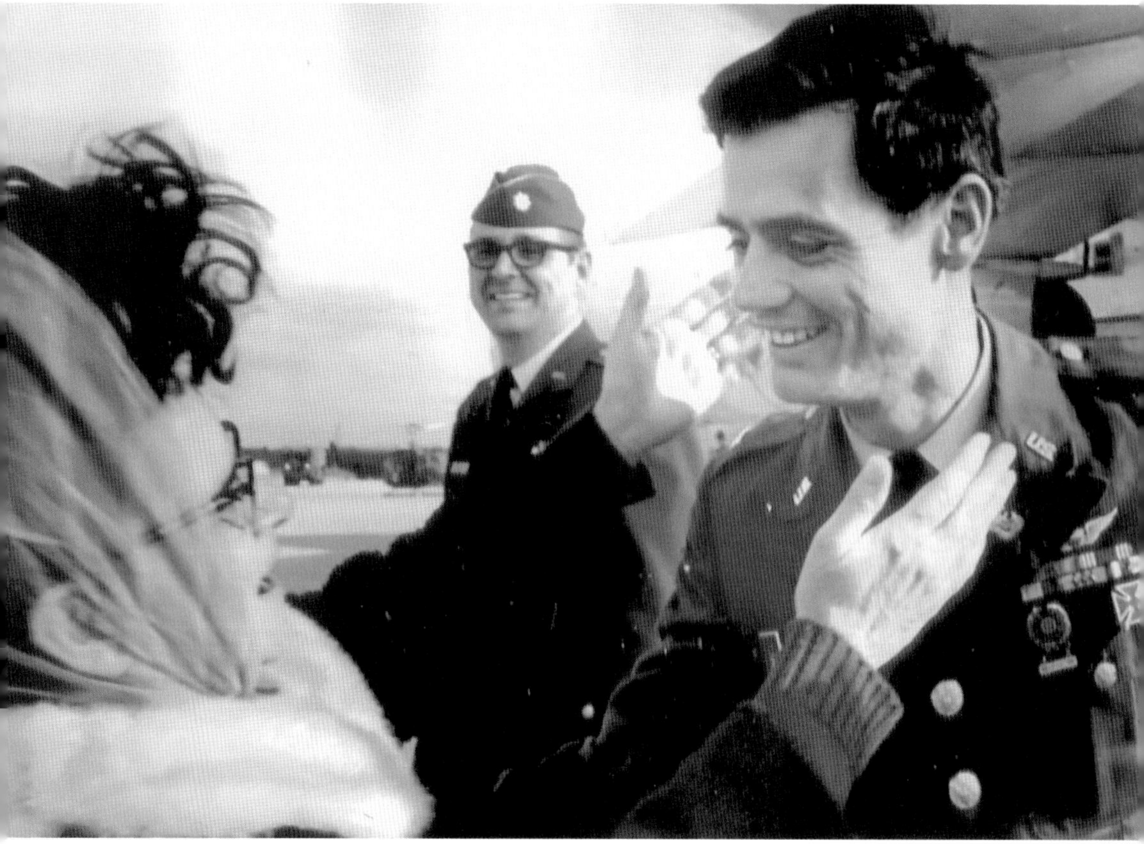

**War Veterans**

Willingboro residents have served their nation with distinction. The township is home to many members of the famed Tuskegee Airmen and Buffalo Soldiers. Frank Anton (right), a US Air Force helicopter pilot, was shot down during a mission in Vietnam in 1968 and held prisoner for five years. More recently, Jimmy Wesley James, a chemical warfare specialist, was killed in the Persian Gulf War. S.Sgt. Terry Hemingway and Maj. Dwayne Kelley died in Iraq in 2003 and 2008, respectively. (Courtesy *Burlington County Times.*)

# CHAPTER SIX

# Economic Drivers

## Business and Commerce

When South Korean immigrant Micha Alston opened Kingsway Bagel and Deli 15 years ago, she thought making sandwiches would be a good way to learn English and American culture. Today, she has a loyal following who consider her homemade hoagies the highlight of their day.

Alston is indicative of the many small entrepreneurs who have businesses in Willingboro. Levitt and Sons' neighborhood park design left little room for commerce, and the shops in those areas sometimes struggled. The main business district was on Route 130, with the Willingboro Plaza and the Village Mall. Both were largely vacant and dilapidated by the late 1980s and early 1990s, as commerce shifted to towns like Burlington Township, Moorestown, and Mount Laurel along Interstate 295.

Within the past 10 years, Willingboro has witnessed an economic resurgence. Working with a New York developer, the township converted the plaza into the Willingboro Town Center, anchored by an Express Scripts (formerly Medco Health Solutions) mail-order pharmacy. Express Scripts is the township's largest employer, followed by Lourdes Medical Center of Burlington County.

While Willingboro has attracted its share of national chains, there are many small businesses operated by local entrepreneurs. William C. Fox and Jeff Fante graduated two years apart from Willingboro High School, and each formed successful heating and air conditioning companies serving their neighbors and South Jersey. Fox and Fante are both active in the community, sponsoring sports teams and working with nonprofit groups.

Charlie Quigley gave up a successful career in roofing to purchase Burlington County Bicycle Center. Now in its 50th year, this Willingboro institution attracts biking enthusiasts of all ages, as well as providing and repairing most police bicycles in Burlington and Camden counties.

One of Willingboro's oldest businesses is the *Burlington County Times*. Launched in 1958 by Stanley Willis Calkins Sr., as Levitt and Sons was in high gear building neighborhood after neighborhood, the *BCT* is the newspaper of record for Willingboro news, as well as the entire county. Although the paper has downsized—it is now printed at its sister publication in Bristol, Pennsylvania—the *BCT* successfully publishes six days a week and daily online.

Another business success story is Inductotherm, in nearby Rancocas (which was part of Willingboro until 1956). Founded in 1953 by Henry Rowan, today Inductotherm is the world's leading manufacturer of induction melting furnaces. In 1992, Rowan and his wife, Betty, surprised the world when they pledged $100 million to Glassboro State College. The gift has transformed the college, now Rowan University, into a regional institution.

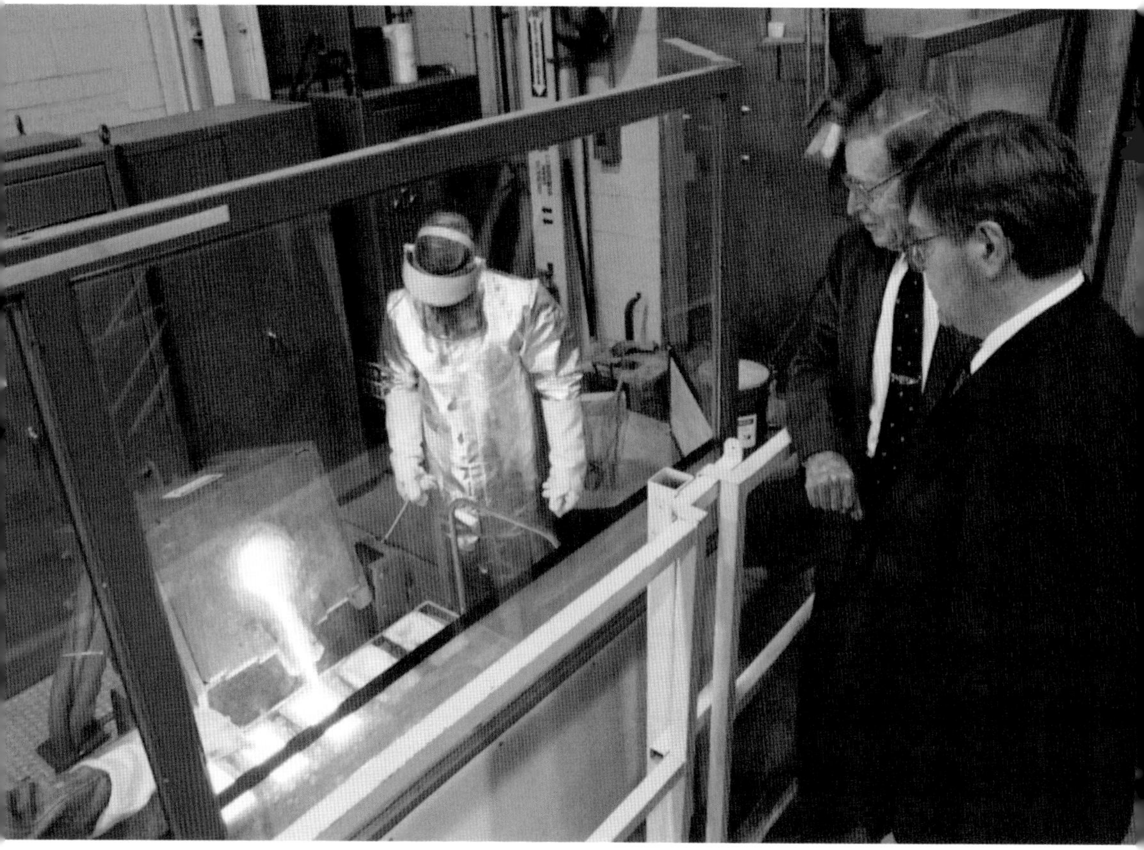

**Henry Rowan** (ABOVE AND OPPOSITE PAGE)
From his earliest years raised by a single mother during the Great Depression, Henry Rowan practiced a doctrine of thrift and self-reliance. With an inner drive that knows no off switch, Rowan (pictured in the center of the above photograph) has thrived on challenges, from seeking dual degrees from Williams College and the Massachusetts Institute of Technology to enlisting in the US Army Air Corps and learning to fly a B-17 bomber, to forming Rancocas-based Inductotherm Industries, Inc.—a multimillion-dollar firm that leads the world in the manufacture of induction melting furnaces. With wife Betty by his side, Rowan risked everything building the first furnace in the basement of a rented house, heating copper over a bonfire in their backyard. Today, Inductotherm Group has 40 subsidiaries with 38 manufacturing facilities in 19 countries. In 1992, the Rowans stunned the nation when they pledged $100 million to tiny Glassboro State College, at the time the largest gift to a public university. The gift has transformed Rowan University, which now has modern buildings and state-of-the-art engineering and medical schools. It also has allowed the children of scores of Inductotherm employees to attend college, a testament to the value he places on his workers. (Courtesy Rowan University/Craig Terry.)

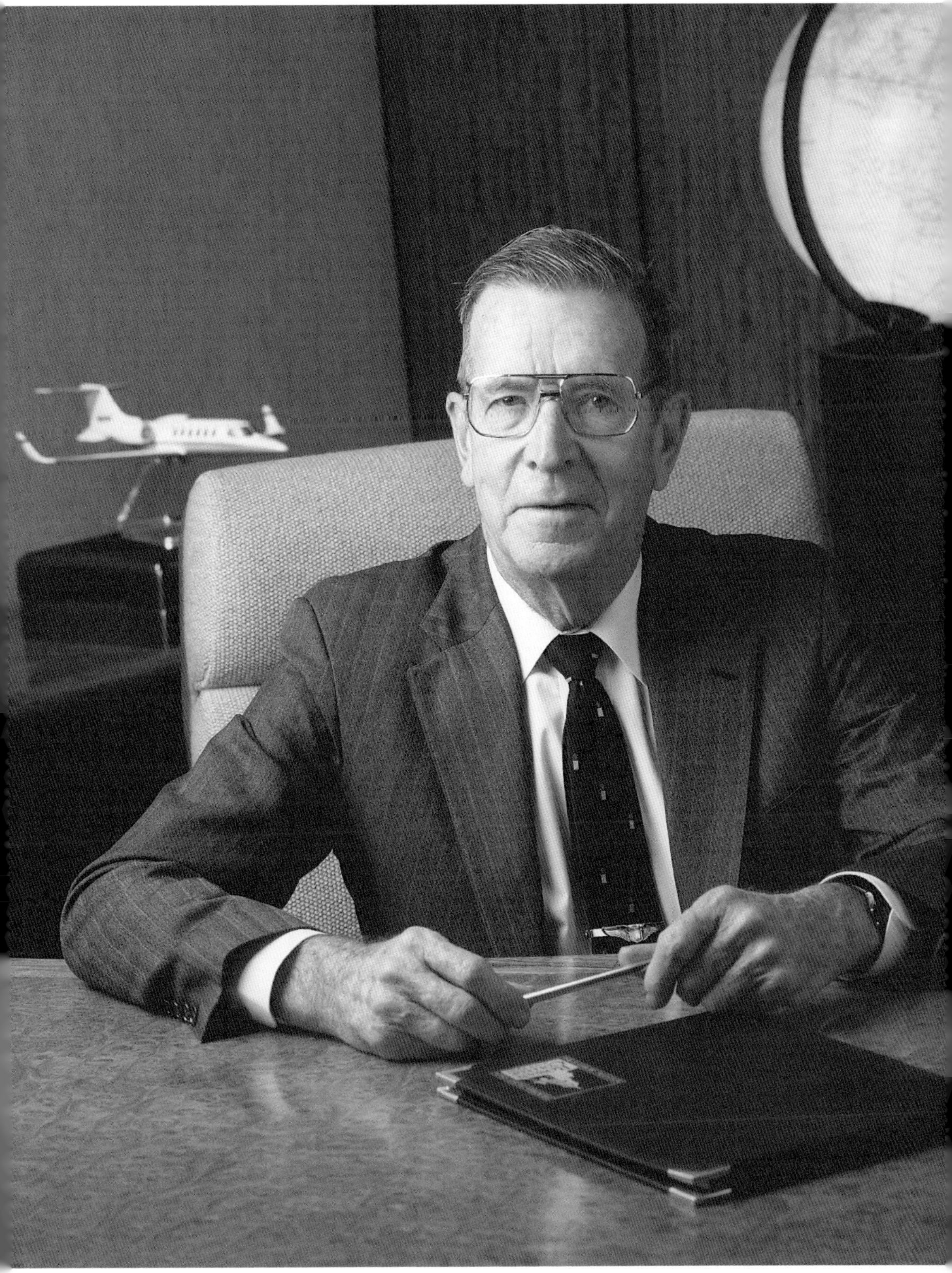

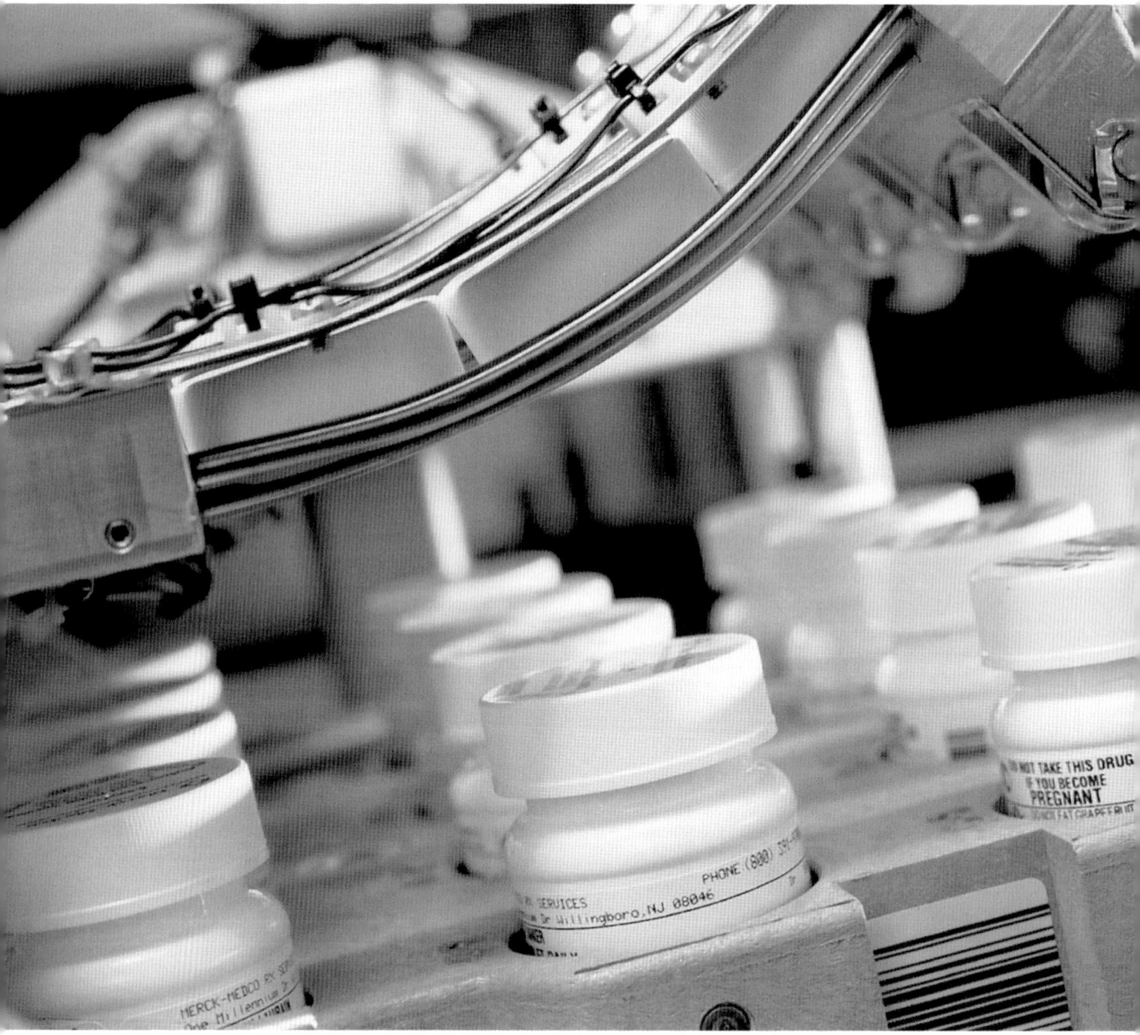


**Calvin G. Wasdyke and Express Scripts**

Calvin G. Wasdyke was a household name. A registered pharmacist, Wasdyke's name was on every bottle that left Medco Health Solutions's automated mail-service pharmacy at the Willingboro Town Center. "I never met another Wasdyke," he told the *New York Times*. "Now the name will be everywhere." Opened in 2001, the 320,000-square-foot facility was the world's largest pharmacy, capable of dispensing more than one million prescriptions each week. With miles of conveyor belts, computers, scanners, and robots designed to speed the filling of prescriptions and reduce human error, the pharmacy is a technical marvel. But it is also an economic engine, helping to jump-start the redevelopment of the former Willingboro Plaza (the building used to house a Boscov's department store) and the Route 130 corridor. The pharmacy is one of the area's largest employers, with about 1,100 people. Express Scripts purchased the pharmacy in 2012 when it acquired Medco Health. (Courtesy the Associated Press.)

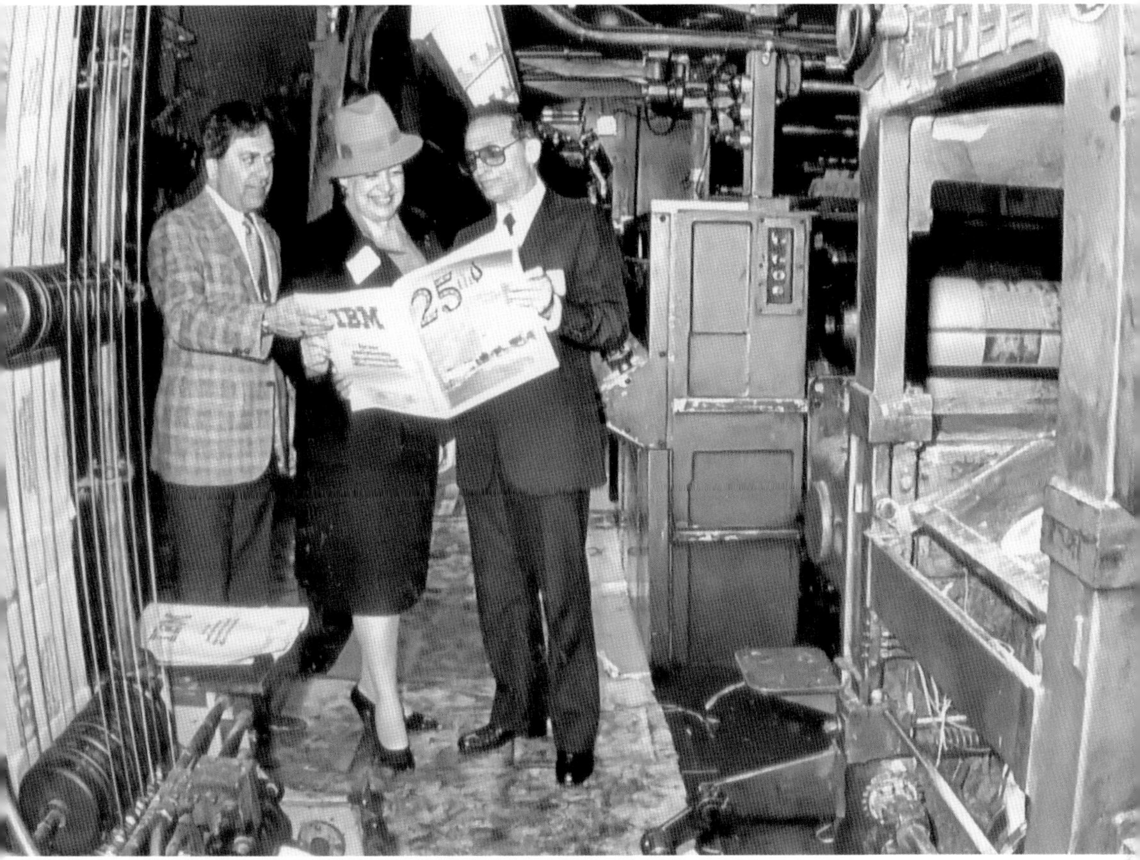

**Stanley Willis Calkins Sr.**

Starting your own company is risky business. Yet Stanley Willis Calkins Sr. was willing to take that leap, and his entrepreneurial spirit, confidence, and determination built a media empire that today spans four states. Calkins purchased his first newspaper in Uniontown, Pennsylvania, in 1937. In 1954, he expanded into the Philadelphia market, acquiring what would become the *Doylestown Intelligencer* and the *Bucks County Courier Times* in Levittown, Pennsylvania. At the urging of builder William Levitt, who was building a new community in New Jersey, Calkins founded the *Levittown Times* in 1958. The paper was renamed the *Burlington County Times* (*BCT*) in 1963 after Levittown residents voted to change the name of their town back to Willingboro. The *BCT* quickly became an integral part of the community. "The newspapers are only as strong as the communities we serve," said Calkins's grandson Stan Ellis, who served as publisher of the *BCT* for many years. "Part of the newspaper's mission is to move forward and prosper, but my grandfather also felt that it's important for newspapers to give back to the communities." Calkins died in 1973 at age 75, and the company remains a family business run by his three daughters. In the photograph above, one of Calkins's daughters (center) celebrates the *BCT*'s 25th anniversary with company executives. Today, Calkins Media owns daily and weekly newspapers, as well as television stations. (Courtesy *Burlington County Times*.)

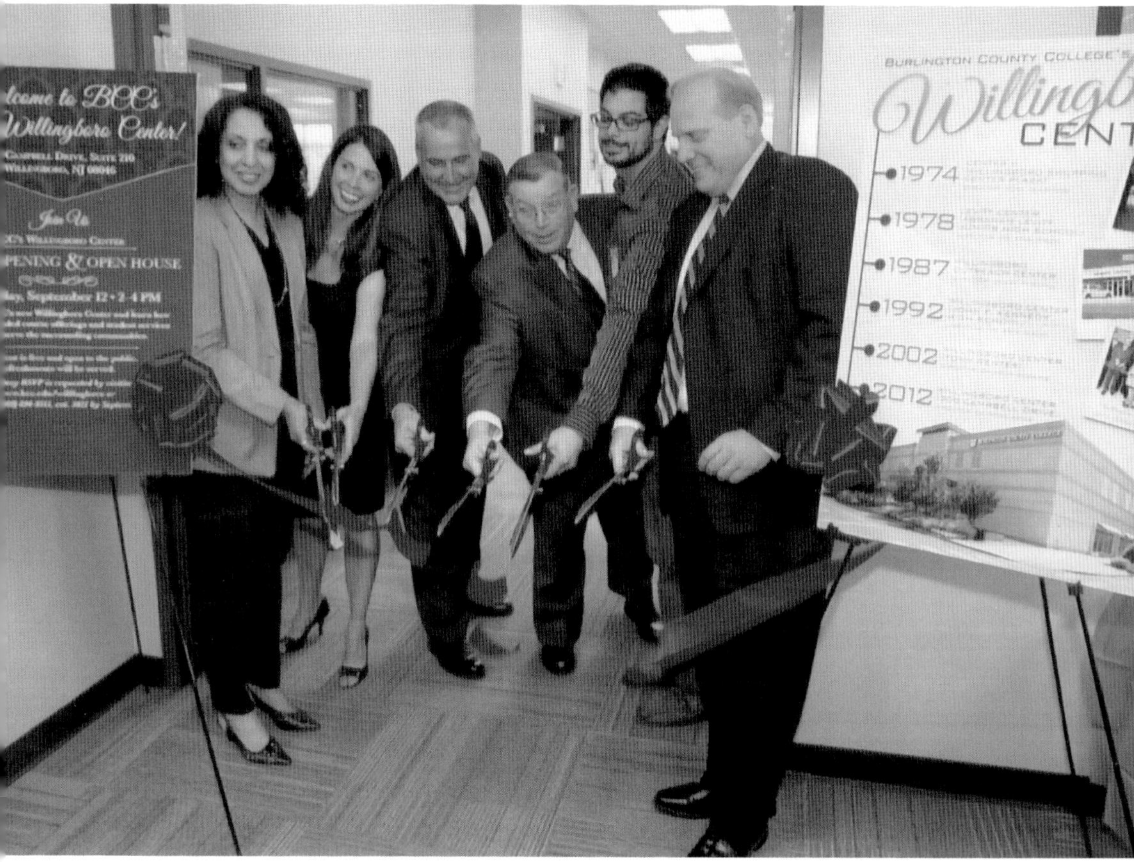


**N. Dean Evans and Burlington County College**

Thanks to the foresight of Dr. N. Dean Evans, Willingboro is a center of higher education. A native of Springfield, Pennsylvania, Evans was the founding president of Burlington County College (BCC), overseeing its development and opening in 1969. A graduate of Ursinus College, the University of Pennsylvania, and Temple University, Evans was a teacher and professor before being hired to lead the two-year community college. The college first held classes at Lenape High School in Medford, before moving to its home in Pemberton Township in 1971. In 1974, Dr. Evans led BCC to open its first major off-campus facility at the Willingboro Plaza. By its second semester, enrollment in Willingboro had doubled.

In 1978, BCC expanded its Willingboro presence, opening a wing at Abraham Levitt Junior High School for adult basic education and other courses. In 1992, the college consolidated its Willingboro campus, which had one of the state's largest dental assistance programs.

Ten years later, under the leadership of Dr. Robert C. Messina Jr. (Evans resigned in 1976), the college moved into a new 18,700-square-foot campus at the Willingboro Town Center. In September 2012, BCC moved into larger, more modern space in the former Sears building at the town center to better serve students living along the Route 130 corridor. Seen here at the ribbon cutting are, from left to right, Willingboro Committee president Patricia Lindsay-Harvey, Burlington County freeholders Leah Arter and Bruce Garganio, BCC Board of Trustees chair Joseph Malone, BCC Student Government Association president Christopher Sanchez, and college president David Hespe. (Courtesy Burlington County College.)

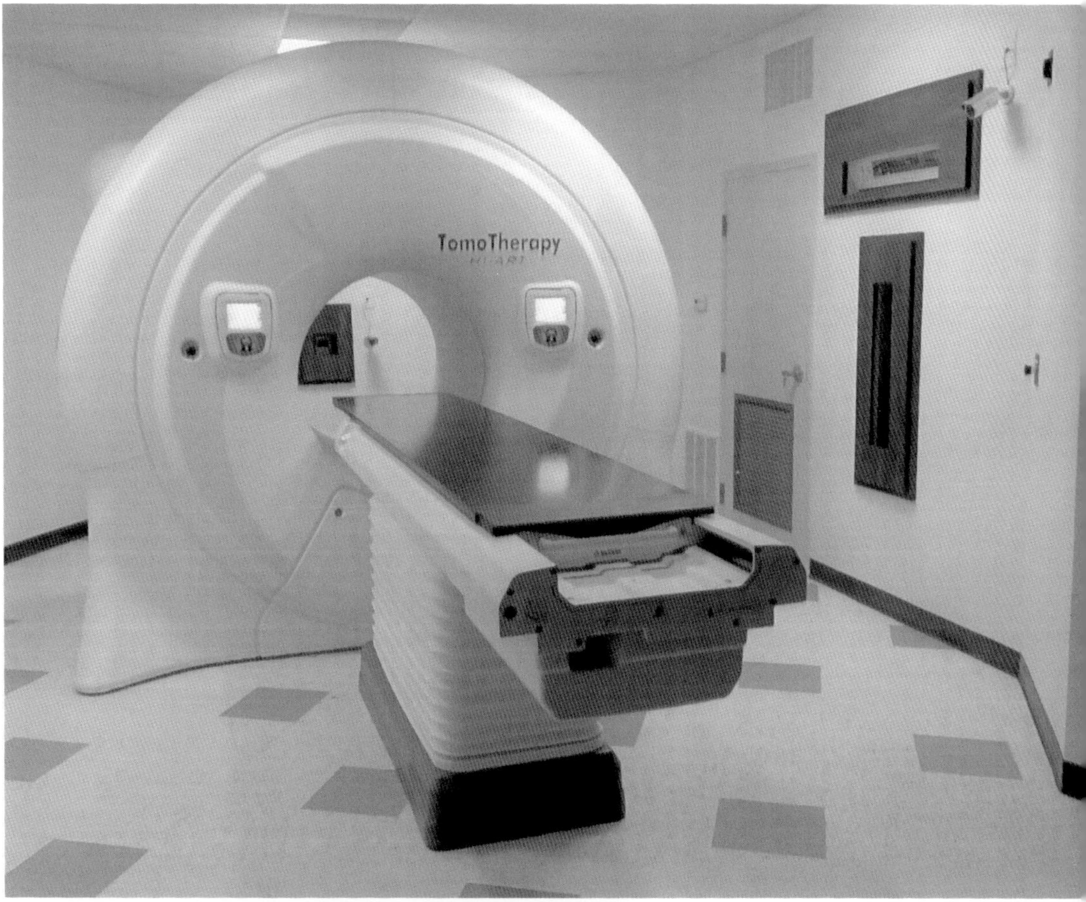


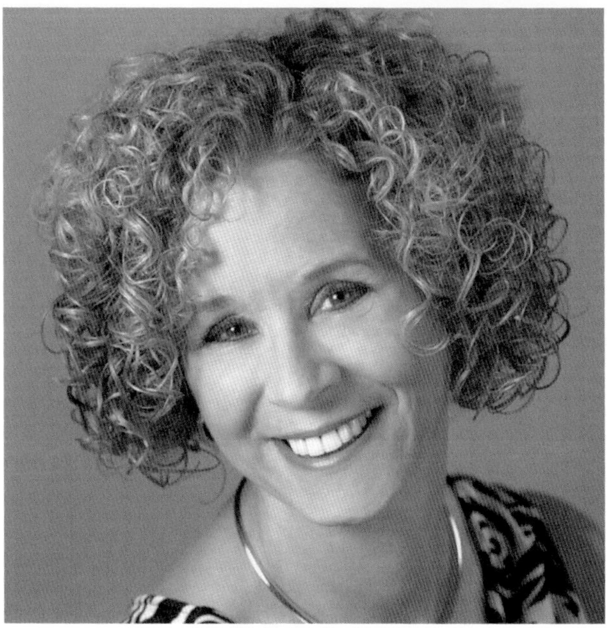

**Dr. Alexis Harvey and 21st Century Oncology**
A lead physician at 21st Century Oncology in Willingboro and three other locations across South Jersey, Dr. Alexis Harvey works closely with other physicians to ensure their patients receive the proper radiologic cancer treatment. A graduate of Villanova University and the Hahnemann University School of Medicine, Dr. Harvey recently was named a "Top Physician for Women" by *South Jersey Magazine*. (Top, courtesy Lourdes Health System; left, courtesy 21st Century Oncology.)

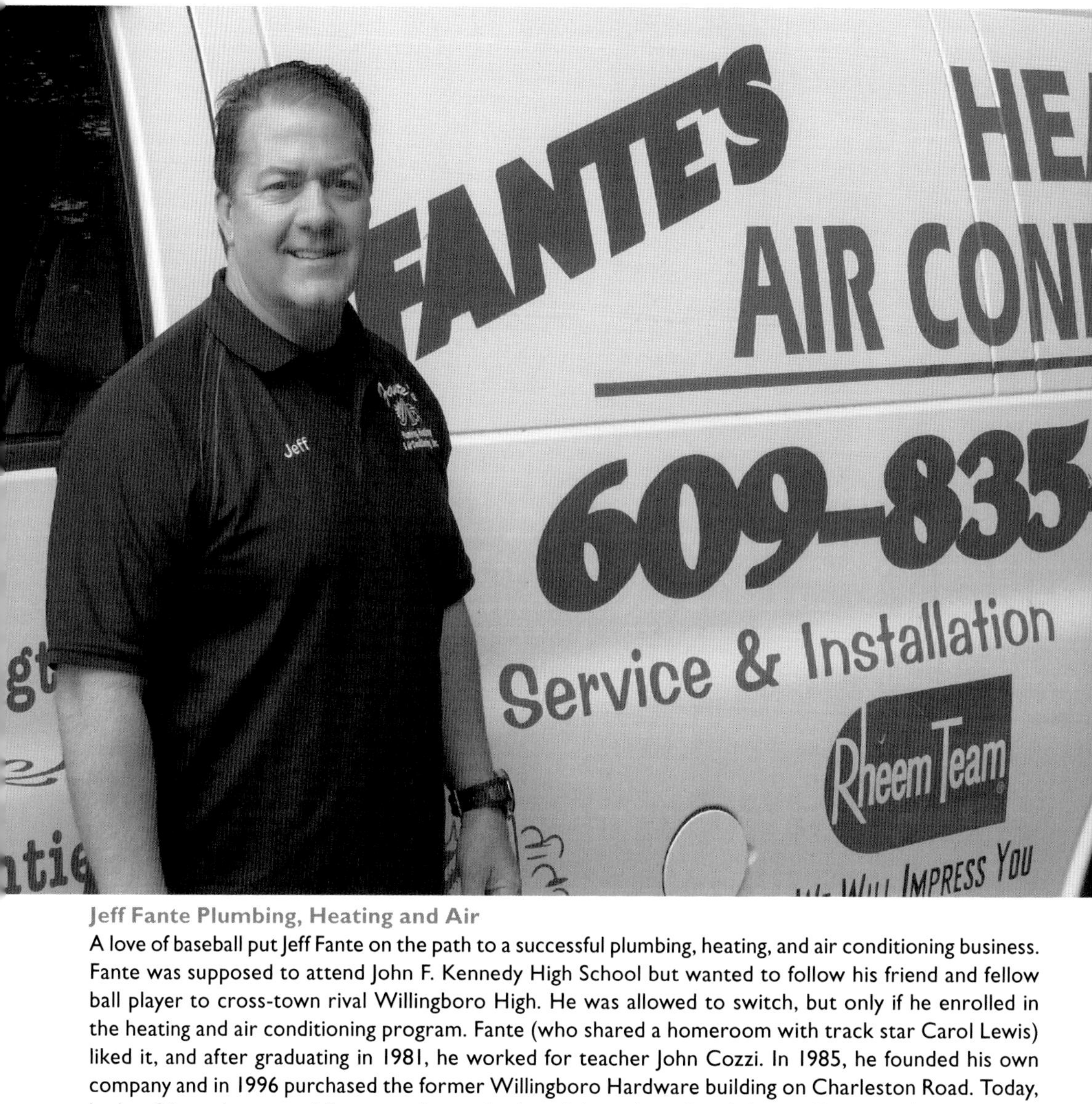


**Jeff Fante Plumbing, Heating and Air**

A love of baseball put Jeff Fante on the path to a successful plumbing, heating, and air conditioning business. Fante was supposed to attend John F. Kennedy High School but wanted to follow his friend and fellow ball player to cross-town rival Willingboro High. He was allowed to switch, but only if he enrolled in the heating and air conditioning program. Fante (who shared a homeroom with track star Carol Lewis) liked it, and after graduating in 1981, he worked for teacher John Cozzi. In 1985, he founded his own company and in 1996 purchased the former Willingboro Hardware building on Charleston Road. Today, he has 26 employees and Fante trucks can be found throughout South Jersey. Despite a busy schedule that has included rehabilitating houses, Fante has not strayed from baseball, coaching and sponsoring teams. Fante is married with three children.

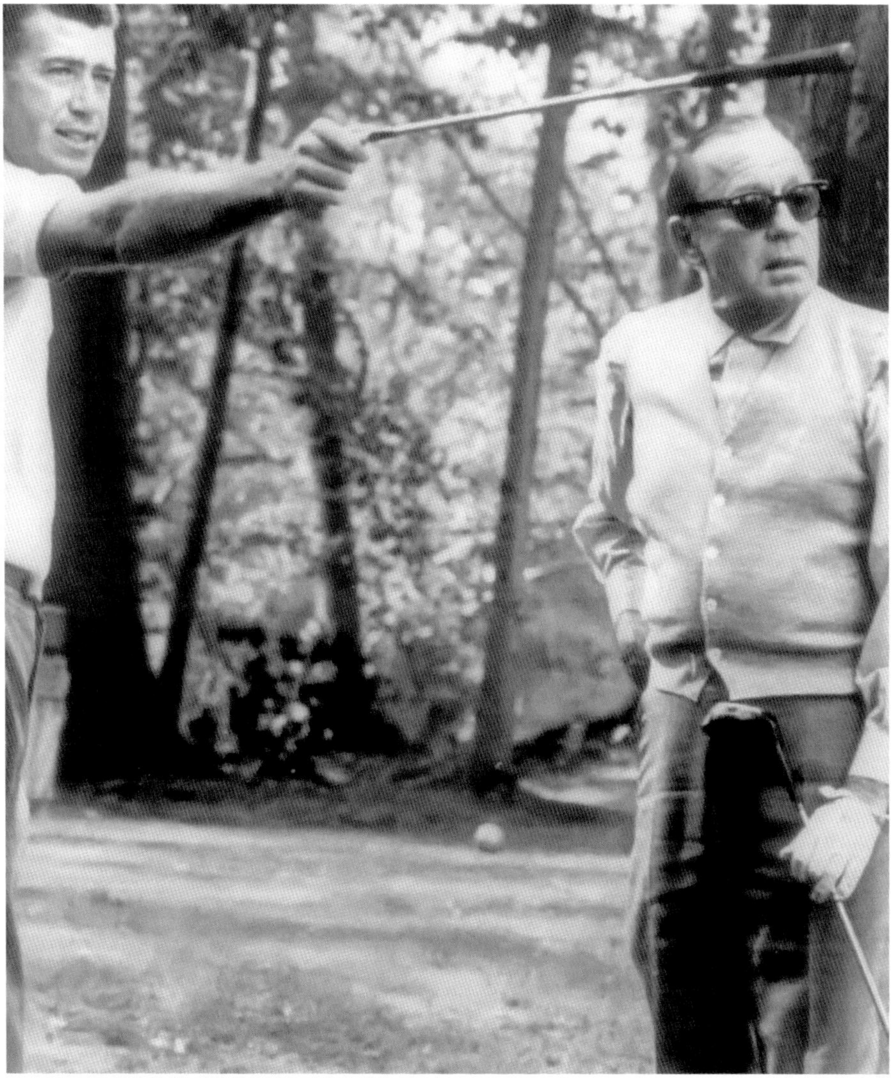

**Robert Trent Jones Sr. and Rancocas Golf Club**
Levitt and Sons hired prolific golf architect Robert Trent Jones Sr. to design the Willingboro Country Club in 1966. A native of Ince-in-Makerfield, England, Jones immigrated to the United States at age five. A skilled golfer, Jones became the first golf professional at Sodus Bay Heights Golf Club, but health problems prevented him from joining tournament competition. Jones attended Cornell University, creating his own course of study to become a professional golf course designer. He went on to design more than 500 courses in 40 states and 35 countries—it's been said that "the sun never sets on a Robert Trent Jones golf course." Jones's courses are noted for their artistic landscaping, innovative use of bunkers, water hazards, and greens that require a high level of strategy. The Rancocas Golf Club's 6,602-yard course is strategically incorporated within the landscape to preserve the area's natural beauty. The front and back nines feature distinctly different characteristics: the front nine is thoroughly bunkered, while the back nine is settled amid tree-lined fairways and rolling hills. The signature 13th hole is a 568-yard par five with a double dogleg uphill to a green guarded by bunkers on all sides. More than 50,000 rounds are played each year at the public course that, over the years, has hosted celebrities like Jack Benny (at right) and scores of tournaments. (Courtesy Willingboro Library.)

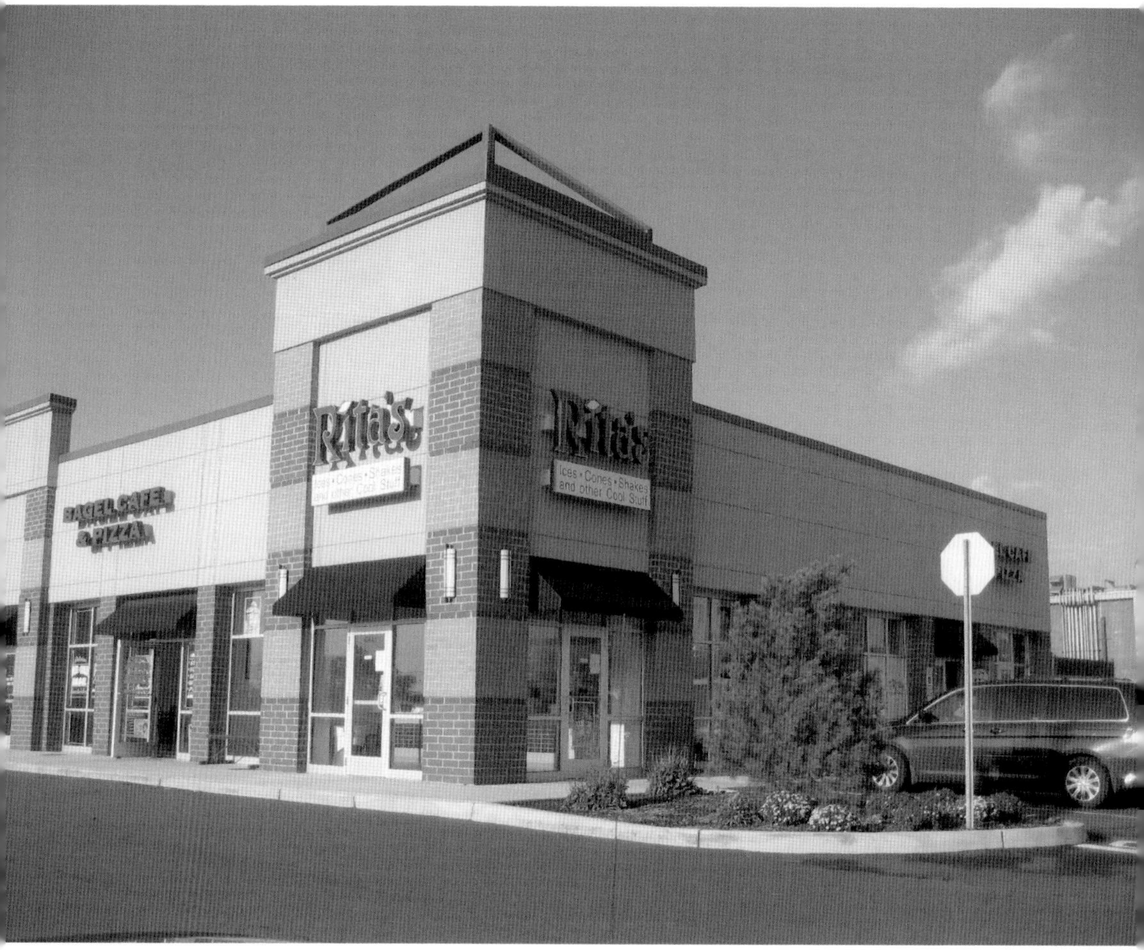


**Robert Stang**

Robert Stang, a third-generation real estate developer with more than 40 years of experience, integrates his passion for the environment and business acumen into sustainable construction and development. Stang founded ReNEWal Realty LLC in 1997 and partnered with Willingboro Township to revitalize the vacant former Willingboro Plaza. Stang envisioned a bustling town center with housing, shopping, restaurants and a library. New Jersey Future honored Stang and the center with its 2002 Smart Growth Award, and today the center is home to a mail-order pharmacy, apartments, two colleges, small stores, and the library.

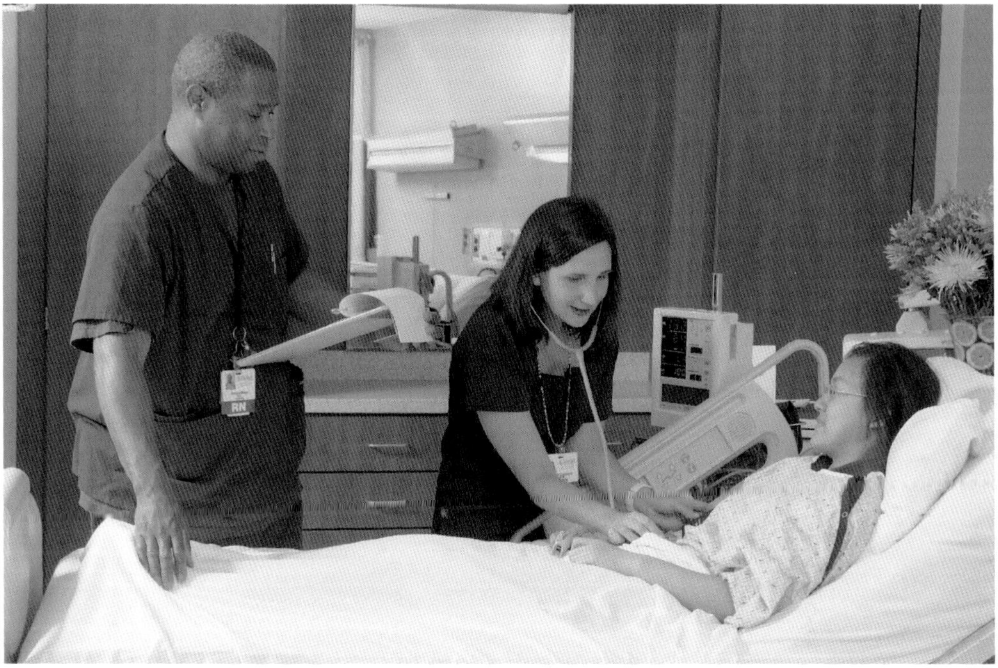

**Alexander J. Hatala and Lourdes Medical Center of Burlington County**
Alexander J. Hatala learned early on that one person could make a significant difference in people's lives, tagging along with his father as they helped fellow parishioners in their church. As president and chief executive officer of Lourdes Health System, he continues his work caring for others. A graduate of Rutgers University and the University of Florida and a fellow of the American College of Healthcare Executives, Hatala assumed leadership of the former Rancocas Hospital when Our Lady of Lourdes purchased it in 1998. Since then, he has tirelessly worked to grow the facility into a comprehensive medical center, offering high-quality care, from surgery to long-term acute care. In 2011, he was honored with the March of Dimes's Born to Shine Award. (Courtesy Lourdes Health System.)

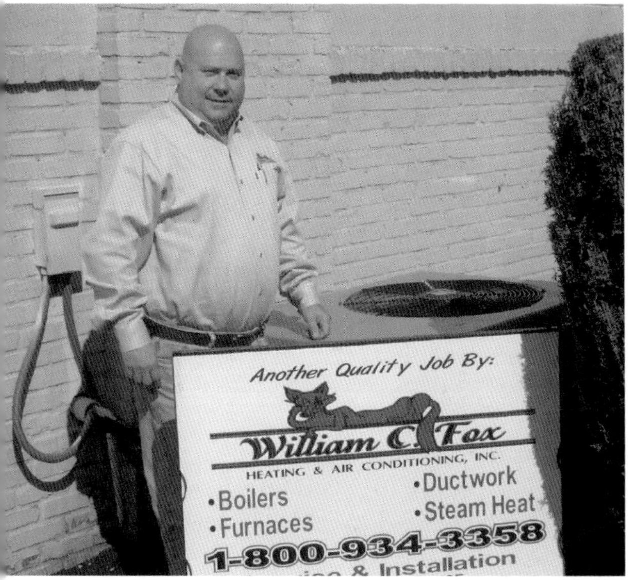


**William C. Fox Heating and Air Conditioning, Inc.**
William C. Fox's ties to Willingboro run deep. One of the first 100 families to move into the new Levittown, Fox was a volunteer firefighter and Boy Scout. In 1979, he graduated from the vocational education program, and the next year started running his heating and air conditioning business out of his parents' Somerset Park home. While growing his business to serve South Jersey and Bucks County, Fox has rehabilitated township homes and served as 1998 president of the Willingboro Rotary. "Willingboro has been good to me in school and in my early career," he said. "Where else would I go?" Fox is married with two children.

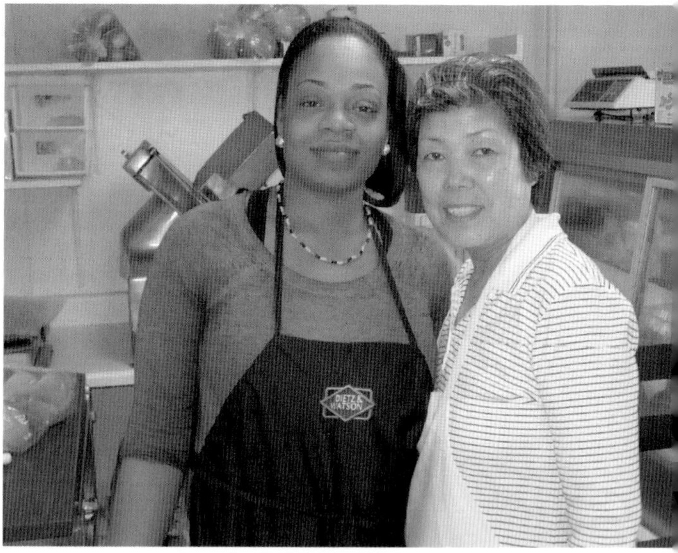

**Micha and John Alston**
Micha and John Alston met while he was stationed with the US military in South Korea. She immigrated to the United States in 1974, and 15 years ago opened Kingsway Bagel and Deli on Charleston Road near Route 130. Micha (at right with employee Stacy Shields) is known for making hearty, affordable sandwiches, remembering a customer's favorites—even if she has not seen him or her for several years. Micha says having the deli gives her the opportunity to meet many people and learn American culture.

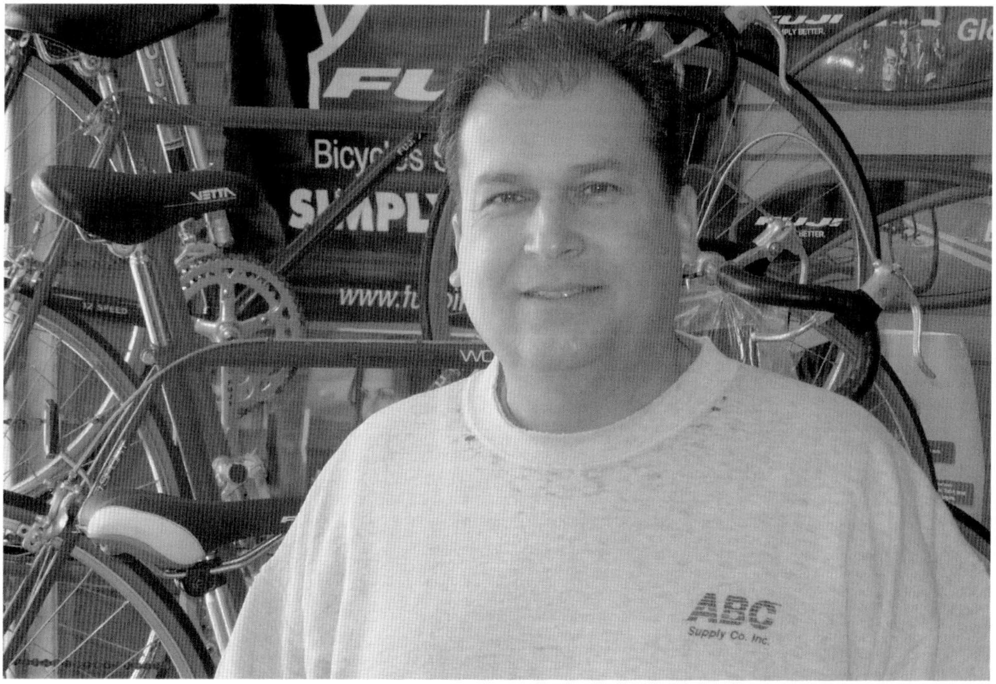


**Charlie Quigley and Burlington County Bicycle Center**
If there's a large building in the area, Charlie Quigley likely was involved in its construction. Yet in 2006, the union roofer switched gears and purchased Burlington County Bicycle Center. Founded in 1963 in a garage on Sedgwick Lane, Quigley has built upon the shop's excellent reputation, selling and repairing bicycles for both recreational and avid riders. As the store celebrates its 50th anniversary, the Bucks County native and married father of two hopes to expand to the Jersey Shore. "Every day you ride a bike in the parking lot or up and down the road making sure everything functions. What's more fun than riding a bike for a living?"

# INDEX

Abdul-Malik, Karen (Queen Nur), 78
Abrams, Dr. Meyer, 90
Adamo, Mark, 73
Allen, Diane, 28
Alston, Micha and John, 126
Anderson, Priscilla, 26
Anton, Frank, 114
Ayrer, James, 33
Baskies, Dr. Arnold, 95
Belford, Tyrone, 56
Bell, Marie White, 27
Best, Hosey, 42
Blackstone, Adam, 76
Blank, Dr. Andrew, 90
Blank, Dr. Bernard, 91
Bowman, Sgt. Eric, 104
Braxton, Director Benjamin, 105
Brunson, Kendall, 87
Burlington County College, 120
Burnett, Anthony, 110
Calkins, Stanley Willis Sr., 119
Campbell Jr., Eddie, 32, 34
Campbell, Doreatha 7, 34
Cantwell, Capt. Brian, 106
Cheeseman, Norman, 107
Cintron, Edgardo, 86
Coan, Father Francis P.J., 44
Conners, Jack, 48
Costa, Catherine, 28
Crews, Tiffany, 52
Dash, Ron, 38
Davis, Aaron M., 63
Day, Alma, 86
Derr, George, 108
Dey, Lt. Joseph, 101
Dimitri, Capt. Donna, 107
Duccilli, Charles, 64
Epps, Jesse, 31
Express Scripts, 118
Fante, Jeff, 122
Fernandez, Dr. Eduardo, 94
Fox, Willliam C., 125
Franklin, William, 11
Friedman, Sally, 84
Friedman, Victor, 32
Gama, Millie, 36
Gammage, Jeff, 85
Gans, Herbert J., 17
George, Freddie, 57
Gray, Jim, 47
Hamaty, Dr. John, 91
Harvey, Dr. Alexis, 121
Hatala, Alexander J., 125
Hatten, Addie, 2
Helem, Lisa, 87
High School Bands, 80
Hill, Christine M., 83
Huddleston, Marion, 35
Jackson, Lydia, 16
James, Rev. Willie, 13
Johnson, Lavonne, 33
Jones, Robert Trent Sr., 123
Kalik, Barbara, 29
Kearns Jr., William J,. 25
Kelly, Edward, 23
Kendall, Harry, 83
Kent, Bill, 82
King, Christine, 88
Krane, Paul, 24
Langhorne, Crystal, 50, 51
Lesser, Jeffrey, 79
Levine, Rabbi Richard A., 45
Levitt and Sons, 12
Lewis, Carl, 53
Lewis, Carol, 54
Lewis, Cleveland, 65
Lewis, William and Evelyn, 67
Logan, Kelly, 39
Logan, Latrece, 39
Maier, Gus, 111
Marella, Robert James (Gorilla Monsoon), 68, 69
Marshall, Marilyn, 40
McFarland, Harry, 20
McGrath, William, 35
McHugh, Jack, 19
McKenzie, Kareem, 62
McMillan, Dr. Sean, 98
Messey, Dr. Edwin, 93
Mest, Dr. Stuart, 97
Minkins, Josh, 57
Miscavige, David, 46
Morris, Lizzie, 30
Moses, Dezman, 60, 61
Nelinson, David, 109
Olive, Thomas, 8
Ortiz, Claudette, 74
Pardlo, Gregory, 81
Pardlo, Robbie, 75
Payne, Delbert, 37
Penn, William, 10
Perzin, Dr. Adam, 98
Peterson, Gervase, 77
Petroski, Dr. Donald, 97
Phillips, Shaun, 58, 59
Quigley, Charlie, 126
Ramsey, Jeffrey, 47
Randall, Capt. Michael, 102
Reynolds, Margaret, 41
Richardson, George, 113
Rodriguez, Jr., Patrolman Mario, 103
Roser, Chief Marshall, 100
Rowan, Henry, 116, 117
Rucker, Director Gregory, 106
Ruvolo, Dr. Louis, 95
Ryan, Lt. Timothy, 103
Sbraga, Kevin, 72
Singleton, Troy, 48
Smith, Lamont, 55
Stang, Robert, 124
Stephenson, Dr. Ann Marie, 92
Stephenson, Paul, 43
Stringfellow, Brendan, 112
Stringfellow, Janine Maier, 112
Strother, Capt. Kenneth Jr., 102
Stuart, James Cresswell,15
Talone, Dr. Albert, 96
Tegley, John, 21
Thomas, Madison, 16
Toby, Ryan, 75
Valenta, Capt. Gerald, 101
Van Sciver, Charles, 18
Van Sciver, Chief Richard, 104
Van Sciver, Edwin, 100
Vermes, Peter, 66
War Veterans, 114
Whittaker, Celeste, 70
Whittaker, Chester M., 22
Williams, Vera and Charles, 14
Willingboro Fire Department, 1